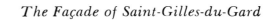

The Façade of Saint-Gilles-du-Gard

The façade of Saint-Gilles-du-Gard, the central portal, John and Peter.

The Façade of Saint-Gilles-du-Gard

ITS INFLUENCE ON FRENCH SCULPTURE

by WHITNEY S. STODDARD

WESLEYAN UNIVERSITY PRESS *Middletown, Connecticut*

Grateful acknowledgment is made to Fordham University Press for permission to quote passages from the article "Peter of Bruys, Henry of Lausanne, and the Façade of St.-Gilles" by Marcia L. Colish, from the journal *Traditio* (Volume XXVIII, 1972).

Library of Congress Cataloging in Publication Data

Stoddard, Whitney S.
    The façade of Saint-Gilles-du-Gard.

    Bibliography: p.
    1. Saint-Gilles, France (Gard). Church.
2. Sculpture, Romanesque—Saint-Gilles, France (Gard).
3. Sculpture—Saint-Gilles, France (Gard). I. Title.
NB543.S79   731'.54   72-3696
ISBN 0-8195-4056-0

Manufactured in the United States of America
First edition

In Memory
of
Wilhelm Koehler

Contents

Illustrations

ALL illustrations are from photographs by the author unless otherwise indicated. The author wishes to thank the following for permission to reproduce photographs: Bernard Martin, Arles; Richard E. Evans; Foto-Marburg; Orlandini, Modena.

Parts of portals are designated by letters and numerals. For example, *CP.L 2* designates central portal, left side, second jamb or second figure from the door.

Acknowledgments

RESEARCH for this book, aided by an Advanced Research Fulbright, began too long ago. In the intervening years, this material has been discussed with colleagues at Williams College and at other institutions as well as with Williams undergraduates in courses and seminars in medieval art. To all of them I wish to express my deep appreciation for their reactions and suggestions. But errors, omissions, or misinterpretations are mine alone.

The majority of the photographs were taken by the author and catalogued by his wife. Bernard Martin of Arles photographed some of the capitals of the Arles cloister, took aerial photographs of Saint-Gilles, and developed and printed with great care many of my negatives. Richard E. Evans of Fort Lauderdale, Florida, took several photographs of the superstructure of Saint-Gilles portals. Howard Levitz of the Williams College Photographic Facility and Ernest Le Claire of Williamstown aided greatly in the preparation of the photographs for the illustrations. To all of them I extend warm thanks.

Detailed measurements of the portals of Saint-Gilles were made by the author and his wife with the aid of a long fish pole. Using these measurements, Jeffrey L. Walker, Williams '68, drew the elevations of the Saint-Gilles portals (figs. 5, 6, 10) and the elevations of the three portals (fold-out 1). Professor H. Lee Hirsche of Williams College made the drawing of the Arles cloister, based on Revoil (fold-out 2).

Freeman Foote, Professor of Geology at Williams College, very kindly made a careful analysis of the different kinds of stones on the façade of Saint-Gilles. His conclusions helped to clarify the changes in the construction and design of the portals as work progressed. I thank him sincerely for his help.

Victor Lassalle's splendid book *L'influence antique dans l'art roman provençal* appeared after this manuscript had been submitted to the publisher. Most of the illustrations of Roman and Early Christian sculpture, which this author selected, appear in his book. It was possible to add several footnotes referring to this book, to clarify the possible sources of the Saint-Gilles sculpture.

I wish to express special appreciation to colleagues at Williams, Professors E. J. Johnson and Ronald Malmstrom, who made important observations. Professors Meyer Schapiro, François Boucher, and Alan Borg tempered several of my conclusions. The unknown reader for Wesleyan University Press, whom I think I know, submitted many valuable suggestions, all of which have been incorporated. Jean-Maurice Rouquette, Conservateur des Musées d'Arles, made my study of the Arles cloister much easier.

Galleys were proof-read by Margot Archer and my colleague Sheila Somers Rinehart, both of whom I sincerely thank. The manuscript was carefully typed in several versions by Kay Hall. Nancy MacFadyen of the Williams College Library staff procured on interlibrary loans many articles necessary for my research.

Finally, I wish I could now thank Bill Koehler again for the many hours he spent studying photographs of Saint-Gilles and Arles, listening to my conclusions, and offering sensitive observations. His encouragement, enthusiasm, and acute critical judgment were of inestimable help to me in this project as well as in previous research. I dedicate this book to his memory.

Williamstown, Massachusetts

Introduction

THE façade of Saint-Gilles-du-Gard (figs. 1, 2) is the most important medieval sculptured monument in southeast France and perhaps the most controversial of the Middle Ages. The Saint-Gilles façade has been dated as early as after 1096 and as late as after 1209. The dating of Saint-Gilles concerns more than merely a date per se, since the whole evolution of Provençal Romanesque sculpture is involved. Indeed, the whole chronological relationship between the Romanesque of Provence and of other regional styles is implied.

During the past century some scholars have attempted to date Saint-Gilles by comparisons with sculpture outside Provence in Italy and in southwestern and northern France. Others have concentrated on locating the façade in time by analysis of the Saint-Gilles crypt, choir, and upper church. A third basis involves deduction from historical events of the twelfth and thirteenth centuries, and more specifically from documents referring to a sculptor named Petrus Brunus. Finally, another solution focuses on the dating of epitaphs in the crypt and the stylistic connection between dated Provençal manuscripts and the façade sculpture. The fact that Saint-Gilles is the climax of the proto-Renaissance spirit of the region within a medieval context confuses rather than clarifies the problem of dating.

The unfinished condition of the central portal of Saint-Gilles (figs. 1, 2), with projecting pedestals and paired columns supporting nothing, has led scholars to search for the original design of the façade before the program was enlarged to include

1. Saint-Gilles-du-Gard. Air view.

2. Saint-Gilles-du-Gard. Façade.

the upper friezes. For these critics the somewhat chaotic state of the façade presupposes a second design following the first scheme.

In 1934, Richard Hamann published two reconstructions of the first design of the façade of Saint-Gilles, one with and one without tympana and lintels.[1] He included no archaeological evidence, such as measurements, to prove his theory that the paired columns and double socles were originally in the splays of the central portal and were moved to their present location on a new projecting pedestal after the program changed. Since the four apostles were carved for the splays of the central portal and since the low-relief sculpture on the projecting portals is the oldest sculpture on the

---

1. R. Hamann, "The Façade of Saint-Gilles: A Reconstruction," *Burlington Magazine*, LXIV (January 1934), 19–29.

façade and could not have been added during the second campaign, Hamann's reconstructions are incorrect. Hamann argued that the façade was begun after the consecration of 1096 with a second campaign after 1116, with work largely finished by 1129. In the opinion of this author this dating is much too early.

Walter Horn's book (1937), the first scholarly study of Saint-Gilles, disproved the reconstructions of Hamann.[2] Horn's reconstruction of the first scheme of the façade included only a single portal with the projecting pedestal and paired columns supporting a portico, which was later suppressed when the upper frieze was added. However, much evidence exists in the actual construction of the portals to prove that the façade contained three portals from the very beginning. Horn dated the portals between 1125 and 1145, or for sure between 1116 and 1152.

Marcel Gouron (1951) also argued for a single central portal, flanked by the twelve apostles on the front plane of the façade. Like Horn, he thought that the first scheme did not include the heroic Roman columns which are, however, completely integrated with the structure of the whole façade. Gouron, relying on documents mentioning a sculptor, Petrus Brunus, argued that the façade was begun in the 1180's and completed after 1209.[3] In his book of 1955, Hamann published the same two reconstructions which appeared in his article in 1934.[4] He failed to answer the criticisms of Horn, offered no new evidence to substantiate these reconstructions, and repeated the early dating of the façade. Thus in spite of the existence of Horn's book, which has only seven plates, and Hamann's book, which is profusely illustrated but appears to be wrong in so many aspects, including the dating of the façade and the reconstructions of the first campaign, a new study of Saint-Gilles is in order. Measurements of each portal, a study of the construction, including a geological survey of the kinds of stone employed, an analysis of the different sculptors involved in carving the apostles, reliefs on the bases, and the sculpture of the superstructure will all be included. A detailed iconographical study of the sculpture is outside the scope of this book; yet a section on iconography is included as it relates to the dating of the façade. Following Part I on Saint-Gilles, Part II will focus on four monuments which exhibit different relationships to Saint-Gilles: the frieze of Beaucaire, the cloister and portal of Saint Trophîme at Arles, the portal of Romans, and the cloister of Saint-Guilhem-le-Désert. The dating of these monuments and stylistic connections with dated North Italian monuments will in turn establish the *terminus ante quem* for the façade of Saint-Gilles.

---

2. W. Horn, *Die Fassade von St. Gilles. Eine Untersuchung zur Frage des Antikeneinflusses in der südfranzösischen Kunst des 12, Jahrhunderts* (Hamburg: Paul Evert, 1937).

3. M. Gouron, "Saint-Gilles-du-Gard," *Congrès archéologique de France*, CVIII (1951), 104–119.

4. R. Hamann, *Die Abteikirche von St. Gilles und ihre künstlerische Nachfolge* (Berlin: Akademie-Verlag, 1955).

PART I

The Façade of Saint-Gilles-du-Gard

CHAPTER I

Construction of the Portals

THE façade of Saint-Gilles (figs. 1, 2) preserves one of the largest ensembles of sculpture on the exterior of a Romanesque church. Eight apostles are located on the front face of the façade between the central and side portals, four apostles stand on the inner splays of the central portal, and angels appear on the extremities of the façade (see fold-out, labeled elevation of Saint Gilles). The friezes and tympana of Saint-Gilles comprise an extraordinary iconographical unity which challenges, in its completeness and consistency, High Gothic façades. The Passion of Christ begins in the left tympanum with the Virgin and Christ Child enthroned, flanked by the three Magi bearing gifts and the Angel appearing to Joseph in a dream and telling him to flee to Egypt. The frieze and lintel of the left portal depict the Entry into Jerusalem. The Passion resumes in the upper frieze of the central portal. From left to right we see the Payment of Judas, Christ purging the Temple, and the Raising of Lazarus. The frieze continues in the central portal with Christ prophesying the Denial of Peter, Christ washing Peter's Feet, and the Last Supper on the lintel, and the Betrayal on the right. The right-hand side of the upper frieze is decorated with the following scenes: Christ before Pilate, the Flagellation, and Carrying the Cross. The Passion sequence next moves to the tympanum of the right portal with the Crucifixion. On the left side of the portal are located Christ meeting two Disciples on the Road to Emmaus, *Noli me tangere*, Christ anointed by Mary. On the lintel appear the Holy Women buying Spices and the Holy Women at the Sepulchre, while the right frieze is decorated with Christ appearing to the Holy Women. (See Notes, Chapter 1, Restorations.)

3. Saint-Gilles. Left portal, left splay (LP.L).   4. Saint-Gilles. LP.L, reconstructed.

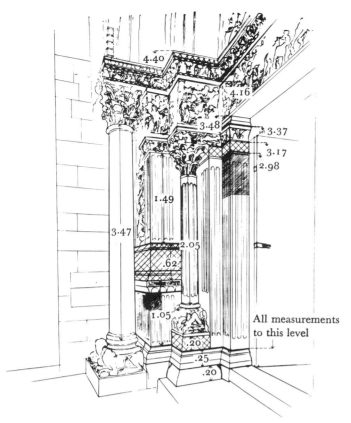

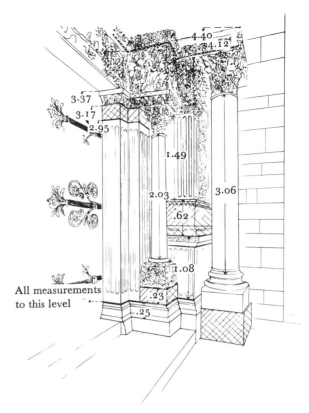

5. Saint-Gilles. LP.L, measured drawing.

6. RP.R, measured drawing.

7. RP.R.

8. RP.R, reconstructed.

The large monolithic columns of the façade (fig. 2) support the front planes of the side portals and the superstructure which projects over the apostles. These columns, with the exception of the one restored in the nineteenth century (LP.R), are Roman.[1] All have entasis, but vary in size and in type of stone (see Notes, Chapter 1, Geology). The organization of the splays of the side portals (figs. 3, 7) is logically integrated with sculptured frieze and the archivolts. The inner jamb serves as impost for the lintel, while the inner column supports the first section of the frieze, and this area, forming a right angle, is echoed by the inner archivolt. The smaller, outer section of the frieze is supported by the wall of the façade and crowned by the undecorated part of the second, major archivolt. The freestanding columns support the remaining half of the archivolt, which is ornamented with a scotia, torus, dentil, and egg-and-dart molding. The continuity between columns, walls, frieze, and archivolts seems to prove that these monoliths were part of the original design.

In spite of the apparent clarity and consistency of the design of the side portals, certain ambiguities exist. Why should the angels and the apostles on the front plane of the façade stand on two tiers of bases? Why are there undecorated blocks under the inner socles and under the lintels of the side portals? These ambiguities, together with the original function of the paired columns, flanking the central portal and presently supporting nothing, must be explained by a study of the masonry. The type of stones employed, their different surfaces, and the measurements of each portal—all help clarify the procedures of construction of the façade as well as prove that the design changed as work progressed. (See Notes, Chapter 1, Measurements.)

Measured drawings of the splays (see figs. 5, 6, 10) exhibit a consistent pattern of interlocking blocks in each course of masonry across the entire façade (see fold-out, scaled elevation). Measurements on the left side of the left portal, LP.L (fig. 5). correspond exactly with the opposite splay, LP.R. The right portal has slightly different measurements for individual sections, but the two sides correspond. In spite of the projecting pedestals which differentiate the central portal from the side portals, the central portal is built up of the same series of horizontal, interlocking courses of masonry (see fig. 10).

The bases of the left side of the left portal, LP.L (figs. 3, 5) consist of two courses of masonry, the lowest .20 meters high and the other .25 meters with three torus and two scotia moldings. The upper course is one block, extending from the doorway to a joint under the statue of Saint Michael, while the lower consists of three dovetailed

---

1. Parts of portals are designated by letters. For example: LP.R: left portal, right side. Measurements of the six monolithic columns (not including bases and capitals) are as follows: LP.L, 3.47 meters; LP.R (modern), 3.49 meters; CP.L, 3.47 meters; CP.R, 3.66 meters; RP.L, 3.66 meters; RP.R, 3.06 meters.

blocks (see fig. 5). The bases of the opposite splay correspond in both plan and elevation. Further, the bases of the right portal correspond in plan and in height, but the interpenetration of blocks of masonry at the re-entrant angles differs slightly. On these bases of two courses of masonry rests the entire façade except the outer, western face, which is supported by the large freestanding columns (figs. 3, 7, 9).

Above the bases rise two channeled sections (fig. 3). The inner section (doorjamb) consists of a double jamb extending from the bases almost to the lintel. (The doorjamb of LP.L has been patched with a modern piece at the top.) Behind the sculptured socle of the first jamb (LP.L) is another channeled block, .85 meters high (fig. 3). These channeled blocks are extremely fine-grained, cream-colored lithographic limestone. (Professor Freeman Foote, a geologist, made a study of the rocks of the façade for me. See Notes on Chapter 1.)

Directly above the channeled section and extending behind the small inner columns is a thin course (.20 meters) decorated with a frontal acanthus and meander patterns (see LP.L—figs. 3, 5). This strip, which is of very fine-grained white marble, serves as a crowning element of the pedestal of the entire façade (fig. 2).

Directly below the carved socle of the LP.L, which supports the inner column, is an undecorated square block. This block is .20 meters high, which corresponds exactly to the height of the unadorned block between the top of the channeled doorjambs and the floral abacus under the lintel. These blocks are found on all four splays of the side portals, although on the right splay of the right portal the blocks below the socle and over the doorjambs are .23 meters. These four blocks under the inner columns of the side portals are of coarse-grained, cream-colored, fossiliferous limestone. The blocks above the doorjamb have the same pitted surfaces, but are probably a different rock.

Continuing upward, the next section consists of two courses of eroded, coarse-grained limestone like the blocks under the inner columns (see LP.L—figs. 3, 5). The lower, smaller course is capped by a torus-and-scotia molding, while the larger is plain except for the top, which is decorated with bead-and-reel and egg-and-dart moldings. These two courses, varying in height between .62 and .60 meters, extend across the whole façade, with the exception of the inner splays of the central portal (fig. 9). In the case of the latter portal, the four lion socles beneath the four apostles correspond in dimensions and position in elevation to these two courses.

These two courses have the same pitted, rough surfaces as the blocks under the socles and over the doorjambs (fig. 3). As stated, the rock is coarse-grained limestone, like the pieces under the inner columns. It is the same local stone used to build the entire abbey. The function of these two courses under the monumental apostles would seem to duplicate that of the channeled sections directly beneath them. Indeed, from

14. Saint-Gilles. Back of lion socle under John (CP.L 2).

15. Back of lion socle under Paul (CP.R 2).

16. Façade, reconstructed.

The total width of the portal, measuring from the outer corners of the projecting pedestals supporting paired columns, is 7.28 meters. The width of the projecting section of the crypt (see plan—fig. 171) is 9.40 meters. Thus the present, existing design of the central portal would seem to be related to and physically supported by the extension of the crypt.

In spite of damage and subsequent patching, a careful study of the masonry of the central portal (fig. 10) reveals that the bases and low-relief sculpture have never been changed or altered in any way. Since the reliefs on the bases are among the oldest carvings on the façade, it follows that the present design of the central portal, at least in the lower parts, is the original one. If the diagrammatic drawing of the CP.L (fig. 10) is compared with the view of the left splay (fig. 9), it is clear that courses of masonry overlap re-entrant angles in three different levels. The course with torus-and-scotia moldings, which incidentally corresponds to the design at this level on the rest of the façade, overlaps the concavity to the left of the relief of the Murder of Abel. The same dovetailing of structure occurs in the acanthus-and-meander molding which crowns the pedestal. The facts that the matrix of these bases is interlocked structurally, that the decoration moldings of the bottom and top of the pedestals are continuous across the whole façade, and that the dimensions of the projection of the portal correspond to those of the crypt extension—all point to the conclusion that the existing pedestals of the central portal belong to earliest work on the façade and were not added at a later date.

The Cain and Abel reliefs on the left (fig. 9) are .85 meters high, while the sculpture in the rondels on the right (fig. 13) are .88 meters in height. This slight difference is consistent with the rest of the façade, since the channeled sections, to which these reliefs correspond, are .85 meters high on the left portal and under the left four apostles and .88 on the right portal and under the right apostles. This small change in dimensions thus occurs in the middle of the façade.

The massive lion socles under Saints John, Peter, James, and Paul (CP.L 1, 2 and CP.R 1, 2—figs. 9, 13) correspond in height (.60 meters) and in placement in elevation to the two courses of masonry which have been added to the side portals and to the pedestals under the other eight apostles. Details of the bulbous base on which Paul stands (figs. 11, 12) reveal that its lower half has been transformed with lions' hair to harmonize with the lion socle. Thus the block from which the Paul was carved includes the convex base which has been recarved in a different profile with bunches of hair to make the transition from apostle to lion socle. Furthermore, the back of the lion socle under Paul (fig. 15) is unfinished and therefore implies that it was a later addition. Since the socles are the same height as sections added to the side portals and since their completion necessitated the recarving of the already finished

Paul, it can be concluded that the central portal underwent a transformation exactly like the rest of the façade. With the increase in height of the socles, new corbels with angels were placed on top of the doorjambs and the lintel was raised.

At some point during construction it was decided to raise the whole façade. The most obvious reason was certainly the desire of the clergy to expand greatly the sculptural program. As a reconstruction of the façade without these added blocks reveals (fig. 16), the apostles and angels do not project into the zone of the frieze. It is impossible to say how far work had proceeded when the change was made, but it is obvious that blocks could not physically be inserted. Rather the portals would have to be partially dismantled and rebuilt. Other Romanesque portals seem to have evolved over a period of time. At Vézelay the tympanum of the narthex portal was raised by the insertion of blocks containing the four apostles on the jambs and by the complete redesigning of the trumeau.[2] The John the Baptist of the trumeau supported the lintel, when the whole superstructure was at a lower level; now the John the Baptist projects up into and damages the continuity of the lintel. At Moissac the floral lintel was added to the portal when the porches were constructed. Thus there is precedence for this kind of change in important Romanesque monuments. Perhaps it might be said that this procedure is more typical than unusual.

Before leaving the construction of the Saint-Gilles façade, mention should be made of the superstructure (figs. 2, 16). The upper frieze and cornice, supported by corbels, corresponds at its sides with the break in the plane of the upper façade. This slight projection or central pavilion corresponds to the nave of Saint-Gilles and, before the religious wars, was capped by a pitched roof, different in elevation from the roofs over the aisles.

NOTES—CHAPTER I
Construction of the Portals (figs. 2–16)

Restorations

The restorations of the façade, following the religious wars in the seventeenth century and following the French Revolution, bear directly on any analysis of the masonry. The Protestants attacked the town and monastery in 1562, and as a result the vaults of the nave collapsed. In 1622 the arrival of royal troops prevented the complete demolition of the monastery. Notary acts place the restorations involving the new vaults for nave and choir, the closing of the side portals, and the construction of stairs in front of the central portal

---

2. F. Salet, "La Madeleine de Vézelay, Notes sur la façade de la nef," *Bulletin monumental*, XCIX (1940), 223–237. Also F. Salet, *La Madeleine de Vézelay* (Melun, 1948), 42–45.

between 1650 and 1665. C. Nicholas (1895) quoted the contracts and the raising of funds in 1650: "Bail a pris faict de la grand ésglise de Saint-Gilles pour le seigneur abbé, chapitre et communauté dud. Saint-Gilles passé à Jean Gabriel et Pierre Daudet Mes massons et Jean Girardeau charpentier."[3] The destruction of existing stairs, the construction of oval stairway, and the closing of the side portals followed:

> Thumber les escalliers qui servent de monter à lad. ésglise et à l'endroit de la grand porte d'icelle et les reffaire en perron les mettre à quatre ponces et demy hauteur et de largeur un pan et demy et thumber la muraille qui est du côsté du marin pour plus facilement faire lesd. escalliers.
>
> Plus reffaire lad. grand porte servant dentrée à lad. ésglise, y mettre au milieu un pillier et audessus pour couvert une pierre ou faire servir les vielhes en case se trouveront soutenir les ares et murailles qui sont audessus de lad. porte, bâtir aussi les deux portes en suivant les deux portes en suivant le vieux dessain; Plus hausser les murailles métresses du vaut droit et marin de l'hauteur du premier pillier . . .[4]
>
> In 1900 C. Nicholas summarized the documents:
>
> (1) De faire un perron pour monter et entrer à l'église et de le faire en rond pour en faciliter l'entrée. (2) De faire à la grande porte, servant d'entrée à la dite église, un pilier au milieu pour la séparer en deux. (3) De fermer les deux portes qui sont à droite et à gauche de la grande porte. (4) De voute la dite église, depuis la grand porte, jusqu'au milieu et tambour du sixième pilier . . .[5]

Another note by C. Nicholas was added to the article of 1900.[6]

M. Gouron (1951) added information concerning the restoration of the lintel of the central portal and the refurbishing of the right pier of the central portal.[7] The patching of the lintel and right-hand frieze of the central portal is clearly revealed in the third figure from the left in the Last Supper (fig. 120) and in the Betrayal (fig. 133). It is impossible, however, to agree with Gouron's conclusion that the entire Betrayal scene was carved in the seventeenth century. The damage to the lintel obviously necessitated the introduction of the trumeau.

The damage to Saint-Gilles during the Revolution seems to have been more extensive than that incurred during the religious wars. The existence of a print of the façade (fig. 202), dated 1833, shows a missing monumental column and no paired columns with capitals surmounting the pedestals of the central portal. This print reveals the oval staircase and walled-up side portals and at the same time indicates what areas will have to be restored in the nineteenth century.

---

3. C. Nicholas, "Documents inédits sur Saint-Gilles," *Bulletin du Comité de l'art chrétien du Diocèse de Nîmes*, VI (1895), 448.

4. *Ibid.*, 450.

5. C. Nicholas, "Construction et réparations de l'église de Saint-Gilles," *Mémoires de l'Académie de Nîmes*, XXIII (1900), 121.

6. C. Nicholas, "Notes de M. Delmas sur l'église de Saint-Gilles 1843," *Mémoires de l'Académie de Nîmes*, XXV (1902), 95–122.

7. M. Gouron, "Saint-Gilles-du-Gard," *Congrès archéologique de France*, CVIII (1951), 117–118.

The nineteenth- and twentieth-century restorations are preserved in Paris[8]. Some of the relevant items are as follows:

1842–1843: purchase of houses attached to façade.
1844: destruction of houses which blocked central portal.
1844 (estimate of 17 May and passed 24 May):
   sculpture: two capitals for columns of central portal; repair of cornice angle on right side of central portal; new cornice on left side.
   materials: four granite columns, copper covering for protection of capitals.
   masonry: cornice for left side of central portal; a piece for right cornice; several pieces for the right pedestal of the central portal.

The rest of the document deals with transportation and scaffolding.

1844: (letter from Charles Questel, dated 17 May 1844) states that excavations made in 1840 unearthed capitals, which seemed to fit the central portal, and a fragment of the cornice. All were so worn that it was decided not to use them.
1846: opening up of side portals.
1847: money voted to carry out restorations.
1862: appreciation extended to H. Revoil for his report on the sculpture and inscriptions on the façade.
1866: letter to the Marshal of France describing the discovery of the tomb of Saint Gilles in excavations in the crypt.
1876: separation of house from cloister.
1917–1918: demolition of houses to the north in order to drain area and keep the crypt dry.

It is difficult to relate the documents of the 1840's with the print of 1833 unless the artist removed the structures from the central portal or unless these structures did not exist in 1833. The print does, however, show the damage described in the contracts: no columns on the pedestals of the central portal, damage to the west sides of the pedestals and to the right cornice.

A study of the façade reveals the two distinctly different periods of restoration, the seventeenth and nineteenth centuries. The upper cornice above Christ's Prophecy of Peter's Denial and above the Betrayal (with metal covers), and the four columns and capitals with patched sections of cornice, are nineteenth-century (figs. 113, 133). The restoration of the outer half of the right rondel can be seen in a detail of the pedestal (fig. 13). The pedestals themselves show patching which seems to date from both periods (see figs. 50, 51). The repairs of the seventeenth century are visible on the lintel of the central portal and in the relief of the the Betrayal (figs. 120, 133). Documents describing the construction of the present stairs over a half-barrel vault are missing from the files. Nicholas (1900, p. 132) stated that they were constructed between 1842 and 1845.

---

8. Saint-Gilles, Église 1er Dossier, Gard 506, Monuments historiques, 1839–1883 (1926).

Measurements of the Façade of Saint-Gilles

In order to follow a uniform procedure in measuring the façade and in order to avoid the discrepancies in levels of the worn and often patched stairs, all measurements were calculated from the bottom of the horizontal course of masonry which rests on the doorsill. The measurements of the left side of the left portal appear in figure 6. The right splay of the left portal has the exact same measurements in every course of masonry. Both splays of the right portal are identical in their system of construction and measurements in elevation, but the whole portal, from the top of the fluted doorjamb to the sill, is slightly lower (3.25 meters to 3.20 meters for the right portal).

The dimensions of the taller central portal are illustrated in figure 10 (CP.L). Again the opposite splay is identical in division of courses and major dimensions. The heights of the doorjambs are, however, slightly different. The left doorjamb is 3.94 meters tall, as opposed to the right one of 3.92 meters. This slight discrepancy in height, which is corrected in the size of the capitals supporting the lintel, seems to relate the left side of the central portal to the left portal and the shorter right side of the central portal to the right portal.

The plan of the façade was measured from the bottom of the course of masonry resting on the doorsills (see plan at bottom of fold-out elevation). As can be seen from the plan, the left portal is slightly wider than the right or south portal, but the dimensions of the splays remain practically uniform. The central portal is obviously considerably wider. The projecting pedestals as well as the dimensions and arrangement of the splays are entirely different. This width of the façade between the projecting pedestals of the central portal and the side portals is different (4.11 meters from the north side of the left pedestals of the central to the left portal, as opposed to 4.31 meters from the south face of the right pedestal to the right portal).

Because of extra blocks inserted under the lintel of the left portal, the bottom of the lintel is 3.74 meters above the doorsill. On the right portal a very thin block raises the lintel above the abacus on the left side, while no block is inserted between lintel and doorjamb on the right side. The result of these differences is the lower height of the lintel of the right portal, 3.66 meters, as opposed to 3.74 meters for the left portal.

The dimensions of the monumental statues are as follows: Michael (2.0 meters), Matthew (2.05), Bartholomew (2.01), Thomas (2.01), James the Less (2.01), John (2.03), Peter (2.03), James (1.99), Paul (2.0), CP.R 3 (1.98), CP.R 4 (1.98), CP.R 5 (1.98), CP.R 6 (1.99), archangels (2.0 meters).

Geology of the Façade

In November of 1967, Freeman Foote, Professor at Williams College, found Saint-Gilles to be "a geologist's paradise." His summary of the different types of rock on the façade follows:

1. Channeled pedestal, which extends across the front face of the façade: extremely fine-grained, cream-colored, lithographic limestone.

2. Narrow, carved course above No. 1: very fine-grained white marble.

3. Apostles and their framing pilasters: very fine-grained white marble like No. 2.

4. The two courses of masonry between the pedestals and the apostles, added after work began on the façade: coarse-grained, cream-colored, fossiliferous limestone.

5.   Blocks under the socles supporting the inner columns of the side portals: same as No. 4. This rock, used to construct the outer walls of the entire abbey, probably came from a local outcrop.

6.   Carved double socles of central portal: fine-grained white marble.

7.   Four small columns in splays of side portals: marble.

8.   Large Roman columns (from left to right): dark-colored granite; light-colored granite (nineteenth-century column); fossiliferous limestone, similar to courses and blocks added to façade; very fine-grained fossiliferous limestone; very fine-grained rock (about 10 percent black mineral and 90 percent white mineral) on each side of the right portal.

The fact that the majority of the carved stones are marble, while the stones which are added are limestone, is further proof of a change in the design of the façade as work progressed. The variety of types of rock in the colossal columns, together with differences in size and design, helps prove that all are Roman.

CHAPTER 2

Apostles and Angels

THE twelve apostles and two angels are all approximately two meters in height and carved in very fine-grained white marble. Matthew is signed *Brunus me fecit* in the upper left-hand corner, but the adjacent Bartholomew has lost its Brunus signature. Except for these two, the remaining twelve can be associated with artistic personalities only by stylistic analysis and comparison. Five sculptors carved these fourteen life-size figures, and three of them were responsible for most of the sculpture on the tympana and friezes of the superstructure. (Rather than include in the text the divergent opinions of many scholars who have written about Saint-Gilles, this writer will omit references to previous literature but include a summary of each author's conclusions in Notes, Chapter 2.)

BRUNUS MASTER: Matthew and Bartholomew

Two apostles, Matthew and Bartholomew (CP.L 6 and 5—fig. 17), appear to be inspired by Early Christian sarcophagi depicting apostles in niches framed by pilasters (figs. 18, 20) or by Roman sculpture. The sarcophagi, formerly in Saint-Honorat-des-Alyscamps at Arles, only twelve miles from Saint-Gilles, are now exhibited in the Musée d'Art Chrétien at Arles (see Notes, Chapter 2). Heavy, voluminous costumes, sandaled feet, and architectural frames are common character-

17. Saint-Gilles. Matthew and Bartholomew by Brunus (CP.L 6, 5).

istics of these Christian heroes of both Saint-Gilles and the Early Christian reliefs.[1] Yet here the similarities cease. The Early Christian apostles stand firmly in niches with space around them. Gestures, anatomical articulation, and a freedom of pose give each figure an individuality within a spatial ambience. In their frontality the two Saint-Gilles apostles, standing precariously on steep conical socles, echo the plane of the framing pilasters, and movement is denied. Articulation is merely suggested by the slightly swelling folds over knees, while the anatomy is disjointed in arms and wrists. Whether Brunus was inspired by Early Christian monuments in which the Roman tradition still strongly prevailed or by local Roman monuments no longer extant need not concern us, since it is clear that Brunus transformed his models into a mural, architectonic statement which is Romanesque, albeit an unusual Romanesque. Brunus related these apostles both to the pilasters which tightly frame them and to the walls behind them of which they are an integral part.

The figure of Matthew (fig. 17) is heavy and square in silhouette. Drapery falls in weighty folds. Matthew's bodice is animated by a horizontal band across his neck and by sagging folds with marked juxtapositions of convexities and concavities. In the concave areas the surface is further articulated by parallel incisions which follow the dip of folds. More elliptical folds cover his left leg, and gentle zigzag folds terminate the outer silhouette. The total impact of the figure is one of almost brutal monumentality and stark heaviness.

Bartholomew (fig. 17) is more frontal and stiffer than Matthew. Over his chest, the drapery is similar to Matthew's, except that the collar is not a flat area but is folded. The center section has elliptical folds getting more pointed in a rhythmical fashion near the bottom. The undergarment over his right leg has drilled, elongated teardrop patterns, while the area over his left leg displays graceful curved folds similar to those on the Matthew. The same extraordinary archaic ruggedness and the same transfixed spirit permeate both Matthew and Bartholomew.

THOMAS MASTER: Thomas and James the Less

Thomas (CP.L 4—fig. 21) is more elongated, more sinuous, and more freely conceived than the Brunus Master's apostles (fig. 17). In spite of the fact that the crossed legs accentuate the animation of the figure, there is more grace and

---

1. V. Lassalle in *L'Influence antique dans l'art roman provençale*, Revue archéologique de Narbonnaise, 2 (Paris: Editions E. de Boccard, 1970), 93–105, points out the stylistic connections between Roman sculpture and Early Christian sarcophagi and Provençal Romanesque sculpture, especially the Saint-Gilles frieze, the Beaucaire frieze, and the cloister and portal of Arles (see Lassalle, Plates XXXVIII–XLVII).

18. Early Christian Sarcophagus. End of fourth century. Arles, Musée d'Art Chrétien, 10.

19. Early Christian Sarcophagus about 400. Arles, Musée d'Art Chrétien, 17.

20. Early Christian Sarcophagus. End of fourth century. Arles, Musée d'Art Chrétien, 6.

21. Saint-Gilles. Thomas and James the Less (CP.L 4, 3). Thomas Master.

22. Angoulême. Lunette, Apostles.　　23. Angoulême. Angel of spandrel.

24. Saint-Gilles. Head of Thomas.　　25. Souillac. Head of Isaiah.

movement in Thomas when contrasted with the more lithic Matthew and Bartholomew. Thomas' silhouette is less square; it curves toward and then breaks away from the framing pilasters. The hair and beard flow more freely than the remaining curls of Matthew. Cuffs and top of bodice are ornamented with a bead-and-reel border. The undergarment is accentuated by eyebrow folds over the abdomen and S-shaped terminations across the knees and over the feet. The whole statue possesses a strange combination of flatness and implied movement. Not only the crossed legs but the rhythmic undulation of silhouette and drapery manifest a spirit different from that of the Brunus Master. The style of Thomas is, at once, more linear and less massive.

As pointed out by previous critics (see Notes), Thomas and other reliefs on the façade (to be discussed later) have a close stylistic relationship to sculpture on the façade of the Cathedral of Angoulême in western France (figs. 22, 23). If the Saint Peter or the other apostles of one of the lower lunettes of Angoulême (fig. 22) were compressed between two classical pilasters, the similarity with Thomas would be striking. The treatment of drapery, both in the arrangement of folds and the design of hems, the ornamented bodices, and their animated poses—all exhibit a marked affinity. Furthermore, the angels in higher relief in the upper zone of the façade of Angoulême (fig. 23) are in many respects closer in style to the Saint-Gilles apostle. However, none of the Angoulême heads have flowing beards like that of Thomas; nor do any of the Angoulême figures suggest the weight and monumental scale of Thomas. Indeed, the treatment of Thomas' head and the scale of the Saint-Gilles apostle recall the Prophet Isaiah of Souillac of the 1130's (fig. 25). It is possible, however, to suggest that Thomas was carved by a sculptor who worked earlier in his life on the façade of Angoulême. However, the classical nature of the design of the façade of Saint-Gilles forced him to compress his figure into a more strict ambience.

James the Less (CP.L—fig. 21) is more closely related to Thomas than to any of the other apostles. In general characteristics, such as elaborately bordered nimbus, relation of feet to socle, and over-all flatness of relief, James resembles Thomas. Ornamented cuffs and borders and the treatment of sleeves over the wrists echo the Thomas statue. The statue is, however, much more static than Thomas with its implied movement of crossed legs and animated drapery; yet the rather dull symmetry would be alleviated if the staff or crozier he held was restored. This same juxtaposition of V folds and curved folds can be seen in the lower abdomen of Thomas. The hands, like those of Thomas, are large and accentuated by raised ridges marking the tendons. The carving technique and the general format are much closer to Thomas than to the Brunus apostles.

In his transformation of Early Christian models, Brunus with his Apostles Matthew and Bartholomew established a new local tradition, while Apostles Thomas and James the Less, which reveal close stylistic parallels with Angoulême and other monuments in western and southwestern France, were carved by an outsider, summoned to Saint-Gilles-du-Gard.

FOUR UNIDENTIFIED APOSTLES

The four unidentified apostles to the right of the central portal (CP.R 3, 4, 5, 6—figs. 26, 27) possess some features characteristic of Brunus and the Thomas Master. All four have their heads placed against capitals which are backed by a plain nimbus similar to Matthew and Bartholomew. The figures are part of plain panels which are crowned by simple moldings like the left four apostles. Characteristics which differentiate these four from the left apostles are the concavity and flare of drapery at the level of the ankles and feet, and the drapery style.

SOFT MASTER: CENTRAL PORTAL, RIGHT 3 AND 4 APOSTLES

The left apostle (CP.R 3—fig. 26) does not project the crispness of carving or massive weight and stiffness of Matthew and Bartholomew. The statue appears to be pushed into the block, more in the manner of Thomas and James the Less. The modeling is softer. Hands are limp and inarticulate. Over the feet the garment flares out and terminates in tonguelike folds. The head (fig. 47) is the best preserved of any of the apostles. The hair undulates around the prominent ears and flattens out on the nimbus. Beard and mustache emphasize the rectangularity of the face. Eyebrows are prominently marked with thick, convex projections. The whole spirit of the head is one of brooding seriousness. From the point of view of quality, the head seems superior to the somewhat ambiguous and soft figure.

The next apostle (CP.R 4—fig. 26) is very close stylistically to the one just described. The crossed legs and greater emphasis on smaller folds give the lower part of the figure a slightly different feeling, but the upper part has the same soft, concave folds. This figure with its crossed legs corresponds in location on the façade to the crossed-legged Thomas on the other side of the portal. If we look at these two unidentified apostles together (CP.R 3, 4—fig. 26), it is possible to conclude that they were carved by the same artist. Heavy, stiff hands, decorative collars, and drapery folds over their left shoulders and upper arms are found in both statues. A new feature is the greater articulation of anatomy through thin, clinging folds. The quality is less sensitive. Certainly a third sculptor carved these two apostles.

26. Saint-Gilles. Unidentified Apostles (CP. R3, 4). Soft Master.

27. Saint-Gilles. Unidentified Apostles (CP.R5, 6). Hard Master.

HARD MASTER: CENTRAL PORTAL, RIGHT 5 AND 6 APOSTLES

The extreme right two apostles (CP.R 5, 6—fig. 27) have certain features which are related to the two apostles just discussed, yet were certainly carved by a different hand. In contrast to CP.R 3 and 4 by the Soft Master, the drapery is much heavier. All the folds are more plastically conceived, like Roman sculpture. In the CP.R 5 apostle the whole treatment of the drapery is more ponderous than on any of the other apostles. Its monumentality resembles the Brunus statues; yet the drapery extends out from the body more than in the Matthew, but, at the same time, the figure does not seem to weigh as heavily on the socle. There seems to be an ambiguity between a sense of weight and suspension.

The extreme right apostle (CP.R 6—fig. 27) is clearly by the same hand as CP.R 5. The starkness of Bartholomew has given way to heavy, undercut folds. Certain details are entirely new, such as the spiral fold over his right breast and the confused treatment of his left knee with convex folds indicating the kneecap.

Since the Soft Master (CP.R 3, 4—fig. 26) was responsible for most of the sculpture of the left portal, while the Hard Master (CP.R 5, 6—fig. 27) was in charge of creating the right portal, these four unidentified apostles were carved by two distinct personalities. If there was an interval of time between the left apostles by Brunus and Thomas and the right unidentified apostles, it was a very short one. Thus on the front face of the façade we have eight apostles and four sculptors.

JOHN, PETER, JAMES MAJOR, PAUL (SPLAYS OF CENTRAL PORTAL)

The four apostles on the splays of the central portal (figs. 28, 29) seem to be elaborations either of Brunus' or the Thomas Master's styles. This suggests a stylistic evolution in time. In two of the apostles strong overtones of Roman sculpture are apparent. If it is assumed that the original inspiration for the Saint-Gilles apostles was Roman or Early Christian sculpture, the evolution might be reversed, moving from a more classical position of some of the apostles such as James Major or Paul to a more archaic point of view of the Brunus statues. This question of chronology can be answered only after each of the four apostles is analyzed.

PETER (CP.L I)

Peter, holding the keys (figs. 28, 32), exhibits marked connections with the Thomas Master, especially his James the Less (fig. 21). Peter's general flatness, double V folds on chest and over ankles, raised drapery over shoulders, S-shaped terminations of folds, simple concave fold between legs, drilled and ornamented hems and borders, position and treatment of hands, halo decorated with bead-and-reel—all are characteristics seen in James the Less by the Thomas Master. The hair in tight curls is similar to the treatment in the apostle Thomas. Furthermore, the arrangement of folds across the ankles is close to the gnomelike figure between the bears on the socle of the right portal (fig. 58), which was carved by the Thomas Master. Even though Peter has thinner proportions than James the Less, the style of Peter has so many features related to James the Less that it can be concluded that the Thomas Master carved the statue of Peter. As already stated, Thomas came originally from western France. Thomas is responsible for the reliefs of Cain and Abel on the pedestals of the central portal (see figs. 52, 54, 55), to be discussed in Chapter 3, which bear the closest connection with Angoulême. Since he must have carved these reliefs on the lowest parts of the façade before the apostles Thomas and James the Less, it follows that we have a chronological sequence of the work of one sculptor: the low reliefs of the projecting pedestals of the central portal and socles of the right portal, Thomas, James the Less, and Peter.

PAUL (CP.R 2) and JOHN (CP.L 2)

The outer apostles of the central portal (Paul on the right and John on the left—figs. 28, 29) both reveal strong connections with the two Brunus statues (fig. 17), yet at the same time appear more complex and more Roman in spirit. All four apostles have many similar motifs of drapery. Paul and John appear more three-dimensional, although the absence of framing pilasters may accentuate this difference. A much freer treatment of drapery, greater resilience, and more implied movement can be observed in the Paul and John than in the Matthew and Bartholomew by Brunus.

The elaboration of the Brunus formula is clearly manifested in the apostle Paul (CP.R 2—figs. 29, 33). Paul's bald head (fig. 33) is set against a capital with ornamented abacus and is framed by a wide, plain nimbus, which is slightly concave. His brow is animated by three ridges, and eyebrow and cheeks are strongly demarcated. Prominent ears are surrounded by flowing hair, and beard and mustache encase the chin, giving a striking transfixed character to the face as a whole. Whereas the eyes of Peter (fig. 32) appear to be single drill holes surrounded by oval eyelids, Paul's eyes are more elongated and undercut at the side, giving them a sense of stark actuality. The ruggedly modeled hands hold the scroll which crosses his chest. Again Paul's hands and fingers consist of evenly rounded surfaces, not flat surfaces accentuated by raised tendons as in the hands of Peter and James the Less by the Thomas Master. The mantle with its decorated hems falls from both shoulders. The bottom part of the figure seems to be an elaboration of Matthew in the raised drapery re-

28. Saint-Gilles. John and Peter (CP.L 2, 1). Brunus and Thomas Master.

29. Saint-Gilles. James Major and Paul (CP.R 1, 2). Brunus.

vealing the ankles. Minute folds are animated with convex ridge moldings in contrast to incisions on Matthew (fig. 17). Greater surface animation with ornament on borders of mantle has replaced the severity of Matthew and Bartholomew.

Paul seems to be the work of Brunus and to have been carved after he finished Matthew and Bartholomew. The impact of Roman sculpture, such as the relief from the Augustan Arch in Arles (fig. 30) or a figure like those from the Arles theater (fig. 31) (the latter not unearthed until the nineteenth century), seems to have intensified as Brunus' style evolved. Since there is a panelled backdrop behind Paul, as opposed to the plain backdrops on all other apostles except James Major, the apostle adjacent to Paul, and since Paul seems to be the Brunus formula made more complex, it is impossible to argue that Matthew and Bartholomew were completed after Paul.

John (CP.L 2—figs. 28, 32) is so closely related to Paul in pose and in style of drapery that one must conclude that this figure was also carved by Brunus. The hooked folds which appear on Bartholomew's right leg are repeated on John's right leg. Incised lines, accenting the lower drapery of the apostles signed by Brunus, are now raised ridges like those on the apostle Paul. Both John and Paul were designed for their present location on the corner of the splay, since their outer sides are flush with the outer face of the façade, and their front planes echo the right-angled nature of both splays. The stone slab, of which John is an integral part, is not paneled, as in the case of Paul. Rather, the plain background, similar to that of the eight apostles on the front face of the façade and that of Peter, is continued. John's head turns toward Peter, which proves that Brunus and the Thomas Master collaborated on the design of the left side of the central portal. Furthermore, the halo with bead-and-reel as well as the decorated cushion socle are similar to those features in the Peter statue. Thus it would seem as though the Brunus Master changed halo, socle, and axis of the head of John in order to bring about a more harmonious relationship with the Peter which was already completed or was being created simultaneously.

JAMES MAJOR (CP.R 1)

James Major (CP.R 1—figs. 29, 33) is the most fluid and agitated of all the Saint-Gilles apostles. Further, as a comparison with a Roman sculpture in Arles (figs. 30, 31) clearly reveals, James Major possesses more pagan overtones than any of the other monumental figures. The thin, clinging drapery over stomach and legs in the Roman statues appear on James's right leg, while the freedom of the cloak on the sides of the Roman statues has its counterparts in the flaring yet congealed draperies on each side of the James Major. The Romanesque sculptor, however, has frozen the action, flattened the mass, and related James to a specific architectural frame.

Many stylistic features, such as the exposed ankle, unevenness of drapery over the

30. Arles, Nymph from a Roman Triumphal Arch. Musée Lapidaire.

31. Arles, Nymph from the Roman Theatre. Musée Lapidaire.

32. Saint-Gilles. Heads of John and Peter. Brunus and Thomas Master.

33. Heads of James Major and Paul. Brunus.

34. Saint-Gilles. Detail of Matthew (CP.L 6). Brunus.

35. Detail of Bartholomew (CP.L 5). Brunus.

36. Detail of Thomas (CP.L 4). Thomas Master.

37. Detail of James the Less (CP.L 3).
Thomas Master.

feet, slightly pinched waist, and outward flare of the mass over the thighs, relate James Major to the other four apostles by Brunus. In spite of the damaged nature of James Major's head (fig. 33), the eyes with drill holes for iris and at the corners, the structure of the eye socket, the treatment of the hair, beard, and ears—all reveal a marked similarity to the nature of Paul's head. Thus, James Major would seem to be the fifth apostle by Brunus. The chronological order of these five statues is difficult to determine, but a case can be made for the following: Matthew, Bartholomew, Paul, James Major, and John.

DETAILS OF THE TWELVE APOSTLES

Details of drapery by the four artists, each of whom carved two apostles on the front face of the façade (figs. 34–41), reveal a distinct stylistic difference in the arrangement of folds and treatment of surfaces. Within the rigidity of pose and squareness of silhouette, Matthew and Bartholomew (figs. 34, 35) exhibit a contrast between loosely handled mantle and minutely incised undergarment. On the other hand, Thomas and James the Less (figs. 36, 37) possess an abstracted system of alternating flat and curved folds which terminate in rhythmical running S's at the hems. The unidentified apostles (CP.R 3 and 4—figs. 38, 39) by the Soft Master do not suggest the heaviness of Matthew or Bartholomew nor the animated flatness of Thomas. Their silhouettes undulate, and the crispness of carving so apparent in both Matthew and Thomas gives way to a softer technique. Although the fourth artist (see CP.R 5 and 6—figs. 40, 41), the Hard Master, seems related to the sculptor of the CP.R 3 and 4 in the inward curve at the level of the ankles, the thick, heavy, and looping folds mark him as a distinct personality. Large looped folds are not continuous curves of profile, but have edges which indicate the shifting planes.

Details of the lower half of the four apostles on the splay of the central portal prove that these have no stylistic connection with the Soft or Hard Master. The treatments of John, of Paul, and of James Major (figs. 42, 43) are closely interrelated, while the Peter (fig. 42) is entirely different. John, Paul, and James Major have many features in common with Matthew by Brunus; but in each instance these three apostles of the central portal reveal a decided transformation of the Brunus format as incised folds become projecting ridges and greater surface animation transpires. Peter has so many details which are similar to the Thomas Master that it is possible to conclude that the Thomas Master carved Peter. Thus Brunus carved five apostles, while Thomas was responsible for reliefs on the lower parts of the central and right portals and Thomas, James the Less, and Peter.

MICHAEL MASTER

Although Saint Michael trampling and transfixing a winged dragon (LP.L—figs. 44, 46, 48) presents a different and more complicated sculptural problem than the placement of single figures in niches, there remain many stylistic relationships both with the Brunus apostles, especially John (fig. 28), and with the Soft Master (fig. 26). Head set against a plain capital and undecorated nimbus, with plain molding—both are features found in the Matthew and Bartholomew by Brunus and the four unidentified apostles. The flat upper part of Michael's bodice and cloak, as well as the ridge folds over his right knee, resembles corresponding areas in John. On the other hand, the arrangement of garment across Michael's stomach, the scooped-out folds over his ankles, and the extension of the cloak behind the figure resemble the Soft Master (fig. 26). Also the anatomical articulation of the legs recalls the crossed legs of CP.R 4. Since it is apparent that Brunus and the Soft Master are two distinct personalities, it would appear that the Michael Master, perhaps a younger man, is influenced by both Brunus and the Soft Master. Michael is no longer emerging through silhouette and surfaces; calligraphy has given way to articulated forms.

The most surprising stylistic analogy is the similarity between Michael's head (fig. 46) and the well-preserved apostle head (CP.R 3—fig. 47). Both heads have the same square silhouette and similar treatment of hair. Eyes have the same convex roll, indicating the eyebrow. The shape of the eyes, with drilled pupils and the curving edge of the lower eyelids, is identical. Although these two are related in general shape to the head of Paul by Brunus (fig. 33), Paul's eyes have drill holes at the sides as well as for the pupils.

The archangels and Satan on the extreme right of the façade (fig. 45) present a more difficult problem of design than Michael slaying the Dragon (fig. 44). The pose of the archangels appears somewhat congealed and awkward when compared with Michael; yet many details of drapery, such as the loop folds between the legs and the straight group of ridge folds over the knees, are similar. In motif only, the lateral folds across the stomach resemble this area of Michael, but the alternating concavities and convexities of the archangels are changed to multiple ridges in Michael. The surface textures of the archangels exhibit relations with the right four apostles, such as the flat ornamented bodice of the Soft Master and the confused folds over the left knee of the Hard Master. These stylistic connections with the unidentified apostles, plus the more minute rendering of folds reminiscent of Paul and John, suggest that the sculptor of these two statues on the extreme sides of the portal is eclectic. It can be argued with some validity that the Michael Master carved the archangels and Satan first and then evolved a more individual style when he created Michael and the dragon.

38. Saint-Gilles. Detail of unidentified Apostle (CP.R 3). Soft Master.

39. Detail of unidentified Apostle (CP.R 4). Soft Master.

40. Detail of unidentified Apostle (CP.R 5). Hard Master.

41. Detail of unidentified Apostle (CP.R 6). Hard Master.

42. Saint-Gilles. Detail of John and Peter (CP.L 2, 1). Brunus and Thomas Master.

43. Detail of James Major and Paul (CP.R 1, 2). Brunus.

44. Saint-Gilles. Saint Michael (LP.L). Michael Master.   45. Archangels (RP.R). Michael Master.

46. Saint-Gilles. Head of Michael.

47. Head of unidentified Apostle (CP.R 3). Soft Master.

48. Detail of Michael. Michael Master.

49. Detail of Archangels. Michael Master.

Since the Hard Master is responsible for most of the tympanum, lintel, and right frieze of the right-hand portal and was probably assisted by the Michael Master, and since the Soft Master carved most of the sculpture of the left portal and was also assisted by the Michael Master, it follows that the Michael Master is the fifth sculptor involved in the creation of the twelve apostles and two angels.

A summary of the individual sculptors responsible for the fourteen monumental figures would seem to be:

Brunus: Matthew, Bartholomew, Paul, James Major, John (possibly in that order).

Thomas Master: Reliefs on pedestals and socles, Thomas, James the Less, and Peter (in that order).

Soft Master: CP.R 3, CP.R 4, and then the left portal (see Chapter 4).

Hard Master: CP.R 5, CP.R 6, and then the right portal (see Chapter 4).

Michael Master: Archangels killing Satan, Michael slaying the Dragon, and assistant to both the Soft Master and Hard Master (see Chapter 4).

NOTES—CHAPTER 2
Apostles and Angels (figs. 17–49)

Critics have differed considerably in the attribution of the apostles to specific hands.

R. de Lasteyrie (1902) has the apostles carved by three sculptors under the supervision of Brunus.[2] Brunus carved the four apostles on the splays of the central portal beside Matthew and Bartholomew. One assistant created Thomas and James the Less, while a second was responsible for the four right, unidentified apostles. Lasteyrie, believing that the apostles were carved contemporaneously, noted that the two angel statues were more expressive than the apostles. He assigned them to a fourth hand and dated them contemporaneously with the apostles. Because of marked stylistic differences between the Brunus and Thomas Masters it is difficult to conclude that Thomas is an assistant of Brunus. It is true that the four right, apostles bear some connections in style with Brunus; yet two different artists must have carved them. Certainly, the Thomas Master carved Peter.

A. K. Porter (1923) also found three hands at work.[3] His Angoulême Master carved Thomas and touched up the draperies of James the Less (CP.L 3); Brunus created Matthew, Bartholomew, and then the four apostles on the central portal in a more advanced style. According to Porter, a third hand, who was Burgundian, did the four unidentified apostles

2. R. de Lasteyrie, "Études sur la sculpture française au moyen-âge," Académie des inscriptions et belles-lettres, Fondation Piot, *Monuments et mémoires*, VIII (1902), 104–107.

3. A. K. Porter, *Romanesque Sculpture of the Pilgrimage Roads*, 10 vols. (Boston: Marshall Jones, 1923), vol. 1, 273–279.

to the right and James the Less. He refined these conclusions by stating that Brunus touched up the two extreme right apostles (CP.R 5, 6) and by establishing the chronological order of the four central apostles as follows: James Major, Peter, Paul, and John. Porter saw an evolution in the style of Brunus. The notion of one artist putting finishing touches on another artist's statue is reminiscent of workshop practices in the Renaissance. Porter related the angels to the tympana and friezes of the side portals and dated them about 1180.[4] Again, Peter is related to the other statues by the Thomas Master, while the heads of Michael and the CP.R 3 apostle are contemporary.

W. Horn (1937) differed somewhat with Porter in his analysis of the artists of the apostles.[5] Matthew and Bartholomew by Brunus, Thomas by a second artist, and James the Less (CP.L 3) by a less gifted hand, combining Brunus and Thomas styles, are the oldest figures on the façade. He further argued that the four central apostles are later and are products of the Brunus workshop. During this interval of time the influence of Byzantine ivories had made itself felt. James Major and Paul he considered by Brunus, while the John and Peter were carved by an assistant. He reasoned that the four south apostles (CP.R 3, 4, 5, 6) represent a sharp fracture in style which was synonymous with a break in time. A new phase has been inaugurated along with the side portals since he saw a connection between the right two apostles and the south portal. He further saw two hands in the four apostles. He concluded that the four north apostles were carved first; then the south four later and in a different style, after the new program including the side portals with frieze and tympana had been begun; finally the four central apostles still later, but delivered by the Brunus workshop. He related these conclusions to the architecture by reasoning that the moldings which flank the unidentified apostles to the right are later. Like Porter, Horn saw some Burgundian features in the right apostles, especially in the CP.R 4.

W. Horn's argument of a third hand for the James the Less (CP.L 3) is plausible; yet it can be stated with equal validity that it was carved by Thomas, but influenced in pose and in certain details of drapery by Brunus. The fact that there are stylistic connections between the right two apostles and the south portal sculpture does not necessarily prove that they are later. Top moldings of the panel, nimbuses, heads against capitals, and the socles of all four resemble the Matthew and Bartholomew of Brunus. It can be reasoned that all eight apostles on the front face of the façade are roughly contemporary. Horn saw some relationship between the right four apostles and the archangels, but was not sure whether the Michael was carved by the same hand.[6] He suggests the possibility of a development from archangel to Michael and an influence of the four central apostles and Burgundy making itself felt in the later work of Michael. He stated categorically that Michael has no connection with Chartres.

M. Gouron (1951) did not attribute the apostles to different sculptors, but he did believe that John and Peter were destroyed during the Albigensian heresy and remade after 1209.[7] Since Gouron dated the decoration of this portal of the first campaign between 1185 and 1195, this recarving of the two apostles is possible; yet if it is argued that the first campaign

---

4. *Ibid.*, vol. 1, 290.

5. W. Horn, *Die Fassade von St. Gilles* (Hamburg: Paul Evert, 1937), 28–32.

6. *Ibid.*, 34.

7. M. Gouron, "Saint-Gilles-du-Gard," *Congrès archéologique de France*, CVIII (1951), 113–114.

took place in the 1140's, these two apostles could not have been carved in the thirteenth century.

R. Hamann (1955) disagreed with all previous writers and evolved an elaborate system of attribution around basic Provençal styles and influences from outside regions.[8] Only two apostles, James Major and Thomas, were carved before 1116, his date for the plan change. According to Hamann, James Major (CP.R 1) was carved by the "Classic-Imitative Master" who was the designer of the first campaign and the originator of the proto-Renaissance. The style of James, which he considered the most progressive but the oldest in date, combined energetic action and archaic majesty or baroque Romanesque with a flat, static quality. His style, which appeared on several socles, was based on antiquity. Paul (CP.R 2) was carved by a different hand after the plan change and made to match James, when the latter was moved to its present location. Both Peter and John were created after the commencement of the second campaign for their present location on the left splay of the central portal.

Hamann's second sculptor was the Angoulême Master who carved the Thomas during the first campaign and was responsible, directly or through his workshop, for the James the Less after the plan change.[9] Matthew and Bartholomew by Brunus combined elements of both the Classic-Imitative Master and the Angoulême Master and were carved after 1116. Most details, according to his theory, originated in James Major and were part of the general development of style. He related the Bartholomew to James Major and to James the Less, carved by the Angoulême Master or his workshop in the second campaign.

The third sculptor associated with the apostles was the "Burgundian Master" or Michael Master who, according to Hamann, played a leading role in the second campaign.[10] This eclectic youth borrowed from the classic-imitative sculpture, but knew the Burgundy of pre-Autun times, such as the outer tympanum of Vézelay, fragments of which are located south of the abbey. He carved the Michael on the left side of the façade during the second campaign. His curvilinear forms and anatomical feeling through fine-lined drapery influenced the sculptors of the CP.R 3 and 4 apostles. But those apostles also displayed a stylistic connection with Paul. The two extreme right apostles (CP.R 5, 6) were attributed by Hamann to an eclectic helper of Brunus who evolved out of Brunus, but restudied the antique. The archangels were carved by a less sensitive sculptor under the influence of the Michael Master and the Thomas Master.

Hamann considered the Michael superior to the four unidentified apostles and concluded that the sculptor who carved Michael became the Headmaster of Chartres.[11] Further he claimed that the sculptor of John (CP.L 2), who he believed represented a stage toward Chartres, studied the Michael statue. John could not have been carved by the Master of Michael because the sculptor of John was too closely related to the Angoulême Master who created the Thomas. Also, for the same reasons, Peter was not the work of the Michael Master,

---

8. R. Hamann, *Die Abteikirche von St. Gilles und ihre künstlerische Nachfolge* (Berlin: Akademie-Verlag, 1955), 110–120.

9. *Ibid.*, 121–131.

10. *Ibid.*, 131–143.

11. *Ibid.*, 131–136.

but was carved by the hand of the Angoulême Master. Hamann thus has only the Thomas and the James Major for his first campaign.

It is difficult to follow Hamann's argument that James Major is earlier than the apostles signed by Brunus. He based his conclusions on the comparison with Roman sculpture and interpreted the rest of the apostles as a kind of stylistic interaction between a classic-imitative point of view and the flat and more Romanesque style of the Angoulême Master. These two styles were then permeated with a Burgundian element. He failed to recognize that the James Major represents an elaboration of the Brunus formula. It cannot be said that Matthew and Bartholomew are the result of the style of James toned down by the influence of the Angoulême or Thomas Master, since both the Matthew and Bartholomew and the Thomas and James the Less appear to be the work of two distinct personalities. Hamann's method seems extremely devious and complicated. The integrity of individual carvers gets lost in a morass of influences and counterinfluences. It is also highly problematical, to say the least, that the Michael is an early work of the Headmaster of the Chartres Royal Portals.

Early Christian Sarcophagi

Six of the seven sarcophagi illustrated in this book are on exhibition in the Musée d'Art Chrétien in Arles. All have been published in E. LeBlant, *Étude sur les sarcophages chrétiens antiques de la ville d'Arles* (Paris: 1878), in J. Wilpert, *I sarcofagi cristiani antichi*, 4 vols. (Rome: 1929), and in F. Benoit; *Sarcophages paléochrétiens d'Arles et de Marseille* (Paris: 1954).

Figure 18: Eucharistic Sarcophagus, end of the fourth century, local workmanship and Saint-Béat marble, from the crypt of Saint-Honorat where it was used as tomb of Saint Dorathia (Arles no. 10; Wilpert I, 234, Pl. 38, and III, 25; Benoit no. 9, 37, Pl. VI, 2, Pl. VIII, 4, Pl. XI, 1).

Figure 19: Christ giving Law to Peter, around 400, Carrara marble (Arles no. 17; Wilpert I, 21, 22, 52, 161, 180, Pl. XII, 1, 2, 4; Benoit no. 5, 36, Pl. IV, 2 to 4, Pl. V).

Figure 20: Hydra Tertulla, around 340, from crypt of Saint-Honorat where employed as tomb of Saint Genest (Arles no. 6; Wilpert III, 50, 315, Pl. XXXII; Benoit no. 2, 34, Pl. II).

Reliefs of Bases and Socles

A considerable amount of small-scaled, figured sculpture is located on and above the projecting pedestals of the central portal and on the socles which support the columns of the side portals (figs. 50–74). Since this sculpture would have had to be carved and put in place before the erection of the upper parts of the portals, it follows that this sculpture is contemporary with or more probably earlier than the apostles. On the other hand, the lion socles under the statues of James Major and Paul were carved after the apostles which they support. (Conclusions of other critics appear in Notes on Chapter 3.)

BASES OF CENTRAL PORTAL

The Cain and Abel scenes on the left bases of the central portal (figs. 50, 52) manifest a distinct style which can be associated with sculpture by the Thomas Master (figs. 21, 36). The Offerings of Cain and Abel (Gen. iv, 3–7—fig. 52) depict Cain on the right extending a sheaf of wheat, while Abel's offering of a baby lamb is being accepted by the hand of the Lord. This subject appears on Romanesque capitals in both Spain and France, but is found in reliefs on façades only at Modena and Saint-Gilles and frequently on Early Christian sarcophagi, several of which are at Arles. In the Early Christian examples Cain and Abel are nude, presenting their gifts. The Modena relief (fig. 53), depicting the figures in short skirts presenting their offerings to God in a mandorla, reveals stylistic connections with the Saint-Gilles

50. Saint-Gilles. Bases and socles of CP.L.

51. Bases and socles of CP.R.

52. Saint-Gilles. Offerings of Cain and Abel (CP.L 1). Thomas Master.

53. Modena, Cathedral. Offerings of Cain and Abel.

54. Saint-Gilles. Fragment from CP.L 2, Maison Romane, Saint-Gilles.

55. Saint-Gilles. Murder of Abel (CP.L 1). Thomas Master.

56. Angoulême. Left spandrel above central window.

57. Angoulême. Right spandrel above central window.

Cain and Abel relief, especially in the treatment of folds over the abdomen of Abel.[1] The Saint-Gilles figures are, however, contained by two low arches supported by channeled columns and appear pressed into the block. Repeated S-shaped folds on the hems, paired incised folds and V folds over the groin, and flying mantles animate both the Thomas and the Saint-Gilles Cain and Abel. If this relief is compared with a lunette of Angoulême (fig. 22) or the spandrels above the central window of Angoulême (figs. 56, 57), the origin of the Thomas Master becomes apparent. However, the sculpture by Wiligelmo on the façade of the Cathedral of Modena, probably completed by 1117 or 1120, seems to have influenced work on the façade of Angoulême, carved in the 1130's.[2] Therefore, stylistic relationships between Modena and Saint-Gilles can perhaps be explained by the intermediate role of western France.

The Murder of Abel by Cain (Gen. iv, 8—fig. 55), adjacent to the offering scene, exhibits a slightly higher relief and more cramped and violent action. Cain, on the left, with devil's mask behind his head, is pulling Abel's head by the hair and cutting his throat. Abel's soul is issuing from his mouth and being crowned and pulled upward by two angels which, with their wings under curving clouds, fill the upper part of the panel. The dramatic action is controlled within the frame by major vertical and horizontal axes. Cain's arrangement of drapery over abdomen and between legs resembles Abel's on the other relief. Clouds recall those over the hand of God in the offering scene. The bearded head of Cain with round drill holes for eyes is very similar to Peter's head, also by the Thomas Master (fig. 32).

A fragment, now in the Museum, located in La Maison Romane in Saint-Gilles and unfortunately recently encased in plaster, depicts sections of two arches springing from the remains of a capital (fig. 54). Under the left arch are the head, forearm, and wing of an angel. In the spandrel is a contorted man. Enough of the drapery of the angel and man is preserved to illustrate its stylistic connection with Thomas. The low arches springing from a capital, plus the estimated measurement of this fragment, if completed, corresponds to the Offerings of Cain and Abel. Thus this fragment once adorned the south face of the left outer bases (fig. 50). This scene probably is the Annunciation

The interlocking rondels on the north faces of the right bases (fig. 51) depict a centaur shooting an arrow at a stag on the left, and Samson and lions, and a lioness

1. G. Sanover, "Iconographie de la Bible d'après les artistes de l'antiquité et du moyen-âge," *Bulletin monumental*, LXXX (1921), 212–238.

2. A. K. Porter, *Romanesque Sculpture of the Pilgrimage Roads*, 10 vols. (Boston: Marshall Jones, 1923), vol. 1, 308–310, considered the Angoulême sculpture to have been "executed about 1110 or soon thereafter." With this too early date as a basis, he argued for a two-way influence between Italy and Angoulême.

nursing her cubs on the right. These two panels have profiled frames which are identical to the top and bottom moldings of the Offerings of Cain and Abel and the fragment in the Museum. The relationship between figures and ground and the positive voids are related to the Cain and Abel scene opposite. The bead-and-reel design of the left relief appears on the halos of Thomas and James the Less, while the circles with dots of the right jamb are also found on the neckband and cuffs of Thomas and James the Less. The gracefully rhythmic movement of the hunting scene carries one visually into the lion and lioness rondels; action starts with the cut-off, left edge acting as the point of departure and terminates with the same chamfered edge and turned pose of the lioness at the extreme right. Because of the moldings on the edges of these reliefs, they must have been carved for their present location.[3]

Balaam riding his Ass and stopped by the angel before the city gate (west side of base between two reliefs just discussed—fig. 51) has a composition similar to the Murder of Abel. Its badly mutilated surface does not allow analysis. Only the feathered wings of the angel and the undulating clouds remain for comparison with the murder scene.

Both sides of the base of the central portal originally had a unified design with similar compositions on their south and north faces and their west faces (figs. 50, 51). These reliefs rest on blocks of masonry which continue around the re-entrant angles. This interlocking system, found on the ornamented cornices above the reliefs as well, proves that this part of the façade was always in this form and never underwent any alteration. Further, since these scenes were carved by the Thomas Master, it follows quite naturally that they were part of the earliest work on the façade.

SOCLES OF THE RIGHT PORTAL

Each side portal has two pairs of columns flanking the entrance. On the right portal, the outer, large columns have no ornamental bases, while the inner columns are sustained by carved socles. The left one (figs. 58, 59) consists of three seated bears framing two frontal, crouching men, perhaps reflecting a traveling circus. The bears, by the silhouette of their backs, by the placement of tails and head at the corners, and by the erectness of their pose, give an extraordinary architectonic character to the socle. The little men appear squeezed between the voluminous bears. The treatment of folds of the man on the west face (fig. 52) is reminiscent of Abel's drapery (fig. 52) as well as the lower section of Peter's (fig. 28). The little man

----

3. The right-hand section of the right rondel is nineteenth-century. It is missing in the print of the façade of 1833 (fig. 202).

58. Saint-Gilles. Socle of RP.L (west face).
Thomas Master.

59. Socle of RP.L (south face). Thomas Master.

60. Socle of RP.R (north face). Thomas Master.

61. Socle of RP.R (west face). Thomas Master.

62. Saint-Gilles. Socle of LP.L.

63. Socle of LP.L (south face). Soft Master.

64. Socle of LP.R (north face).
Soft Master.

65. Socles of LP.R.

on the south face (fig. 59) has a long, flowing beard similar to Thomas' plus straight falling ridge folds which flank V folds like those on the legs of James the Less by the Thomas Master.

The right socle (figs. 60, 61) shows three telamones contorted to fit the square block. An ingeniously structural design results. The handling of the stomach of the left figure resembles the same area in Abel in the scene of offering (fig. 52). The hem of the garment with drilled holes is like Abel's cape, and the chevron pattern on the figure's mantle appears on Thomas and James the Less (fig. 21). These figures move freely in space and possess more plasticity than the figures of Cain and Abel. In many respects this socle is closer to the sculpture at Modena than to reliefs at Angoulême. Although the pose of the left-hand figure (see fig. 60) recalls the telamones on the façade portal of Modena, the drapery style resembles more closely the telamones of the Porta Pescheria of Modena of about 1130.

Do these two socles have any iconographical meaning beyond their decorative and structural function? Bears and apes were known to be the most popular pets in the twelfth century. The telamones might reflect the "jongleurs" who toured Europe.

SOCLES OF THE LEFT PORTAL

The inner socles of the left portal, depicting lions forcing a draped figure to the ground on the left side (figs. 62, 63) and a lion and a goat fighting on the right (figs. 64, 65), are not by the Thomas Master. The figures stand on bases of two torus moldings and a scotia, which are more elaborate and three-dimensional than the bottom of the telamon socle on the right portal (fig. 60). Animals and figures project outward in a more plastic manner and are more freely posed than the bears of the south portal. There is more interest in a free treatment of textures of fur. The drapery of the figure on the south face of the left socle (fig. 63) has broad, flaring, indented folds which are not related to the Thomas Master, but do seem to have a kinship with the drapery of the Soft Master (see figs. 26, 38). Since the Soft Master, after carving the CP.R 3, 4 apostles, was the major artist of tympanum, frieze, and lintel of the left portal, it is possible to argue that he is responsible for the two inner socles on the same portal.

Paired crouching lions support the large outer columns of the left portal (figs. 62, 65). This motif is Italian in origin. The lions, being paired with heads turned, point to a mid-twelfth-century date. In contrast to the right-hand inner socle, in which bunches of fur are depicted by lines incised on the rounded surface, the manes of the paired lions on the bases of the outer columns are conceived in three-dimensional, projecting bunches. Thus, they would seem to have been carved by a different sculptor or at a later date. It has been suggested that the location of lions as symbols of authority and justice flanking a portal, *inter leonese*, marks the place where jurisdictional matters were judged.

Are these two lion bases the only two preserved of the six which once supported all the large columns across the entire façade? It would not seem to be the case, since it is obvious from the shape of the bases of the columns of the right portal that paired lions could never have supported them. Perhaps these paired lions of the left portal were originally carved for the central portal, to cap the projecting pedestals? Their width of .60 meters is better related to the width of the pedestals (.80 meters) than are the smaller double socles of .50 meters, which presently surmount the pedestals. If their planned location was on the central portal, it follows that the original concept of this portal involved somewhat taller single columns on each side of the entrance, instead of the present paired columns.

LION SOCLES UNDER APOSTLES OF THE CENTRAL PORTAL

The four socles under the apostles of the central portal portray lions clawing and biting men or animals (figs. 66, 67). Since the heads of each pair of lions turn inward and since each pair is practically a mirror image of the other, it can be concluded that these socles were designed for this location as supports for the apostles. As discussed in Chapter 1, alterations were made to the bulbous cushions on which the apostle Paul stands, so that a better junction could be made between apostles and bases. The outer socles on each side have been completed along their western flanks (figs. 50, 51). On their rear sections, however, the blocks have been left unfinished (figs. 14, 15). This unfinished character can be interpreted as further proof of the late installation of these supporting socles.

The style and scale of these socles is consistent with their role of supporting the apostles. In spite of their damaged surfaces, it is possible to find certain characteristics which are related to other sculpture on the façade. The ropelike folds of the legs of the man under Peter (fig. 66) and the undercut curved folds between his legs can be found on the frieze, especially the upper frieze to the right of the central portal. Also accented bone structure, like the clawed figure under James, is seen in this same section of the frieze, especially in the Flagellation scene. The three-dimensional emphasis of the ram's coat (see socle under Paul—fig. 67) is entirely different from the incised surfaces of animals on the inner socles of the left portal (figs. 62, 65). Thus these lion socles appear to be later than the socles of the side portals and the reliefs on the projecting bases of the central portal. Furthermore, the socle under Paul

66. Saint-Gilles. Lion socles (CP.L 2, 1).

67. Lion socles (CP.R 1, 2).

68. Saint-Gilles. Double socle (CP.R), Calling of David (north face).

69. Double socle (CP.R), Winged griffin (west face).

70. Double socle (CP.R), David slaying Goliath (south face).

(fig. 67) was carved after the Paul statue was completed, whereas the socles under John and Peter (fig. 66) seem to be contemporary with the apostles they support.

DOUBLE SOCLES OF CENTRAL PORTAL

Two double socles, each supporting two columns, crown the outer projection of the central portal (figs. 50, 51). The double socles (figs. 68–74) possess a decidedly different style when contrasted with the socles of the side portals (figs. 58–65). Figures and animals are more plastically conceived and are set against a channeled ground which gives an illusion of space. In contrast to the relief sculpture on the bases of the central portal (figs. 50, 51), the contours of forms are rounded off gradually and do not have abrupt edges perpendicular to the ground. The problem of decorating these small socles differs somewhat from the more mural requirement of the much larger bases; yet these socles are obviously the work of a different hand.

On the north or inner face of the right socle (fig. 68) is depicted the Calling of David: the angel comes from the left and stands before David, who is seated on a stump, holding his lyre. His flock and a schematized tree fill the right section. This subject appears to be unique in Romanesque sculpture. The whole quietly animated scene takes place on inclined ground and against a channeled background. Drapery falls in loose ridge folds and reveals anatomy of legs, stomach, and chest. In the softness of the folds there is a relationship to the apostle CP.R 3 (fig. 26) by the Soft Master and the figure attacked by a lion in the socle of the left portal (fig. 63). It is necessary to jump ahead to the upper frieze to find the closest parallel in the Payment of Judas on the upper left of the central portal (fig. 136).

The west or outer side of this socle (fig. 69) depicts a griffin whose wings extend into the corner of the north face. The south side (fig. 70) shows David slaying Goliath, a subject depicted on capitals in Burgundy and Vienne. In this subtle composition, Goliath has been driven to the ground, and his bowed and contorted arms repeat the shape of his shield. The relief as a whole is slightly flatter; yet the drapery of David resembles the treatment of costume on the two figures on the opposite side. The entire socle is certainly the work of one hand.

The double socle on the north or left side of the central portal (figs. 71–74) depicts on its south face a lion and two men fighting. The bearded man on the left continues around from the west side (fig. 72) and prods the lion from the rear, while a man being clawed on the right thrusts a spear into the lion's chest (fig. 74). The protagonists rest on an inclined plane and against a channeled background, which is more deeply undercut than that of the David and Angel scene on the opposite socle. The spread-eagled figure on the west face recalls the figure on the LP.L socle

71. Saint-Gilles. Double socle (CP.L), Apes and camel (north face).

72. Double socle (CP.L), Figure (west face).

73. Double socle (CP.L), Lion and humans (south face).

74. Double socle (CP.L), Detail.

as well as the drapery style of the Soft Master (CP.R 3, 4—fig. 26). Certainly this double socle, like the David socle, bears no relationship to the Brunus apostles or the sculpture by the Thomas Master.

A pair of apes, struggling against their bonds, and a camel appear on the north face of this socle (fig. 71). Like the south side of the David socle, the relief appears to be flatter. The paneling of the background is wider and rises diagonally to the left. H. W. Janson connected these figures with the "sinner-apes" of Spanish Romanesque and, following a suggestion of M. Schapiro, discussed an additional, zoological significance of apes and camel as a reflection of commercial ties between North Africa and Provence.[4] The connotation of evil appears on the other side in the struggling lion and men.

In summary, the Cain and Abel reliefs and rondels of the projecting pedestals of the central portal (figs. 50, 51) and the socles supporting the inner columns of the right portal (figs. 58, 60) seem to be the creation of the Thomas Master, who carved Thomas, James the Less, and Peter (figs. 21, 28). The inner socles of the left portal (figs. 63, 64), more plastically conceived, appear to be closer stylistically to the Soft Master (CP.R 3, 4 apostles—fig. 26). The lion socles under the apostles John, Peter, James, and Paul of the central portal (figs. 66, 67) are later in date and display relationship in style with the upper frieze of the central portal. Finally, the double socles supporting paired columns (figs. 68–74) manifest common denominators with the upper frieze of the central portal in their greater illusion of space, established by the figures set against a channeled ground.

NOTES—CHAPTER 3
Reliefs of Bases and Socles

(1) *Reliefs of Bases of the Central Portal* (figs. 50–55)
A. K. Porter (1923) attributed the Offerings of Cain and Abel and the Murder of Abel to his "Angoulême Master" or Thomas Master.[5] M. Gouron (1951) pointed out that M. Formigé had interpreted the cutting off of the right rondel with the lioness and her cubs to mean that this panel originally was placed on the left side of a portal with the cut section next to the entrance.[6] Gouron concurred with this assumption and stated the possibility that these reliefs, which he dated in the thirteenth century, once adorned transept portals. As already

4. H. W. Janson, *Apes and Ape Lore in the Middle Ages and the Renaissance* (London: 1952), 47, fn. 87. See also F. Kobler, "Das Pisaner Affenkapitell in Berlin-Glienicke," in *Minuscula discipulorum; Kunsthistorische Studien Hans Kauffmann zum 70. Geburtstag 1966* (Berlin: Hessling, 1968), 157–164.
5. Porter, *op. cit.*, vol. 1, 273.
6. M. Gouron, "Saint-Gilles-du-Gard," *Congrès archéologique de France*, CVIII (1951), 115–116.

pointed out, the action of this entire right splay is unified with a subtle, rhythmic movement from left to right. These clipped-off ends have terminal moldings and start and stop this action. Further, by giving the outer circles the effect of a low arch, the designer brought about a harmonious relationship with the Cain and Abel scene and the fragment now in the Museum, on the opposite embrasure (figs. 51, 52). W. Horn (1937)[7] agreed with R. Hamann (1934)[8] in his attribution of these reliefs to the Master of Thomas. However, he thought that the two workshops which were active before his plan change were those of Brunus and Thomas. Horn pointed out that the masonry was continuous through these bases, and therefore he included this section of the central portal in his reconstruction of the first campaign.

R. Hamann (1955) attributed these reliefs to the sphere of the Thomas Master: Offerings of Cain and Abel very close, Murder of Abel by his workshop more plastic, and the others related to Thomas but possessing more movement.[9] On the other hand, he placed them after the change of plan of 1116. In his opinion these reliefs were part of the expansion of the central portal, necessary for the substructure of the four apostles which were originally planned for the front of the façade. Thus they were not part of his first campaign. The whole nature of his first design hinges on the interpretation of these reliefs and the construction of the areas of which the sculptures are a part. The dovetailing of blocks between the outer-projecting base and inner base, the harmonious design of the entire splays, and the style of the reliefs associated with Thomas who along with Brunus represents the oldest styles of Saint-Gilles—all point to the conclusion that these base reliefs were part of the earliest work on the façade and have not undergone any alteration.

(2) *Socles of Side Portals* (figs. 58–65)

W. Horn (1937) did not include the side portals in his design for his first plan of the façade.[10] He interpreted the socles of the south portal as being related to the Cain and Abel reliefs, but more plastic because of the continuation of the Brunus workshop. The socles of the north portal he characterized as displaying much higher relief with the animals emancipated from the block. R. Hamann (1955) saw two styles in these socles: one, an archaic style related to the reliefs of the central portal, and the other, a baroque and classic style connected with the Classic-Imitative Master or the Master of James Major.[11] He believed that the archaic style was later since it exhibited an influence from the other style. He divided the socles as follows: bear socle (RP.L) by the Thomas Master; telamone socle (RP.R) also by Thomas workshop; lions striking down man (LP.L) by the Classic-Imitative Master of James Major; lions and goat socle by the sculptor of the bear socle trying to emulate the socle opposite. In their chronological order, Hamann placed the side-portal socles earlier than their related apostles and earlier than the socle and bases of the central portal. Hamann has the

---

7. W. Horn, *Die Fassade von St. Gilles* (Hamburg: Paul Evert, 1937), 28.

8. R. Hamann, "The Façade of Saint-Gilles: A Reconstruction," *Burlington Magazine*, LXIV (January 1934).

9. R. Hamann, *Die Abteikirche von St. Gilles und ihre künstlerische Nachfolge* (Berlin: Akademie-Verlag, 1955), 127–128.

10. Horn, *op. cit.*, 33.

11. Hamann, *Die Abteikirche*, 101–107, 121–128.

bear socle carved by the Thomas before he carved the Thomas, and the lion-killer socle (LP.L) prior to the apostle James Major and before the David scene on the double socle of the central portal. Also the left double socle (CP.L) was, according to Hamann, carved by a member of the archaic workshop under the influence of the Classic-Imitative Master. There Hamann argued that the socles of the side portal were earlier than those of the central portal and that they, along with the inside and west faces of the double socles of the central portal, were carved before this plan change of 1116, while the base reliefs of the central portal and the socles under the four central apostles were carved during the early years of his expanded, second campaign.

It is difficult to agree with Hamann's conclusions. Obviously, they are tied up with his reconstruction of the first campaign. His design for the first campaign shows the socles of the side portals in place, the double socles of the central portal supporting double columns in the splays of the central portals, not on the projecting pedestals as now located, and all the twelve apostles in niches on the front plane of the façade. The bear socle and especially the telamone socle (RP.L and R) seem later than the Cain and Abel reliefs on the central portal, while the lions and man socle (LP.L) does not seem to be related to the Brunus and the Thomas Master, but to the right apostles (CP.R 3, 4), which appear to be somewhat later in date. This disagreement with Hamann's theme, however, does not preclude the possibility that the first design involved three portals, but it does take exception to his reconstruction of the central portal.

(3) *Four Lion Socles of Central Portal* (figs. 66, 67)

W. Horn's reconstruction (1937) shows these four socles in place under the apostles.[12] Horn thought that the four apostles of the central portal were planned for their present position, but were not put in place until the second expanded program had begun. Thus, in his opinion, four socles and four apostles were carved during the second campaign, but included in the design of the first. M. Gouron (1951) claimed that these socles originally supported four large columns framing two portals and were reused in the thirteenth century following the carving of two apostles and the general reuse of older materials in the reconstruction of the portals.[13] The manner in which these blocks have been carved, with plain joints where they join each other on each splay and with the outer ones projecting westward out beyond the square blocklike support, precludes Gouron's conclusion. These lion socles must have been carved to support the four apostles. R. Hamann (1955) related these socles stylistically to the rondels of Samson and the lioness and her cubs.[14] He considered that they were carved during the second campaign to support the four apostles which were planned for the front face of the façade. His conclusion is, of course, based on his reconstruction of the first design.

As already stated, there exists the possibility of another interpretation. At the start of the work on the façade, the four apostles (John, Peter, James Major, and Paul) were designed to stand directly on the pedestals with the Cain and Abel and rondel reliefs. Paul and James Major were completed by the Brunus Master for the right splays with no supporting socles.

---

12. Horn, *op. cit.*
13. Gouron, *op. cit.*, 114.
14. Hamann, *Die Abteikirche*, 128.

When the decision was made to heighten the portals, the four lion socles were carved with the resulting recarving of some of the bases of the apostles (see Paul—figs. 29, 11, 12). The fact that the socles under John and Peter (fig. 66) seem to fit together suggests that by the time Brunus carved the John and Thomas carved the Peter, the decision had been reached to raise the whole façade.

(4) *Double Socles of Central Portal* (figs. 68–74)

These two socles are intimately tied up with the varying solutions of the first design of the façade as opposed to the expanded program. R. Hamann (1934) placed these two double socles in the splays of the central portal in the position now occupied by the apostles, with only their inner and west faces carved before his plan change.[15] He placed, in his first plan, Paul and Peter in the areas now occupied by the acanthus panels, but pushed this section back flush with the rest of the apostles. John and James Major were planned originally for the extremities of the façade. His evidence for this conclusion was based on the difference in carving of the side of the socles and the prominent edges of the block (especially to the right of the Goliath scene and to the left of the ape and camel relief—see figs. 70, 71). He assumed that these edges and the flatter carving of these sides, plus the shift along the eastern face of the lion socle to a more linear style, were evidence of later work after the socles had been moved to their present position. The lack of relationship in size between the extended bases and these double socles would seem to back up Hamann's argument, since the projecting bases are (left and right) 1.00 and .85 meters on the same axis. On the other hand, if the four apostles were planned from the beginning for the splays of the central portal and if the deep bases with their projections were part of the original design, as their construction would lead one to believe, Hamann's theory is disproved. The sharp contrast in style between these socles and the base relief, plus their relative smallness in contrast to the size of the projection, might possibly suggest that they, together with the double columns, were not part of the original design at all and some other superstructure was planned for these projections.

W. Horn (1937) disagreed with Hamann and argued that the difference between the south and north sides of the left double socle was caused by weathering.[16] These sides are related iconographically, since they represented basic instincts: lion (devil), 2 apes (devil), and camel (wrath). He further argued that it was impossible to prove that the Goliath scene is later than the David scene.

R. Hamann (1955) added little to his previous analysis of these socles.[17] He did, however, conclude that only the inside and west faces of these double socles and the apostles Thomas and James Major were completed before his plan change of 1116. He linked the socles, especially the David one, with the Classic-Imitative Master of the James Major. If it is assumed that the James Major Master worked during the first campaign, it follows that Hamann's conclusions were justified. On the other hand, if the style of James Major is interpreted as an evolution of the Brunus formula of Matthew and Bartholomew, and if the construction of the bases is considered, Hamann's conclusions are erroneous.

---

15. Hamann, "The Façade," 19–29.
16. Horn, *op. cit.*, 49–51.
17. Hamann, *Die Abteikirche*, 105–107, 128.

CHAPTER 4

Sculpture of the Superstructure

THE friezes and tympana of Saint-Gilles comprise an extraordinary iconographical unity (see fold-out elevation and fig. 2). The sequence of scenes, according to the Gospels, is generally followed, although certain liberties are taken in order to fit scenes into different-shaped areas on the superstructure. The only scene which is far removed from its place in the Gospels is Christ anointed by Mary in the house at Bethany. This scene should follow the Raising of Lazarus on the left side of the central portal; rather, it is located on the left side of the right portal. In all instances, these sequential changes relate to the number of figures involved in each episode and to the desired compositional balance of each portal. Indeed, on the basis of the number of figures on the corresponding sides of the left and right portals, it seems that consideration was given to the total balance of the entire façade.

Several scenes are unique in Romanesque sculpture, while others appear only at Saint-Gilles and in monuments influenced by Saint-Gilles. Some episodes are found exclusively in Romanesque capitals. Several of the episodes appear only on Early Christian sarcophagi, which could be studied at Arles. This dependence on Early Christian monuments for subject matter has its parallels in the style of the apostles and the sculpture on the superstructure.

LEFT PORTAL

The tympanum of the left portal (fig. 75) contains the Madonna and the Christ Child enthroned. On the left are the three Magi bearing gifts, while on the right side an angel appears to Joseph. The only extant tympanum which combines the Madonna and Child Enthroned with the three Magi and the Dream of Joseph is the portal of Notre-Dame de Malpas at Montfrin (Gard—five miles northwest of Beaucaire). The tympanum of Montfrin, probably dated between 1178 and 1181, is a reflection of the original portal of Beaucaire, which, in turn, was based on the left portal of Saint-Gilles.

The central block of the tympanum depicts the Madonna and Christ Child inside a badly damaged tabernacle (figs. 75, 76). The Virgin and Child are enveloped in soft, voluminous drapery. The general flatness of the figure and the softness of folds are reminiscent of the CP.R 3 and 4 apostles by the Soft Master (figs. 26, 77). The loop folds over her chest, the mantle falling from her right arm, the articulation of legs through thin garments, and incised folds—all can be seen on the niche apostle CP.R 3 (fig. 77). Folds cover the feet and touch the ground, as on the CP.R 3 apostle. The Soft Master, the author of the CP.R 3 and 4 apostles, is certainly responsible for the Madonna and Child of the tympanum.

The frieze and lintel of the left portal depicts the Entry into Jerusalem. On the left side (figs. 78–80) is the preparation for the Entry (total of ten figures). The apostles proceed from left to right, and the one nearest Christ unties the reins of the donkey, which Christ prepares to mount. Certain details of figures, such as the oval folds across the chest, accordionlike treatment of upper arms, ponderation pushed downward and outward, and treatment of drapery over the ankles, resemble the Soft Master of CP.R 3 and 4 (figs. 26, 77). The folds extending down between the legs and pulled over the right ankle can be found both in the fourth, sixth, seventh, and eighth apostles and in the large apostle (CP.R 3). Perhaps more important than these stylistic parallels is the actual technique of carving. The detail of CP.R 3 (fig. 38) exhibits the softness of surfaces, yet the importance of edges to demarcate the folds. This same technique appears on the LP.L frieze. It can be concluded that the Soft Master, the author of the CP.R 3 and 4 apostles, carved this section of the frieze as well as the Virgin and Christ on the central block of the tympanum.

On the lintel under the tympanum (figs. 81, 85–87) is depicted the scene of the actual approach to the gate of Jerusalem by Jesus and his disciples. The diagonal and impelling action is carried through Christ and is only stopped by the reverse action of people spreading their cloaks in front of Christ, dropping palm fronds from trees, and watching from the city walls. To keep the action under control, the sixth, eighth, and eleventh figures turn their heads to the left. The figures have the same relatively squat proportions and relaxed poses as those in the left side of the frieze (fig. 78). Right legs of all figures are emphasized by curving mantles, and waists are accented

75. Saint-Gilles. Left portal, tympanum, Magi, Virgin and Christ Child, Dream of Joseph.

76. Left portal, Virgin and Christ Child. Soft Master.

77. Unidentified Apostle (CP.R 3). Soft Master.

78. Saint-Gilles. LP.L, Preparation for Entry into Jerusalem. Soft Master.

79. LP.L, detail. Soft Master.

80. LP.L, detail. Soft Master.

81. Saint-Gilles. LP., lintel, Entry into Jerusalem. Soft Master.

83. Early Christian Sarcophagus. Late fourth century. Arles, Musée d'Art Chrétien, 2.

82. Early Christian Sarcophagus. Arles, Saint-Trophîme. Adoration of Magi and Entry into Jerusalem.

84. Early Christian Sarcophagus. Late fourth century. Arles, Musée d'Art Chrétien, 18.

85. Saint-Gilles. LP, lintel, Entry into Jerusalem. Soft Master.

86. LP, lintel, Entry into Jerusalem. Soft Master.

87. LP, lintel, Entry into Jerusalem. Soft Master.

by horizontal folds. The general animated yet controlled character of the lintel with the dignified but relaxed disciples, slightly overlapping each other, resembles the Preparation scene. It follows, therefore, that the lintel and the left side of the frieze can be attributed to the same sculptor, and more specifically to the Soft Master.

In a convergence of iconography and style the format of the Entry into Jerusalem as a running, narrative frieze and the style of the figures bear comparison with Early Christian sarcophagi from the fourth century at Arles (figs. 82–84). The lower panel of the sarcophagus in Saint-Trophîme at Arles (fig. 82), although a shorter procession, was perhaps the source of the composition of the Saint-Gilles lintel, while other sarcophagi suggest closer stylistic connections (figs. 83, 84). However, the Romanesque relief is much lower and less undercut. Several Italian monuments, such as S. Leonardo al Frigido from Lunigiana (now in The Cloisters in New York), and the portal at Thines, north of Provence, as well as a capital in the east gallery of the Arles cloister, appear to be influenced by the Entry into Jerusalem of Saint-Gilles.

On the right side of the frieze (figs. 88, 90–92), citizens of Jerusalem, carrying palm fronds, approach the city gates. These seven figures, including the child about to climb a tree, are stylistically quite different from the opposite frieze and adjacent lintel. They are thinner, more isolated, and more three-dimensional, and they stand on a more steeply inclined plane. Mantles are buckled over the shoulders and fall straight downward between legs. In spite of the relative thinness of the figures they are more plastic and less relaxed when compared to those on the lintel and the opposite frieze. More movement is implied throughout the entire pose of the figures. These stylistic divergencies do not, however, detract from the compositional harmony between the two sides of the portals.

Another artist with a different artistic background must have carved this section. The pose of the left two figures is reminiscent of the archangel Michael (fig. 89). The arrangement of drapery and the anatomical interest are characteristic of both. The folds over the knee and across the waist of the boy on the right (fig. 92) are seen in the same places on the Michael. Allowing for the decrease in size and the resulting transformations, it would appear that the Michael Master carved the right side of the frieze.

The side blocks of the tympanum (figs. 93, 94), which complete the well-balanced composition of the tympanum, appear to be by a different sculptor than the Soft Master who created the Virgin and Child. Gestures of the Magi are accentuated, while their feet exert little pressure on the inclined plane. Mantles, which are buckled at their shoulders, cascade down the middle of their bodies. Accentuated gestures, elaborate costumes, and emphasis on revealing the body beneath the drapery relate

Joseph and the Angel to the Magi. The curve of the angel's wing and arm and scroll makes a bow with Joseph's arm as the arrow. These curves are echoed in the raised arms of the Magi.

The five figures of the side blocks of the tympanum seem to be the counterpart of the citizens awaiting the entry (LP.R frieze—figs. 88, 90–94). All wear the same costumes and possess the same thinness of mass and the same frozen articulation. The left-hand Magus is the second frieze figure from the left; but his right hand and arm plus the gesture are like the left figure on the frieze (LP.R frieze—fig. 90). The arrangement of mantle and emphasis on folds around the knee are related to the second frieze figure. The kneeling Magus has his counterpart in the two citizens of the extreme sides. The right-frieze figure has cuffs ornamented with jeweled circles, which are found on all three Magi. The ring folds on the boy's right wrist ornament the Magi. The mechanically stiff and disjointed gestures of the Magi appear on the LP.R frieze (compare the right standing Magus with the second citizen from the left) and are of marked contrast when compared with the relaxed gestures of the figures on the left frieze (fig. 78). The greater number and more minute folds are common denominators between the sides of the tympanum and the right frieze. The feet of the tympanum figures on the sides seem to hang on the steep ground like those of the citizens of Jerusalem, while the feet of the Madonna project straight outward on a flat, narrow block which is part of the throne. All these characteristics of the sides of the tympanum are related to the right frieze and are at variance with the Madonna and Christ Child. The Madonna and Child, however, portray many characteristics linking this central part of the tympanum to the left frieze and lintel and to the Soft Master of the CP.R 3 and 4 apostles.

If these stylistic relationships between parts of frieze and tympanum and the monumental statues in niches are valid, the sculptural work on the superstructure of the left portal can be divided between two artists. One carved the left part of the frieze, lintel, and enthroned Madonna and Child and is the Soft Master, the author of the two unidentified apostles (CP.R 3 and 4). The second artist created the right frieze and the two side panels of the tympanum and seems to be related to the Michael Master. The work on the superstructure of the left portal would, therefore, be divided between two sculptors: about two-thirds by the Soft Master and one-third by the Michael Master.

RIGHT PORTAL

On the right portal (figs. 95–110), the Passion of Christ is completed, following the sequence of episodes on the upper frieze of the central portal (to be

88. Saint-Gilles. LP.R, Citizens of Jerusalem. Michael Master.

89. Saint Michael (LP.L).

90. LP.R, detail. Michael Master.

91. Saint-Gilles. LP.R, detail. Michael Master.

92. LP.R, detail. Michael Master.

93. LP, tympanum, Three Magi. Michael Master.

94. LP, tympanum, Dream of Joseph. Michael Master.

95. Saint-Gilles. Right portal, tympanum. Crucifixion.

96. RP.R, frieze, Holy Women meeting Christ. Hard Master.

97. Saint-Gilles. Unidentified Apostle (CP.R 5). Hard Master.

98. RP.R, Christ. Hard Master.

99. RP, lintel, Holy Women buying Perfume. Hard Master.

100. RP, lintel, Holy Women at Sepulchre. Hard Master.

discussed later). On the central block of the tympanum is depicted the Crucified Christ flanked by John and the Virgin with symbols of the sun and moon above. The left-hand block contains the centurion and his assistant and the figure of the Church ("When the centurion and those who were with him, keeping watch over Jesus, saw the earthquake and what took place, they were filled with awe, and said 'Truly this was a son of God'"—Mat. xxvii, 54). On the right hand appears an angel who is pushing the figure of the Synagogue with such force that the latter is losing her crown, which is in the form of a temple.

The Crucifixion (fig. 95) is rarely depicted on Romanesque tympana. It can be seen on the late eleventh- or early twelfth-century portal of Saint-Pons, on the façade of the church of Condrieu, near Vienne, and on the tympanum of Champagne (Ardèche) of the late twelfth century, and on the portals of Berceto and Carpi in Italy. The Condrieu and Champagne portals are obviously influenced by Saint-Gilles. The only relief which contains Christ together with the figures of the Virgin, Church, sun and moon, John, Synagogue being thrust by an angel, is the Deposition in the Cathedral of Parma, dated 1178.

On the lintel appear two scenes (figs. 99, 100): the Holy Women buying Spices and the Holy Women at the Sepulchre (Mark xvi, 1–7):

> And when the sabbath is past, Mary Magdalene, and Mary the mother of James, and Salome, bought spices, so that they might go and anoint him. And very early on the first day of the week they went to the tomb where the sun had risen. And they were saying to one another, "Who will roll away the stone for us from the door of the tomb?" And looking up, they saw that the stone was rolled back; for it was very large. And entering the tomb they saw a young man sitting on the right side, dressed in a white robe; and they were amazed. And he said to them, "Do not be amazed; you seek Jesus of Nazareth who was crucified. He has risen, he is not here; see the place where they laid him. But go, tell his disciples and Peter that he is going before you to Galilee; there you will see him, as he told you."

As already stated, the Holy Women buying Spices from the Merchants occurs on reliefs only at Beaucaire and Arles, both in Provence. The Holy Women at the Sepulchre can be found on many Romanesque capitals and archivolts and on the tympanum of Condrieu, to the left of the Crucifixion, and on the right side of the south transept portal of San Isidoro at Léon, together with the Ascension and the Deposition.

On the re-entrant angle of the left frieze are the figures of Christ and the seated Mary Magdalene (*Noli me tangere*—John xx, 14–17). This scene (fig. 104) occurs on numerous Romanesque capitals, but is rare in larger-scaled compositions. The ad-

101. Saint-Gilles. RP, tympanum, Crucifixion, Church, Mary, John.

102. RP.R, detail, Holy Women. Hard Master.

103. RP. tympanum, Synagogue. Hard Master.

jacent scene (fig. 104) depicts Christ being anointed by Mary Magdalene, an episode which takes place chronologically after the Cleansing of the Temple in all four Gospels and directly after the Raising of Lazarus, found only in the Gospel according to John. Thus this scene should be located on the central portal, although the unusual Johannine chronology places the Cleansing of the Temple, the Raising of Lazarus, and Jesus being anointed by Mary in Bethany before the Entry into Jerusalem. The left figure, Judas, pointing to Christ, and Christ pointing to Mary who is wiping Christ's foot with her hair, would seem to be derived from the Gospel of John, xii, 1–9.

The extreme left-hand scene consists of Christ meeting two Disciples on the Road to Emmaus (Luke xxiv, 13–28—fig. 105). The disciple on the left is only a half figure and is part of the acanthus block directly above the unidentified apostle (CP.R 6). This scene appears in the cloister of Arles and on many Romanesque capitals, especially those monasteries located on the routes to Santiago de Compostela. The traveling disciples were equated with the pilgrims journeying to Spain.

On the right-hand frieze (fig. 98) the episode is either the three Holy Women telling the Disciples of the Resurrection of Christ (Luke xxiv, 10, 11) or Christ appearing to the Holy Women (Matthew xxviii, 9, 10). The corner figure is enthroned, which suggests the presence of Christ; yet he appeared to only two Marys, according to the Gospel of Matthew. The outer part of the frieze reveals two disciples on the west face and Christ with his hand raised in blessing on the north face. This scene is probably Jesus appearing to the Disciples (John xx, 19–22), although the left disciple is turning away from Christ. The figure of Christ is directly opposite the Christ of the *Noli me tangere*.

The seven figures on the right frieze (figs. 96, 98) correspond exactly to the number on the LP.R frieze, containing the citizens of Jerusalem (fig. 88). The figures are short and massive with proportionally large heads and hands accented by incised lines and ridges. Large loop folds of the mantle swing downward across waists. Oval, gouged-out folds indicate breasts. Surfaces are deeply undercut, and the raised folds display pronounced edges, not smooth, continuous curves. This same massiveness and heavy, manipulated folds appear in the unidentified apostles CP.R 5 and 6 by the Hard Master (fig. 97). Details such as the ring folds, jeweled neckbands, and drapery extending down over the feet—all can be found on one or both of the apostles in niches by the Hard Master. It is valid to conclude that the Hard Master who carved two apostles below and to the left of the right portal was responsible for this part of the superstructure.

The Holy Women at the Sepulchre occupies over one-half of the lintel (figs. 99, 100). The sculptor, placing two sleeping soldiers in the middle of the lintel with the three Holy Women moving to the left toward the merchants and to the right toward the angel, has created an extraordinarily sensitive composition. All figures are short and stocky with large, heavy hands and drapery. This lintel echoes the style found in the right side of the frieze, although the relief is not as high. This reduction in the depth of the relief, which can also be seen on the lintel of the left portal, assures the dominance of the tympana.

Since much of the projecting sections of the figures on the tympanum of the right portal (figs. 101, 103) has been broken off, the flatness of the sculpture is accentuated. The Crucified Christ has flowing hair and beard; ribs and navel are accentuated by ridges. His loincloth is ornamented by curving, undercut folds. Mary and the Synagogue are attenuated versions of the third Holy Woman on the right frieze (fig. 102). All details and arrangements of drapery can be seen on the lintel, right frieze, and the two apostles by the Hard Master.

In the three scenes on the left or north side of the frieze of the right portal (figs. 104, 109) there is a total of ten figures. Again we have a repeat of the LP.L frieze with its ten figures. Like the left portal, the frieze is harmoniously balanced left and right of the doorway. The two Christs (figs. 98, 107) appear on the same place and have similar poses. Four figures appear on both sides in the wider panels, if the kneeling sinner is omitted. Christ's gesture on the left side has its parallel in the raised hand of the third Mary.

The figure style of these three scenes (figs. 104–109) is uniform in spite of the differences in costume. Thick folds with accented edges envelop the bodies. Figures are short, but not massive like those on the lintel and right-hand side of the frieze. Heads are more in proportion to the rest of the figures. More drill work appears on the bench on which Christ sits and on jeweled collars and halos. Anatomy is revealed through the drapery, but it is not the heavy, lithic anatomy of the three Marys. The surfaces exhibit a crispness different from that on the lintel and right frieze. A different personality, who carved thinner, lighter, and more sinuous figures, is responsible for the left frieze.

The left-hand panel of the tympanum contains the figures of the Church and the centurion and his companion (fig. 110). The Church figure is similar to Mary in the area of the undergarment and feet, but displays a more curvilinear pose and a highly ornate costume of drilled geometric patterns. The centurion and his companion differ from the sculpture on the rest of the tympanum in costumes and in the treatment of the drapery. The more regular folds, the large amount of drill work, the turbaned head (see Disciples of Road to Emmaus—fig. 105), relate this block to the sculptor who carved the left frieze of the right portal. However, the Synagogue on the right

104. Saint-Gilles. RP.L, frieze, *Noli me tangere*. Christ in the House in Bethany. Michael Master.

105. RP.L, detail, Christ meeting Disciples on Road to Emmaus. Michael Master.

106. RP.L, detail, Christ meeting Disciples on Road to Emmaus. Michael Master.

107. Saint-Gilles. RP.L, detail, *Noli me tangere*. Michael Master.

108. RP.L, detail, *Noli me tangere*. Michael Master.

109. RP.L, detail, Christ in the House in Bethany. Michael Master.

110. RP, tympanum, Centurion and Companion. Michael Master.

(fig. 103) has the same loop folds and accented breasts as the Virgin Mary and thus was carved by the Hard Master.

Thus in the right portal the division of labor would seem to be slightly different than in the left portal. Here the Hard Master carved the central and right block of the tympanum, lintel, and right frieze, while another sculptor was responsible for the left side of the frieze and the left block of the tympanum.

On the basis of comparisons of details (figs. 108, 91) the assistants on the left and right portals seem to be one individual sculptor. The relative thinness of figures, the anatomical articulation, the extensive use of drill work, the drapery forms and treatment of folds, especially the hems, abrupt gestures, and pitted surfaces in concavities—all are characteristics which can be seen on the side blocks of the left-portal tympanum, the right frieze of the left portal (Citizens of Jerusalem), the left frieze of the right portal, and the left block of the right tympanum. Thus the work on the side portals seems to be divided about equally among three sculptors: the Soft Master (LP), the Hard Master (RP), and the Michael Master (on both portals).

It would appear that these side portals were carefully designed as a pair, since the compositions of the tympana are so closely related. In both portals the central panels have strong verticals, while the side sections have curves which echo the bend of the archivolts and countercurves which play against the frame and lead to the central figures. The gestures of the Magi (LP) and the centurion and companion and the bowlike forms of the wing of the angel and scroll in the Joseph's Dream (LP) and the angel's wing and the back of the Synagogue show an extraordinary affinity of design. Furthermore, the number of figures on each frieze corresponds: ten on both left friezes and seven on both right sides. In neither instance is the number entirely determined by iconographical requirements.

Is it possible to see a stylistic evolution in the portals or to date one earlier than the other? The moldings behind the heads of the right frieze consist of the cavetto concavity, but no flat fillets frame this molding, as in the left-portal frieze. Since the work of two sculptors, each of whom carved two apostles, is found on the tympana and since each of them appears to be the major sculptor of the two portals, it seems tenable to argue that work on these two portals was carried out simultaneously. The styles are quite distinctive, just as are the two pairs of apostles, CP.R 3, 4, and 5, 6 (figs. 26, 27). The fact that a third sculptor, the Michael Master, assisted both the Soft and Hard Masters is further proof of the contemporaneity of the two portals. Since there are more stylistic connections between the Michael and the reliefs the Michael Master carved on the left portal than between the Michael and the right-portal reliefs, it can be argued that the Michael Master carved the reliefs for the left portal first and then assisted the Hard Master on the right portal.

111. Saint-Gilles. Upper frieze (CP.L), Payment of Judas, Christ cleansing the Temple.

112. Upper frieze (CP.R), Christ before Pilate, Flagellation, Carrying the Cross.

CENTRAL PORTAL

The extensive frieze of the central portal (figs. 111, 112) is supported by the freestanding columns in front of the apostles in niches and continues along the sides and lintel of the central doorway. The left section (fig. 111), from north to south, consists of the Payment of Judas, Christ purging the Temple, Mary Magdalene and Martha imploring Christ to save their brother Lazarus, and the Resurrection of Lazarus. On the left side of the central portal is depicted Christ prophesying the Denial of Peter, while on the lintel appears Christ washing Peter's Feet and the Last Supper. The Betrayal and Arrest of Christ completes the central portal. The upper frieze to the right of the CP (fig. 112 from left to right) consists of Christ before Pilate, the Flagellation, and Simon carrying the Cross. Since this sculpture exhibits more spatial illusion and appears to have been created by the three evolving artists of the side portals, it follows that this upper frieze is the latest work on the façade.

The relief above the left splay of the central portal (fig. 113) depicts Christ prophesying the Denial of Peter (Mark xiv, 26–31):

> And when they had sung a hymn, they went out to the Mount of Olives. And Jesus said to them, "You will all fall away; for it is written, I will strike the shepherd, and the sheep will be scattered. But after I am raised up, I will go before you to Galilee." Peter said to him "Even though they all fall away, I will not." And Jesus said to him, "Truly I say to you, this very night, before the cock crows twice, you will deny me three times." But he said vehemently, "If I must die with you, I will not deny you." And they all said the same.

The left-hand block (fig. 113) has three figures seated in three-quarter pose facing Christ with four heads behind them, while the right one reveals Peter, the cock, and Christ. Great attention is paid to subtle revelation of anatomy from thighs to ankles. Heads are either beardless with classical profile or covered with full-flowing beards. The drapery is even more animated on Peter. By contrast, Christ seems calm and somewhat stiff. His parallel legs, equally articulated by the drapery, and the position of his body, with right hand raised, bring the entire scene to a subtle climax.

The closest stylistic connections with the side portals seem to be with the apostles of the left-hand frieze and lintel of the left portal by the Soft Master (fig. 114). The arrangement of the upper garments and oval folds over knees, and the straight-falling bundle of folds beside legs—all can be seen on the reliefs of both the central and left portals. The heads, with narrow eyes with sides curved downward, can also be seen (compare extreme left head in left frieze and the two beardless, profile heads on central-portal relief). This scene appears only at Saint-Gilles and Beaucaire, but is represented often in Early Christian sarcophagi in Arles (fig. 115). The Soft Master's renewed contact with Early Christian art perhaps explains the increased suggestion of space and partially accounts for the composition (compare heads in profile at Saint-Gilles and on the Arles sarcophagus).[1]

The lintel of the central portal (fig. 116) has two scenes: Christ washing Peter's Feet and the Last Supper. The former scene (John xiii, 3–12) appears on many Romanesque capitals, on lintels together with the Last Supper at Bellenaves (Allier) and at Saint-Pons, and on Early Christian sarcophagi (fig. 119). The Last Supper is portrayed on the lintels of several churches in France such as Saint-Bénigne at Dijon, Condrieu, Thines, Nantua, as well as in several churches in Italy, such as the "pontile" at Modena. The lintel of Saint-Gilles is about one-fifth narrower than the adjoining side strips of the frieze, forcing the figures into tighter areas. Extensive damage to large sections makes it difficult to analyze. In the Washing scene (John xiii, 3–12—fig. 117) the treatment of the drapery with thick, heavy folds which are modeled by planes separated by several edges on their convexities is similar to the style of the reliefs on the lintel of the right portal by the Hard Master (see details of the merchants, fig. 118) or the Holy Women on the right side of the right portal (fig. 96), also by the Hard Master.

The Last Supper (figs. 120, 121) is badly damaged: the second figure from the left is largely effaced, the third mostly recast in concrete. All but the right two faces are entirely defaced. The same thick folds animate surfaces. The left-hand disciple is close stylistically to the seated merchant on the lintel of the right portal. The carving techniques and surface textures all find parallels in the reliefs by the Hard Master as well as the two apostles by the Hard Master.

Purging the Temple (fig. 122) shows Christ driving out two pigeon merchants, another merchant, a moneylender, two oxen, and two sheep (John ii, 14—17). It is, to my knowledge, the only depiction of this scene in Romanesque sculpture with the exception of a capital at Lubersac. Christ, framed by the largest of the four arches, pushes the nearest merchant with his left hand, while his raised right hand holds a whip. The four animals in the lower right of the scene echo the action of the figures being expelled. The drapery of Christ reveals both knees clearly, and the mantle is looped across the stomach and sags down to the ankles. Halo and border of bodice are animated with drill work. This figure of Christ is almost identical to the Christ in *Noli me tangere* (fig. 123) on the R.P.L by the third sculptor of the side portals, the Michael Master. The four merchants are related to the inhabitants of Jerusalem on

---

1. It is of interest to note that the Raising of Lazarus, which is adjacent to this scene, is depicted on the same sarcophagus in Arles (fig. 115). See V. Lassalle, *L'Influence antique dans l'art roman provençale*, Revue archéologique de Narbonnaise, 2 (Paris: Editions E. de Boccard, 1970), 95/108 and Plates XLV, XLVII for more comparisons between Roman and Early Christian sarcophagi and Saint-Gilles sculpture.

113. Saint-Gilles. CP.L, frieze, Christ's Prophecy of Peter's Denial. Soft Master.

114. LP.L, detail, Preparation for Entry into Jerusalem. Soft Master.

115. Early Christian Sarcophagus. About 325. Christ's Prophecy of Peter's Denial. Arles, Musée d'Art Chrétien, 20.

116. Saint-Gilles. CP, lintel, Christ washing Peter's Feet, Last Supper. Hard Master.

117. CP, lintel, Christ washing Peter's Feet. Hard Master.

118. RP, lintel, Holy Women and Merchants. Hard Master.

119. Early Christian Sarcophagus. About 400. Christ washing Peter's Feet. Arles, Musée d'Art Chrétien, 17.

120. Saint-Gilles. CP, lintel, Last Supper. Hard Master.

121. CP, lintel, Last Supper. Hard Master.

122. Saint-Gilles. CP.L, frieze, Christ cleansing the Temple. Michael Master.

123. RP.L, detail, *Noli me tangere*. Michael Master.

124. LP.R, detail, Citizens of Jerusalem. Michael Master.

the right side of the left portal (fig. 124), also by the third sculptor. The left merchant (fig. 124) is like the third figure with arm raised, and the right-hand merchant resembles other figures on the left-portal frieze in drapery arrangement, stance, and body movement. All the figures have the hems of both front and back of the bottom of skirts showing and the same mantle buckled over the right shoulder.

Mary and Martha beseeching Christ to save their brother Lazarus and the Raising of Lazarus complete the front face of the left side of the central portal (figs. 125, 127). The figure of Christ is a slightly more attenuated version of Christ in the adjacent scene, while the heads are identical. Both kneeling supplicants have the same treatment of drapery as appears on the merchants. Numerous curvilinear folds envelop the forms, and great variety is achieved through the difference in intervals between folds. These kneeling figures are almost exact duplicates of Mary washing Christ's Feet in the RP.L frieze (fig. 126) by the Michael Master. Since this scene is on the same block as Christ purging the Temple and is paralleled stylistically, it is obviously by the same sculptor.

The badly damaged scene of the Raising of Lazarus (fig. 127) has only three figures: Christ on the south face of the re-entrant angle and Lazarus and a man starting to unbind Lazarus on the west face. This episode (John xi, 38–44), which appears often in Early Christian art, especially in sarcophagi, can be seen in Romanesque sculpture only on capitals at Arles, Moissac, Vézelay, Vienne, and on the Chichester reliefs and on the lintel of the south portal of the church of the Holy Sepulchre in Jerusalem.[2] From the evidence of surfaces and the general shape of heads and hair, it would seem to be by the same artist who carved the last two scenes discussed.

The right side of the central frieze on the front face of the façade (fig. 112) consists of three scenes: Christ before Pilate, the Flagellation, and Carrying the Cross.

The whole action of the Christ before Pilate (fig. 128) is gracefully executed with a marked projection of the relief. The humble Christ with bowed body, being pushed and pulled by Pilate's attendants, as contrasted with the regal and authoritarian Pilate, who sits solidly on his throne, is emphasized by the variety of poses of the secondary figures (fig. 128). Drapery is crisp and clearly defined; folds are doubled with extra delineations in their concavities. Is the sculptor who carved this scene a new artist, or does his work appear elsewhere in the parts of the frieze already discussed? It seems quite possible that he is the same person who carved the Purging of the Temple and the Lazarus scenes. If the Christ of the Purging of the Temple

---

2. See A. Borg, "Observations on the Historiated Lintel of the Holy Sepulchre, Jerusalem," *Journal of the Warburg and Courtauld Institutes*, XXXII (1969), 25–40.

(fig. 129) is compared with this Christ, one can see similarities in drapery, proportions, and arrangements of garments; yet the Christ being led to Pilate has a more intense face. The pushing figure is similar to the boy pulling the hesitant Jew on the LP.R. The treatment of feet on the ground line resembles the citizens of Jerusalem (LP.R), the Magi and Joseph (LP tympanum), and details on the RP by the third hand. The subtleties of the treatment of drapery, which distinguish these figures from all others on the frieze, are the extra incised folds in the concavities of the major folds. We find this feature in the apostles signed by Brunus (fig. 17) and in the three apostles on the central portal, which represent an advanced stage of the Brunus evolution. Furthermore, the intensity of the expression on Christ's face and the extra drill holes in the corner of the eyes is reminiscent of the Paul of Brunus (see fig. 33).

It would seem that this sculptor, the Michael Master, carved the inner sides of the side portals (LP.R, RP.L), the side blocks of the left tympanum, and the left block of the tympanum of the right portal, then the Purging and Lazarus scenes, and finally the scene of Christ before Pilate. In his late work the figures project more from the ground, and the stiff, almost frozen attitudes give way to a gracefully rhythmic and interlocking composition. This evolution of the third sculptor's style can perhaps be explained by new contacts with Early Christian art, since this same scene is found on innumerable sarcophagi (fig. 130) and rarely occurs in Romanesque sculpture except at Beaucaire, the church of Champagne, a few capitals, and on the pontile at Modena. In his latest work at Saint-Gilles he may have arrived at a stage where the subtle articulation of forms and the surface vitality of his life-size Michael could be successfully projected in smaller reliefs. On the side portals the Michael Master was assisting the Soft (LP) and Hard (RP) Masters. On the central portal he seems to be responsible for more sculpture than either the Soft or Hard Masters.

The Flagellation scene (fig. 131), which is on the same block as the Christ before Pilate, seems to be by the same hand responsible for the Christ before Pilate just discussed. Garments reveal action of figures, poses are graceful, and gestures seem subtly rendered. The exaggerated anatomy of Christ is similar to the treatment of the man being clawed by a lion on the socle under the Apostle James (fig. 67). The badly damaged Simon carrying the Cross (fig. 132), which decorates a separate block, is closely associated stylistically with the Flagellation scene: same costumes, same carving techniques. These last two scenes of the Passion do not possess the incised extra lines in concave folds, but all other characteristics unite them with the Christ before Pilate relief. Both of these scenes are rarely represented in Romanesque art except in capitals. The Flagellation and Carrying the Cross appear at Beaucaire and at Modena, while the Flagellation appears in the east gallery of the Arles cloister.

125. Saint-Gilles. CP.L, frieze, Raising of Lazarus. Michael Master.

126. RP.L, detail, Christ in House in Bethany. Michael Master.

127. CP.L, frieze, Raising of Lazarus. Michael Master.

128. Saint-Gilles. CP.R, frieze, Christ before Pilate. Michael Master.

129. CP.L, Christ cleansing the Temple, detail. Michael Master.

130. Early Christian Sarcophagus. About 400. Christ before Pilate. Arles, Musée d'Art Chrétien, 17.

131. Saint-Gilles. CP.R, frieze, Flagellation. Michael Master.

132. CP.R, frieze, Carrying the Cross. Michael Master.

133. Saint-Gilles. CP.R, Betrayal. Michael Master.

134. LP.L, Christ meeting two Disciples on the Road to Emmaus. Michael Master.

135. CP.R, Kiss of Judas. Michael Master.

The two blocks on the right-hand splay of the central portal (figs. 133, 135) depict the Betrayal and Arrest of Christ. On the left edge Peter cuts off the ear of Malchus, the slave of the high priest, while the crowds of jeering Jews and soldiers press around Christ, who is being identified for them by the kiss of Judas. These scenes are found on capitals, friezes, and lintels across southern Europe. Both the sections of the frieze on the side splays of the central portal terminate in a profile head looking outward on the edge of the façade. The reliefs thus correspond in compositional design, as did the friezes of the side portals. The drapery of the figures does not possess the softness and slick character of that in the relief opposite by the Soft Master of the left portal. Instead, the treatment of the skirts of the attendant figures and of the long mantles of Christ and Judas have many stylistic parallels with the third side-portal sculptor in such scenes as the Citizens of Jerusalem (LP.R). The placement of feet on the inclined plane and the type of shoe-sock and its treatment are identical in figures on the side portals by the third sculptor. Finally, several of the heads are extremely close to those in the scene of Christ meeting two Disciples on the Road to Emmaus (RP.L—fig. 134). Thus it would seem as though all three sculptors who created the side portals collaborated on the central portal itself: the Soft Master of the left portal carved Christ prophesying Peter's Denial on the left, the Hard Master of the right portal created the lintel of Christ washing Peter's Feet and the Last Supper, and the third sculptor, the assistant on both side portals, was responsible for Christ's Betrayal. Following the completion of the Betrayal panels, this third sculptor completed the scenes of the Purging of the Temple, Raising of Lazarus, Christ before Pilate, Flagellation, and Carrying the Cross—probably in that order.

Two scenes on the upper frieze of the central portal remain to be discussed. On the left side, the Payment of Judas is a double scene (figs. 136, 137), with two Jews arguing about the bribe, and Judas receiving money from the high priest Caiaphas— scenes which are unique in Romanesque sculpture with the exception of reliefs at Beaucaire and Modena. The partially empty arcade divides the two parts of the story. Heads are no longer placed against a concave molding; rather, they are either framed by arches to set them back in space or in front of the supports to suggest their projection from the backdrop. Large feet are placed precariously on the steep ground plane. Five of the seven figures are dressed in short skirts with feet encased in leather shoes. Both Caiaphas and Judas are garbed in long cloaks with round, thick folds accenting the edge of their mantles. The treatment of drapery is more simplified than in any of the figures of the side or central portals. The awkward gestures of both Caiaphas and Judas and the crudely modeled heads impart a kind of frozen intensity. Much of the carving seems low in quality, especially the figure between Judas and Caiaphas. The soft relief style, together with the spatial effect of the protagonists set against an arcade, recalls the Angel appearing to David, the double socle of the central portal (fig. 68). The David socle, however, seems to be superior in quality. This double scene was not carved by any of the three sculptors involved in the side or central portals, but by an assistant who also completed the re-entrant angle on the right side of the central portal (fig. 138). There, the three figures in short skirts are identical with the whispering Jews on the extreme left of the upper frieze.

CONCLUSION:

The Soft Master: Apostles CP.R 3, 4; Virgin and Christ enthroned (tympanum of LP); Preparation and Entry into Jerusalem (left frieze and lintel of left portal); Christ prophesying Peter's Denial (left frieze of central portal).

The Hard Master: Apostles CP.R 5, 6; Crucified Christ, Virgin, John, Synagogue (central and right blocks of tympanum of RP); Holy Women buying Perfume and Holy Women at Sepulchre (lintel of RP); Christ appearing to Holy Women and to Apostles (right frieze of RP); Christ washing Peter's Feet, and Last Supper (lintel of CP).

Third Master (Michael Master): Michael and Dragon, Archangels and the Devil, Citizens of Jerusalem (right frieze of LP); Three Magi and Joseph's Dream (two side blocks of tympanum of LP); Road to Emmaus, *Noli me tangere*, Christ in House in Bethany (left frieze of right portal); Centurion, attendant, and the figure of the Church (left block of tympanum of right portal); Arrest and Betrayal of Christ (right frieze of CP); Purging the Temple and Raising Lazarus (upper left frieze of CP); Christ before Pilate, Flagellation, and Carrying the Cross (upper right frieze of CP).

Fourth Sculptor: Double scene of Judas receiving Silver (left-hand side of CP frieze); three figures (to the left of Christ before Pilate).

FRAGMENTS OF TYMPANA

In the Musée de la Maison Romane at Saint-Gilles are the fragments of a tympanum. One is the central piece of a large tympanum depicting the lower half of Christ enthroned with the kneeling Virgin on the left (figs. 139, 141). Was it originally the Christ of a Last Judgment in the central portal of the façade? The present sculpture (fig. 2) is a baroque restoration and seems to contain no medieval fragments. In spite of its eroded surface, this fragment of Christ possesses an articulation of form and vitality which is lacking in the Madonna and Child on the left portal (fig. 75) by the Soft Master. The garments of the kneeling Virgin are pulled tightly over her legs as ridge folds of different intervals give textural interest. Her mantle falls over both arms and makes curving loops over her stomach. The double cloak

136. Saint-Gilles. CP.L, frieze, Payment of Judas.

137. CP.L, frieze, Whispering Jews.

138. CP.R, frieze, Three soldiers.

139. Saint-Gilles. Fragment of seated Christ. Maison Romane, Saint-Gilles.

140. Paul (CP.R 2), detail.

141. Fragment of Christ, detail.

142. Saint-Gilles. Church of Saint-Martin (?). Fragment of a tympanum of the Last Judgment. Maison Romane, Saint-Gilles.

of Christ reveals the anatomy and extends downward in bunches of raised folds to the feet. The terminations of drapery give a serrated effect. None of these characteristics can be found in the sculpture by the Hard Master or the third hand, the Michael Master. The closest stylistic parallel on the façade would seem to be the apostles Paul and John by Brunus with drapery animated by numerous ridge folds (fig. 140).

The other relief in two fragments (fig. 142) discovered by Marcel Gouron in 1949 in the wall of a house in Saint-Gilles includes four apostles with two angels, one of whom is holding a crown of thorns.[3] This scene is the right-hand section of a Last Judgment. Many characteristics associate these two fragments with the relief of the Christ prophesying Peter's Denial (fig. 113). The diagonal and slightly overlapping placement of figures, legs accentuated by folds drawn tightly over them, undecorated bodices, mantles falling from shoulders over arms, and vertical groups of folds terminating in serrated edges—all find parallels in the Saint-Gilles scene. The closest similarity appears in the heads (compare the head of the extreme right or left apostle on the tympanum fragments with that of the second from left seated apostle on the frieze). Both heads have identical beards falling on receding chins. The youthful head (fig. 142) resembles the classical profile head on the frieze. In spite of all these related features, the surfaces do not reveal the softer, polished, and ivorylike nature of those on the relief of Peter's Denial. The sculptor who carved the fragment is certainly strongly influenced by the Soft Master. The apostles of the relief also are related to the Christ and especially the Virgin of the other fragment (figs. 139, 141): folds over legs, firmly placed feet and pronounced toes, and serrated hems of garments. It would be untenable, however, to argue that this relief and the Christ are part of the tympanum of the central portal, since the present restored surface of the tympanum would have to be pushed back considerably to allow for the depth of the relief, since the type of rock is different, and since placing these pieces on the façade of Saint-Gilles overlooks the possibility of their placement on another portal such as the transept of the abbey or on one of the several parish churches in Saint-Gilles.

NOTES—CHAPTER 4
Sculpture of the Superstructure (figs. 75–142)

R. de Lasteyrie (1902) believed that the frieze and tympana were part of a later campaign.[4] The Betrayal he placed in the thirteenth century or in the restorations of the 1650's or

---

3. M. Gouron, "Découverte du tympan de l'église Saint-Martin à Saint-Gilles," *Annales du Midi*, LXII (1950), 115/120. This relief was exhibited in Cleveland in 1967. See W. D. Wixom, *Treasures from Medieval France* (Cleveland: The Cleveland Museum of Art, 1967), 120–121, 359, no. III 38.

4. R. de Lasteyrie, "Études sur la sculpture française au moyen-âge," Académie des inscriptions et belles-lettres, Fondation Piot, *Monuments et mémoires*, VIII (1902), 108–115.

modern. He found the left side of the central portal of mediocre quality, but the right side better, showing possible influence from Burgundy and the Île-de-France.

A. K. Porter (1923) divided the frieze into two campaigns.[5] The central frieze, he believed, was part of the first campaign and carved at the same time as the apostles. This part of the frieze he attributed to the "St. Gilles Master," although he stated that the entire central frieze was not the work of one hand. This hand, according to A. Priest (1923), carved the south lintel at Chartres after developing his style further at La Charité-sur-Loire and Montmorillon.[6] Porter dated the two side portals and the two angels considerably later and argued that they were carved by a new group of sculptors, whose style, however, was influenced by the earlier work. The fact that the frieze of the central portal was carved by the three sculptors of the side portals and exhibits a stylistic development precludes Porter's argument. Further, Priest's argument that a Saint-Gilles sculptor carved the lintels of the right portal of Chartres is questionable on two accounts: (1) there seems to be absolutely no stylistic connection between the two monuments; (2) the two monuments are roughly contemporary with Chartres, probably finished earlier.

W. Horn (1937) emphasized the iconographical unity of frieze and tympana as part of the second and completely new campaign.[7] He further believed that work started on the south portal, then jumped to the north, and finally ended with the central. Horn opposed critics who thought that the side portals were by different masters. Instead, he reasoned that the side portals were a stylistic unity with different hands executing them, but all reliefs were designed by one leading artist. He argued that the leading artist did the lintel and tympana on the side portals and the lintel of the central portal and that his latest work was the scene of Christ's Prophecy of Peter's Denial. A pupil did the left strip of the central-portal frieze and the rest of the central portal except the right strip. According to Horn, a new and different hand was responsible for the right frieze of the central portal. Horn's argumentation concluded that the three Holy Women at the Sepulchre and the three Holy Women buying Perfume were the most primitive; then the north portal presented a more relaxed and articulated style, as seen in freer folds and greater movement in drapery. He backed up this theory with an analysis of the construction, which seemed to him to be more developed in the north portal than in the south. Details were more clarified in the north portal, and the figures were more pronounced in their three-dimensionality. He finally concluded that certain sections of the portal were by different hands, but that the whole frieze was a continuous development, which was gradual and was not the simultaneous work of different artists, but rather a continuous sequence of development. He reinforced this theory by referring to the development of ornament.

According to Horn, the final phase of construction was the frieze of the central portal.[8] Horn divided the central portal as follows: the Master of the Side Portals carved the central lintel of Christ washing the Feet and Last Supper plus the Betrayal (badly damaged 1562

5. A. K. Porter, *Romanesque Sculpture of the Pilgrimage Roads*, 10 vols. (Boston: Marshall Jones, 1923), vol. 1, 280–290.

6. A. Priest, "The Masters of the West Façade at Chartres," *Art Studies*, I (1923), 28–44.

7. W. Horn, Die Fassade von St. Gilles (Hamburg: Paul Evert, 1937), 35–39.

8. *Ibid.*, 40–45.

and poorly restored 1650–1654) and Christ's Prophecy of Peter's Denial. He attributed the more voluminous folds, greater plasticity, and stronger articulation to the later date of this sculpture. The painterly, illusionistic style started in the side portals and increased in the central. The left strip of the central, Lazarus scenes, Christ cleansing the Temple, Horn connected with the Betrayal, but the Payment of Judas was unrelated to the side-portal frieze. Horn believed that the last work on the façade was by the Master of the Flagellation group whose work was related to the earliest work by Brunus, his Matthew and Bartholomew. This close stylistic relation to Brunus led Hamann and Porter to put this part of the frieze in the first campaign; but Horn thought that this sculpture, including the Christ before Pilate, was the latest on the façade and combined the style of the side portals with details from Brunus and thus could not be contemporary with the apostles, as Porter thought.[9] The Flagellation and Christ before Pilate contained a vitality and sense of dramatic movement not seen in Brunus' work. Horn further speculated either that the Master of the Side Portals died or that differences of opinion arose about the whole treatment or arrangement of the central frieze, with the result that the central frieze could not be contemporary with the apostles and the side portals forty years later, as Porter had argued.

M. Gouron (1951) was inclined to think that parts of the central-portal frieze on the north side are older and originally designed for another place.[10] Gouron further thought that parts of the frieze once decorated areas under a projecting pavilion of the nave, as on the Cathedral of Nîmes. He believed that the later, side portals utilized dismantled pieces plus new ones. The Betraying of Christ he thought was carved in 1655, and all parts of the frieze with undecorated moldings over them were remade.

The iconographical unity of the frieze and tympana plus the strong stylistic relationships between various sections would seem to prove the impossibility of dividing the portals into two quite distinct periods in time. Thus A. K. Porter's theory that the central frieze, because of its reflections of Brunus, is part of the first campaign would seem incorrect, since on the frieze of the central portal there are also stylistic carry-overs from the large apostles as well as from the friezes and tympana of the side portals. For the same reasons M. Gouron's conclusions seem wrong. R. de Lasteyrie placed all the frieze in the second campaign, but had decades separating their completion. Horn, on the other hand, believed that all the frieze was part of one campaign, but the second campaign was not carved at once, but over a period of time with a definite stylistic evolution. It is difficult to follow Horn's evolution from the frieze and tympanum of the right portal to the left portal and then to the central frieze. It is true that the architectural moldings behind the right frieze appear more archaic. But there are so many common denominators in arrangement, number of figures, and style that a more logical conclusion is one contemporary campaign with three different sculptors involved. The Soft Master, the sculptor of the unidentified apostles, CP.R 3, 4, carved most of the left portal, assisted by the Michael Master, while the Hard Master, the sculptor of CP.R 5, 6 apostles, was responsible for the right portal, probably assisted by the Michael Master. Since the third sculptor, or Michael Master, was responsible for about one-third of the sculpture of both side portals, it follows that the work on the side portals was carried on simultaneously.

9. Porter, *Romanesque Sculpture*, vol. 1, 293.

10. M. Gouron, "Saint-Gilles-du-Gard," *Congrès archéologique de France*, CVIII (1951), 115–117.

Further, since all three sculptors of the side portals worked on the frieze and lintel of the central portal, it follows that the central portal is later than the side portals. The clergy certainly determined the iconographical pattern.

R. Hamann (1955) created a theory of complicated interrelationship between three different points of view: the classic-imitative style, the Toulouse archaic-imitative style, and the Burgundian curvilinear style.[11] The entire frieze and three tympana were carved in these three styles (with many influences of one style or another) by different hands, all under the leadership of the Master of the Michael whose style evolved from his Burgundian background and paved the way for the Royal Portals of Chartres, where the Michael Master became the Headmaster and carved the central portal. The Michael Master with a knowledge of pre-Autun Burgundian sculpture came under the influence of the classic-imitative Master of James Major and the archaic-Toulouse Master of Thomas and then evolved toward the monumental style of Chartres.

R. Hamann saw the continuation of the classic-imitative style in its purest form in the scene of the Payment of Judas of the CP.L and the three soldiers guarding Pilate's palace on the CP.R frieze.[12] He thought that these reliefs were not by the Master of James Major, but followed his style. The LP.L frieze was executed, according to Hamann, by the classic-imitative workshop, but exhibited a victory of the fine-line style, which was synonymous with the Burgundian curvilinear point of view of the Michael Master. The lintel of the left portal was carved by the same hand following the overlapping technique of Roman reliefs of processions. The Christ of the Entry he considered somewhat different and possibly by another hand. The citizens of Jerusalem (LP.R) were the only figures carved by the Michael Master. The artist of Christ's Prophecy of Peter's Denial on the central portal grew out of the left portal, but he had studied Roman and Early Christian sarcophagi and the archaic-imitative Toulouse style. He considered the figures of Christ and Peter quite different from the rest of the scene. He related the Betrayal to Christ's Prophecy of Peter's Denial on the grounds of space-composition and drapery, but concluded that one hand did the major figure and another did the rest of the two scenes. He argued against Gouron's conclusions that the Betrayal was seventeenth-century, since the heads were related to those of the Christ and two Pilgrims on the Road to Emmaus, preserved behind the capital on the RP.L frieze. Since both the restorations of the seventeenth century and the nineteenth century can be identified on the panels, it follows that Hamann is correct in this last observation.

The Toulouse archaic-imitative style was found by R. Hamann in the Christ before Pilate.[13] The Toulouse fold style was influenced by the Sarcophagus Master of Christ's Prophecy of Peter's Denial. Pilate reflected the Brunus styles, while Christ was richer than the Christ of the Entry into Jerusalem and the Christ of the central tympanum, which (the latter) he thought was evolved out of the Michael Master. He suggested the possibility that the Michael Master carved the Christ. He discussed the problem of different hands for each figure as opposed to the grades of workmanship, but concluded that the leading artist did

---

11. R. Hamann, *Die Abteikirche von St. Gilles und ihre künstlerische Nachfolge*, (Berlin: Akademie-Verlag, 1955), 121, 172.

12. *Ibid.*, 145–152.

13. *Ibid.*, 153–159.

the planning and workmen used various motifs of different hands in their various stages of development. The Christ before Pilate, according to Hamann, was carved by the Brunus workshop when they were discarding, under the influence of archaic-Toulouse style, the more classic point of view of the Sarcophagus Master and were preparing the way for the austerity of Chartres. The Flagellation and the Carrying of the Cross scenes continued the style of the Christ before Pilate. Although the tympanum of the left portal was designed by the Michael Master, it was carved by the archaic-Toulouse workshop. Hamann utilized this combination of influences to decry the unfortunate cooperation of planning and executing of hands. The crudeness of the Madonna, and yet the connection between the three Kings and Joseph and the Christ of the Christ before Pilate, were considered the product of these unhappy circumstances.

The Burgundian curvilinear style R. Hamann found in the Christ cleansing the Temple and the two scenes of Lazarus (CP.L).[14] These scenes were carved by the Master of the Archangel, who, according to Hamann, was one of the better assistants of the Michael Master. Hamann claimed that both the other workshops of the classic-imitative style and the Toulouse archaic style were found on the central portal, while the more purely Burgundian style, derived from the Michael Master, triumphed on the side portals. The style of these older workshops entered the new Burgundian sphere as artists trained in it then came into the new workshop. The LP.R frieze of the citizens of Jerusalem was therefore close to Michael, while a classic-imitative sculptor modified his style because of the influence of the Burgundian curvilinear style and carved the LP lintel and LP.L frieze. He associated the LP lintel with the Master of CP.R 3 apostle whose figure exhibited the influence of the Michael Master, while the LP.L artist has been influenced both by the Toulouse archaic-imitative style in Christ washing Peter's Feet and the Last Supper on the lintel of the CP. He further stated that the Last Supper reminded him of the CP.R 3 large apostle whom he named the Master of the Entry into Jerusalem.

R. Hamann also argued that the Burgundian style dominated the right portal.[15] He saw a relationship between the Christ of the Emmaus scene (RP.L) and the Christ's head of the Vézelay tympanum. The rest of the RP.L frieze he divided between two hands: one carved the Christ and Mary Magdalene on the re-entrant angle. The scene in the House of Simon resembled the LP.L frieze. The RP.R and the RP lintel were carved by a sculptor influenced by the Brunus style, but the Christ on the extreme right was connected to the same figure on the opposite side of the portal, and the angel on the lintel perhaps was carved by the Michael Master. He reasoned that the tympanum of RP which he related to the frieze was inferior to the LP tympanum. The tympanum derived its expressive power from Byzantium and the proto-Renaissance. The tympanum did not lead to Chartres, but to the late Burgundian portals of Jonzy and Charlieu. The Master of Michael and the Christ fragment from the central tympanum in the Museum of Saint-Gilles led to Chartres.

R. Hamann concluded that the entire frieze and tympana were influenced by the Michael Master, when he was under the spell of the Classic-Imitative Master but discarding his materialistic side by being influenced by the austere-Toulouse style, yet rejecting its flat-

---

14. *Ibid.*, 159–166.
15. *Ibid.*, 167–172.

ness for a more statuesque monumentality.[16] This mélange of influences prepared him for the leading role in the creation of the Royal Portals of Chartres. Thus Hamann saw three basic directions of early twelfth-century sculpture: classic-imitative, Toulouse archaic, and Burgundian curvilinear. All three contributed to the development of Chartres, and all three were found at Saint-Gilles. They were absorbed by the Michael Master, who, in placing four panels on the central portal, created the idea of the Early and High Gothic portals.

This analysis of the frieze and tympana is based on broad generalizations of style. Individual artists are submerged in influences and counterinfluences. The earliest works on the façade are the James Major (classic-imitative artist) and the Thomas (archaic-imitative Toulouse artist). All the rest of the apostles and most of the friezes and tympana are affected by the leadership of a new master (the Burgundian curvilinear Michael Master) who, in turn, absorbs ideas from the two earlier styles.

Is the Master of the James Major the first sculptor of Saint-Gilles, or is he either a follower of Brunus or a developed and later Brunus himself? Since the two signed statues of Brunus, the Matthew and Bartholomew, seem to be the earliest apostles along with Thomas and James the Less, Hamann's first assumption would not seem to be valid. Is the Michael Master, who seems to borrow heavily from the Brunus formula, the great creative artist who designs the entire superstructure and transforms his style in time to voyage to Chartres and take the lead in carving the Royal Portals? Or is he just another artist who worked cooperatively on the sculpture of the superstructure like the Soft Master of the CP.R 3 and 4 apostles, who carved most of the left portal, and the Hard Master of the CP.R 5 and 6, who created the majority of the right portal? From the point of view of quality, it is difficult to see differences between Michael and the right four apostles. The closest affinity between Michael and the frieze sculpture, according to Hamann and to this author, is found in the LP.R frieze, which is certainly not the finest sculpture on the superstructure. It is difficult to imagine what Burgundian sculpture of 1116 and the following few years influenced the Michael Master. Any stylistic connection between Saint-Gilles and Chartres is certainly open to question. As in his analysis of the monumental apostles, Hamann submerges the individuality of artists in a maze of stylistic crosscurrents. The creativity of distinctly different sculptors, which is so apparent in large sculptural ensembles, both Romanesque and Gothic, such as Moissac, Vézelay, Saint-Denis, Chartres, and Reims, is reduced to hypothetical relationships of a "shifting-sands" variety. Since it is possible to find narrative variants of three of the sculptors responsible for the monumental apostles and angels on the frieze and tympana of Saint-Gilles, a more obvious explanation of the nature of the sculpture of the superstructure is to conclude that it was carved by individuals working contemporaneously and following a master plan.

In publishing the fragments of a tympanum (fig. 142), M. Gouron (1950) stated that the stone came from near Aix and is different from that of the Christ fragment (figs. 139, 141).[17] Since these apostle fragments were discovered embedded in a wall about 100 meters from the church of Saint-Martin, Gouron argued that those reliefs cannot be associated with Saint-Gilles. He imagined a lintel with the resurrection of the dead and saw, in the preserved fragments, the Apostles adoring Christ with Angels holding the symbols of the Passion

---

16. *Ibid.*, 172.
17. Gouron, "Découverte du tympan," 115–120.

above. He claimed that the same sculptor who carved the heads in a more rapid style, especially the second head from the left, also carved the Christ heads of the Prophecy of Peter's Denial, Christ washing Peter's Feet, and the Betrayal. In the head of the youth he saw the influence of Chartres and suggested that the same hand created the head of Saint Trophîme in the Arles cloister. He divided the work between a local atelier which created the figures with drapery styles related to other Saint-Gilles sculptures, especially Peter's Denial, and another itinerant atelier which carved the heads on the central-portal frieze, but also worked at Arles, Autun (Lazarus Tomb 1170–1189), and Saint-Guilhem-le-Désert under the influence of Chartres, Autun, and Brunus. He dated these fragments 1183–1190 after the peace between Count Raymond and the King of Aragon.

This notion of seeing a local style in the drapery and an international point of view in the heads is open to question. Both heads and figures are influenced by the Soft Master who carved, as his latest work on the façade, Christ's Prophecy of Peter's Denial.

Provençal Sculpture in Recent Exhibitions

Three recent exhibitions included fragments related stylistically to the façade of Saint-Gilles-du-Gard. Part of a Last Judgment tympanum (fig. 142), discovered by Marcel Gouron in 1949 and now in the Museum of Saint-Gilles, was exhibited in Cleveland in 1967.[18] W. Wixom stated that the relief came from the portal of Saint-Martin of Saint-Gilles and dated it around 1183–1190, following the conclusions of Marcel Gouron.[19] Since these fragments were found in a wall near the parish church of Saint-Martin, Gouron assumed that they came from this church. However, this conclusion cannot be proved, since an equally strong case can be made for the original location on one of the transept portals of the abbey. Wixom dated the apostles of the façade of Saint-Gilles around 1170, a date which will be questioned in Chapter 7.

A small head, loaned by Professor and Mrs. Meyer Schapiro, was exhibited at The Cloisters in 1968.[20] As pointed out in the catalogue, treatment of hair, eyes, and mouth resembles that of the head of Saint Michael on the façade of Saint-Gilles (fig. 46). The weathered surfaces are less crisp than in the Michael. The size of the head, 4⅝ inches, is too small to locate it on the frieze of Saint-Gilles, and furthermore it is in the round, whereas the heads on the frieze are relief. Certainly its style is close to that of the Michael Master. The date of mid-twelfth century seems valid.

Two heads from southern France were included in an exhibition in the Museum of Art, Rhode Island School of Design, Providence, in 1969.[21] S. Scher related the first head, from The Phillips Collection in Washington, to the large fragment of the Last Judgment now in the Museum at Saint-Gilles (fig. 142) and, following Gouron, dated it about 1183–1190 and suggested its original location on the portal of Saint-Martin of Saint-Gilles. This late dating

18. Wixom, *op. cit.*, 120–121, 359, no. III 38.

19. Gouron, "Découverte du tympan," 115–120.

20. C. Gómez-Moreno, *Medieval Art from Private Collections: A Special Exhibition at The Cloisters October 30, 1968, through January 5, 1969* (New York: The Metropolitan Museum of Art, 1968), no. 25.

21. S. K. Scher *et al.*, *The Renaissance of the Twelfth Century* (Providence: Museum of Art, Rhode Island School of Design, 1969), 122–126, nos. 43, 44.

is untenable in the light of the sequence of work on the façade of Saint-Gilles and the relation-ship between Saint-Gilles and other monuments in Provence and Northern Italy (see Chapter 6). Scher's argument for the stylistic connection with relief of the Last Judgment seems valid, although the eyes, with their bulging eyelids, are quite different. The head in The Phillips Collection was recently published by D. Glass.[22] The author related the head to the tympanum fragments from Saint-Martin at Saint-Gilles and to the Michael on the façade. She dated the head tentatively in the middle of the century, but admitted the impossibility of a secure date until further studies of the façade have been completed.

The head from the Cincinnati Art Museum was dated about 1150 by S. Scher and attributed either to the Soft Master, the sculptor of the Saint-Gilles apostles CP.R 3, 4 or the same atelier who worked at Saint-Guilhem-le-Désert (see Part II, Chapter 12). Since it is evident that the Saint-Gilles Soft Master carved at least four of the Saint-Guilhem-le-Désert reliefs, it follows that the Cincinnati head could be from either Saint-Gilles or Saint-Guilhem. On the other hand, if compared to both the reliefs by the Soft Master on the frieze of Saint-Gilles and the Saint-Guilhem reliefs, the Cincinnati head seems to be closer stylistically to the Saint-Guilhem-le-Désert reliefs.

Early Christian Sarcophagi

Figure 82: Sarcophagus in north aisle of Saint-Trophîme at Arles, toward 350, right-hand side with Adoration of Magi and Entry into Jerusalem (Wilpert II, 125, Pl. CXXV; Benoit no. 45, 47–48, Pl. XVII).

Figure 83: Sarcophagus of the Anastasis, end of the fourth century, from the crypt of Saint-Honorat where it served as tomb of Bishop Aeonis (491–502) (Arles no. 2; Benoit no. 58, 53, Pl. XXII, 1, XXIII, XXIV, 2, 3).

Figure 84: Sarcophagus of the Farewell of Christ, first quarter of the fourth century (Arles no. 18; Wilpert, Supplement III, 24, figure 242; Benoit no. 50, Pl. XIX, 2, XX, 1).

Figure 115: Sarcophagus of the Orant, detail of Christ's Prophecy of Peter's Denial, toward 325 (Arles, no. 20; Wilpert II, Pl. CXIII; Benoit no. 52, 51, Pl. XXI).

Figure 130: Christ giving Law to Peter, detail of figure 19 depicting Christ before Pilate (Arles no. 17; Benoit no. 5, 5, 36).

---

22. D. Glass, "Romanesque Sculpture in American Collections. V. Washington and Baltimore," *Gesta. International Center of Medieval Art*, IX, 1 (1970), 58–59.

143. Saint-Gilles. Right portal, right splay.

144. Detail of bases (LP.L).

145. Detail of bases (RP.R).

146. Detail of bases (CP.L).

147. Detail of bases (CP.R).

CHAPTER 5

Ornament

$\mathbf{T}$HE façade of Saint-Gilles possesses a wealth of ornament, the majority of which is based on Roman motifs (fig. 2).[1] Because of this dependence on antiquity combined with the re-use of Roman columns and capitals, the dating of Provençal ornament is difficult. Differences in the treatment of ornament on the façade seem to be qualitative rather than the result of an evolution of forms in time. In other words, the study of ornament reinforces evidence established in the study of figured sculpture that three portals were included in the original project and that sculptors collaborated at the start of the campaign and continued to collaborate until the façade was completed. (See Notes on Chapter 5 for catalogue of ornament.)

BASES

The lowest course of masonry of the entire façade (figs. 143, 3, 7, 9) is crowned by a thinner course (.25 meters in height) with scotia and torus moldings. These moldings have the same profiles across the entire façade. Directly above this course is a channeled section (figs. 2, 3—.85 meters high) which serves as the pedestal

---

1. V. Lassalle, *L'Influence antique dans l'art roman provençale*, Revue archéologique de Narbonnaise, 2 (Paris: Editions E. de Boccard, 1970), 67–85, describes in detail the extraordinary impact of the ornaments of Roman monuments in Nîmes, Orange, Saint-Rémy, Arles, and Carpentras on Provençal Romanesque sculpture.

for the apostles in niches. This course of masonry with the same ornamentation is found on all three portals except the inner splays of the central portal, which have figured panels. The channeling is discontinued behind the inner socles and columns of both side portals (figs. 3, 7). The treatment of this paneling is uniform throughout, while the best-preserved section can be seen on the RP.R (fig. 143).

The crowning block of the channeled section (fig. 143), which is a separate course of masonry (.20 meters high), has a concave molding decorated by frontal floral palmettes and a fillet section animated by geometric motifs. The upper or fillet molding is animated by a meander pattern on all the bases except the one under the CP.R double socle (fig. 147). In this single instance, a more plastic folded ribbon with drill holes ornaments the north side (fig. 147) and a double-ax motif appears on the south side under the relief of David slaying Goliath (fig. 70). There is also more variety in the concave molding of palmettes on this area of the central portal. The LP.L (fig. 144) has frontal palmette patterns with drill holes separating leaves and ridges suggesting the midribs. On the right side of the same portal the frontal leaves are more curved and asymmetrical. This latter arrangement continues under the left four apostles (fig. 17) and around the top of the projecting pedestal. Over the scene of the Offerings of Cain and Abel (CP.L—fig. 146—only the right side is original) the leaves are crisper and more carefully carved. On the right side of the central portal over the rondels of the Centaur and Stag (fig. 51) the filler leaves roll outward into space and animate the surface. The ornament above the ovals of Samson and the Lioness (CP.R—fig. 147) displays an undulating vine with leaves and buds as fillers. It is again on this projecting base that we see the only rupture in the design of the crowning fillet molding. Even the small molding at the bottom, which is a plain torus or bead and reel in the rest of the façade, consists of small floral horseshoes. On the south side of the projecting base (fig. 70), the central leaves are rolled and project like those over the Centaur and Stag. This same treatment continues under the right four apostles and around the left side of the right portal; yet the relief is flatter (figs. 26, 27). Finally, the RP.R (fig. 145) resembles the extreme left side of the façade in its frontality and symmetry. We thus find more variety in the motif and in its treatment in the central portal, especially in the blocks crowning the right projecting base, and the best quality in this portal over the Cain and Abel relief. It is impossible, however, to see stylistic differences which could differentiate the side portals from the central portal in date.

Above these ornamented blocks are two courses of masonry of different stone (.17 and .45 meters high) which have weathered considerably. The crowning molding consists of a bead-and-reel and egg-and-dart pattern (fig. 143) which is treated uniformly under the eight apostles on the front face of the façade and under Michael and the Archangels. As already pointed out, these two blocks and the four lion socles under the four apostles of the central portal were inserted when the entire façade was raised.

ORNAMENT FLANKING AND FRAMING THE APOSTLES

Channeled pilasters frame the angels and the apostles and sustain the lintels of all three portals (figs. 3, 7, 9). On the left portal, a thin block with one channel separates the Michael from the north tower (fig. 44). Corner pilasters, made up of two blocks, separate both Michael and Matthew from the left portal (fig. 148). These paneled members have no base and capitals, but between Matthew, Bartholomew, Thomas, and James the Less (figs. 17, 21, 152, 153) the three channeled supports have rudimentary bases and capitals. To the right of the James the Less the pier appears cut off at the bottom and possesses no molding at the top (fig. 149). The channeling, which continues at right angles, has one channel carved in the north edge of the block containing the acanthus frieze (fig. 149). The pier to the left of the apostle CP.R 3 (fig. 150), like the one beside James on the north side of the central portal, has no base or capital, but does not appear to be cut off at the bottom. The south edge of the vertical block on which the acanthus panel is carved does not have a channel, as does the corresponding block on the north side of the central portal. The three supports separating the CP.R apostles possess more uniformity of molding than those framing the north apostles. The corner support dividing the southernmost apostle from the right portal (fig. 151) is undecorated, while the corner pier separating the archangels from the portal is one block with channels without base and capital. No channels decorate the thin block between the archangels and the south tower.

The essentially uniform treatment of channeled pilasters with bases and capitals occurs only in the six supports which divide the eight apostles on the front plane of the façade. The corner supports on the side portals and those merging with the outer sides of the central portal are either plain or consist of two blocks, and all are minus bases and capitals. The differences between the pilasters between apostles and those on the corners corroborate the changes in the design of the portals when extra blocks are inserted. The convex corners would have to be altered with the addition of the blocks below and the figured frieze above (figs. 3, 7).

The acanthus architrave which crowns the monumental apostles and angels was carved simultaneously with the figured frieze of the side portals, since one half figure of the scene of Christ meeting two Disciples on the Road to Emmaus is part of the ornamental block above the CP.R 5, 6 apostles (fig. 159). The problem of joining the acanthus architrave with the larger figured frieze of the side portals is handled

148. Saint-Gilles. LP.R, Pilasters between LP and Matthew.

149. CP.L, Pilasters between James the Less and CP.

150. CP.R, Pilasters between CP and unidentified Apostle (CP.R 3).

151. RP.L, Pilaster between unidentified Apostle and RP.

152. Saint-Gilles. Ornamental panel above Matthew and Bartholomew (CP.L 6, 5).

153. Ornamental panel above Thomas and James the Less. (CP.L 4, 3).

154. Ornamental panel above John and Peter (CP.L 2, 1).

155. Ornamental panel above James and Paul (CP.R 1, 2).

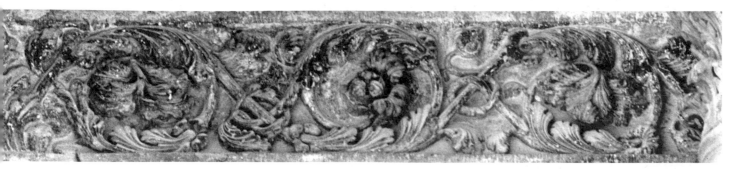

156. Saint-Gilles. Ornamental panel above unidentified Apostles (CP.R 3, 4).

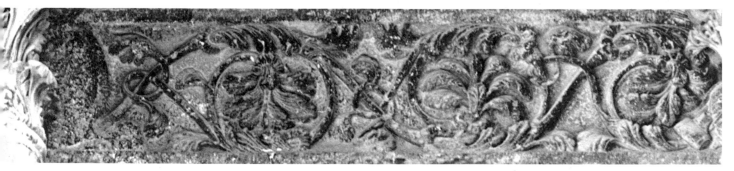

157. Ornamental panel above unidentified Apostles (CP.R 5, 6).

158. Juncture of ornamental panels over CP.R 4 and 5.

159. Panel over CP.R 6, including Disciple and Christ on the Road to Emmaus.

160. Saint-Gilles. Panel under LP lintel.

161. Panel under CP lintel.

162. Panel under RP lintel.

differently at the four corners of the north and south portals. These joints are partially hidden by the large columns with their capitals. On the LP.L (fig. 78), an apostle fills the area to the right of Michael's head, while on the LP.R, vine and leaves, which are part of the acanthus block over the Brunus' statues, abut the extreme right citizens of Jerusalem (fig. 88). On the RP.R, the acanthus block over the archangels starts directly behind Christ's left shoulder.

The acanthus architrave displays undulating vines which give off secondary stems forming ovals filled with leaves, buds, or rosettes. This acanthus motif is very close in format and style to Roman reliefs such as on the frieze of the Maison Carrée at Nîmes. The reliefs over Michael and the Archangels (fig. 89) contain three ovals with floral fillers and rosettes and leaves filling the void of the borders. The architrave over Brunus' Matthew and Bartholomew (CP.L 5, 6—fig. 152) exhibits a more stretched-out design of three and one-half ovals with voids more apparent. The next block over Thomas and James the Less (CP.L 3, 4—fig. 153) has four and one-half floral ovals which are more compressed. The central patterns are sprays of leaves. The acanthus pattern continues over the two vertical panels on each side of the central portal and surmounts the apostles, John, Peter, James Major, and Paul (figs. 154, 155). Two ovals decorate the front plane of the portal and two appear above the apostles. The re-entrant angles at the corners were necessary, when the acanthus panels were placed adjacent to John and Paul; otherwise an awkward and unstructural overhang would have occurred. The relief style is close to the panel over Thomas and James the Less, but has a few refinements such as the bird and little man on the inside edges (figs. 154, 155). Flowing and rolled leaves are crisply carved. Over James Major (fig. 155) the crouching male, grasping leaves, recalls the left-hand figure on the lintel of the façade portal of the Cathedral of Modena; yet the ornamented style is closer to Roman sources.

Over the CP.R 3, 4 apostles (fig. 156) the relief is slightly higher than on the left side of the central portal. The stems are thicker, and the leaves are more three-dimensional. The relief over the right apostles CP.R 5, 6 (fig. 157) is lower, with the left side unfinished and the right side containing a pilgrim of the scene of Christ meeting Disciples on the Road to Emmaus (figs. 158, 159). Differences appear to be the result of varying degrees of quality. The finest sections appear over the central portal and over the nearest pair of apostles (CP.L 3, 4—Thomas and James the Less and CP.R 3, 4).

The acanthus reliefs under the three lintels (figs. 160–162) exhibit essentially a harmonious style with some differences in the extent of the relief and with apparent discrepancies in quality. Of the three, the acanthus panel under the Entry into Jerusalem (LP—fig. 160) is the finest. Leaves are rhythmically arranged and subtly carved. Fillers of rosettes and leaves are gracefully connected with the vines. Edges of the floral ovals extend over the double frame. The acanthus under the right-portal lintel (fig. 162) is more mechanical; the relief is a little lower. The two panels of the central portal (fig. 161), divided by the trumeau, are a more compact version of the right portal.

Again, it is impossible to discover any stylistic evolution which would suggest different dates for these reliefs. Like the acanthus architrave over the apostles, these lintel panels manifest degrees of quality. The workshop practices in the *chantier* can only be surmised. Did the same sculptor carve the lintels and their undersides, or did assistants or specialists carve the ornament? If the former is correct, there would seem to be a possible relationship between figured lintels and acanthus panels, since the left-portal lintel by the Soft Master of the CP.R 3, 4 apostles (fig. 85) is of finer quality than the lintel of the right portal by the Hard Master of the CP.R 5, 6 apostles (fig. 100) and certainly more subtle than the central-portal relief of the Last Supper (fig. 120), also by the Hard Master.

The vertical panels of acanthus on the front faces of the central portal (figs. 163–165) display a style quite different from that of the floral architrave and lintels. The ovals of vines are more tightly formed and the secondary leaves more complicated. Animals and birds help fill the voids along the frames. The stem grows out of a triple frontal acanthus pattern at the base. The numerous filling leaves repeat the surface of the block, and the whole effect of the relief is two-dimensional. Both these vertical panels have unfinished sections on their outer sides and elaborate borders on sides toward the portal. Their dimensions, left 2.04 by .83 meters and right 2.0 by .82 meters, correspond to the height of the apostles (John and Peter—2.035 and James Major and Paul—1.99 and 2.0 meters). But why do they have, on their edges, elaborate borders which vie with the moldings on the west side of the apostles (folded band on John and rounded molding on Paul) and unfinished side to north and south of the right panel? Perhaps they originally framed the doorway of the central portal? Their height would equal that of the apostles without the lion socles, and the width of their carved acanthus panel corresponds to the depth of the bases of .72 meters. If this assumption is possible, we find a connection between the façade of Saint-Gilles and North Italian portals such as at Modena.

ORNAMENT ON SUPERSTRUCTURE

Narrow cornices, framing the frieze, are ornamented by floral and geometric patterns in all three portals. The top abacus surmounts the friezes of the side portals and is carried out over the large freestanding columns. In both side portals this crowning member is decorated with frontal palmettes on the concave molding, framed by classical moldings. The treatment and arrangement consists of frontal, voluted units with the central leaves curved forward in the LP.L (fig. 78). The same motif occurs in the opposite side of the left portal (fig. 88); yet there is more separation between each two units. On the right portal, left side (fig. 104), the same motif is repeated in a less crisp manner, while on the RP.R (fig. 96) the ornament is similar but left unfinished at the re-entrant angle.

The lower ornamental cornice is a double, folded band or waterfall motif on the top molding. On the right portal (fig. 96) the bands or ribbons have ridges with drill holes in the voids. On the left side of the north portal (fig. 78) a smaller border of minute leaves replaces the folded-ribbon motif. The abacus area below has projecting bear heads between leaves on the LP.R (fig. 88) and lion heads and acanthus on the RP.L (fig. 104). On the extreme sides of the façade this area is ornamented with frontal palmettes on the right side (fig. 45) and a freely arranged and sensitively carved acanthus on the left (fig. 44). The quality of this ornamented sculpture is higher on the left portal. On the central portal, the upper cornice is a restoration, while the lower one consists of an acanthus pattern with a meander motif crowning it. In every ornamented section, the quality of the left portal is higher.

The capitals of the Saint-Gilles façade are primarily Corinthian. The four, which crown the inner columns of the side portals, can be seen in figures 3, 7. The capitals of the left portal have three tiers of rolled acanthus leaves. Small volutes converge at corners and in the middle of the bell of the capital. A small rosette ornaments the middle on the LP.L capital. The right-portal capitals (fig. 7) are also of the Corinthian type. Two tiers of frontal acanthus leaves support a larger volute. A single acanthus pattern replaces the rosette and the secondary converging volutes. The much larger capitals on the freestanding columns, which flank the side portals, are also Corinthian, but are Roman (the LP.R capital is nineteenth-century). The LP.L large capital (fig. 3) is similar to the smaller inner capital in its organization; yet the latter has a flaring, un-Roman silhouette and none of the massiveness of the outer Roman capital. The outer Roman capitals flanking the south portal (fig. 7) have three tiers of acanthus, prominent volutes, and large rosettes on the middle of each face. Of the double capitals which surmount the double columns on each side of the central portal, the outer two are nineteenth-century, while the inner ones do not seem to fit.

Two other capitals on the façade follow the Corinthian or composite form, but are ornamented with figures. The middle capital above the left apostles (fig. 166) has two tiers of acanthus leaves and frontal eagles with wings coalescing at the corners, similar to volutes. The eagles, standing on the first tier of acanthus leaves, project outward from the bell of the capital. The other capital above the right, unidentified apostles (fig. 167) has caryatid figures and acanthus leaves. On the left side and front

163. Saint-Gilles. Acanthus panel (CP.L).

164. Acanthus panel (CP.L), detail.

165. Acanthus panel (CP.R).

166. Saint-Gilles. Eagle capital above Bartholomew and Thomas.

167. Atlantes capital above Apostles (CP.R 4 and 5).

168. Angel capital in choir.

169. Capitals in choir.

face, the figures grow upward from the top of the first tier of acanthus, their heads serving as the rosette, while their upraised arms strengthen the corner of the capital. The right or south side has an eagle like the capital just discussed. Other capitals in the choir (figs. 168, 169) resemble the façade capitals in composition and treatment of drapery. Wings, like those in the eagle capital, replace the corner volutes, but the rigid heads with staring eyes and the drapery pulled around the waist and over the arms are related to the caryatid capital.

Finally, there remain the cornice upheld by corbels above the frieze of the central portal and the heads and animals along the cornice directly below the frieze. In figures 2, 111, 112, one can see the siren heads facing the side portals and the variety of animals: bulls, bears, lions, and snakes across the central portal. Both these cornices are balanced left and right by human heads. Crowning the upper frieze of the central portal is an ornamental cornice of bead-and-reel and egg-and-dart moldings. Above this appears a projecting and badly weathered acanthus cornice upheld by corbels (figs. 111, 112). These corbels are found in many Provençal cloisters. From left to right the corbels are as follows: caryatid angel, human head, ram's head, frontal eagle, lion, ox, caryatid figures, acanthus. This cornice does not harmonize with the archivolts of the central portal, but does fit in, at its extremities, with the projection of the middle part of the façade.

The study of Saint-Gilles ornament does help in the comprehension of growth of the façade. The consistency of motif and style of all the bases and their ornamented moldings seems to indicate that from the outset three portals were planned. Stylistic relationships between façade, nave, and choir indicate that all three were under construction at approximately the same time. The finest ornament, from the point of view of quality and variety of motif, is located on the central portal, with the exception of the underside of the lintel, possibly of the Hard Master, while the ornament of the left portal is more crisply executed than that on the right portal. Since the Soft Master, who was in charge of the left portal, seems to be a more sensitive sculptor than the Hard Master of the right portal, it is tempting to argue that these two sculptors carved the ornament on their respective portals.

NOTES—CHAPTER 5
Ornament (figs. 143–169)

I. Ornament on Jambs of Three Portals

    A. Lowest decorated course of masonry (rising above sill—.25 meters high across entire façade) consists of flat fillet, torus, scotia, two small tori, and small scotia (from bottom to top). The profile is the same in all portals (see figs. 62, 65, 143).

    B. Channeled bases on left and right portals and along face of façade under the eight apostles (low-relief sculpture occupies this area on the central portal). Measurements: LP .85 meters, RP .88 meters, CP.L (under Matthew, Bartholomew, etc.) .85 meters, CP.R (under unidentified apostles) .88 meters. Long, thin channeled insets with slightly curved bottoms and semicircular tops.

1. LP.L (fig. 62): west face badly worn, patched at corner, unfinished (no paneling behind carved socle).
2. LP.R (fig. 65): unfinished behind socle.
3. CP (fig. 2): badly worn across face of façade and patched with restoration along splays.
4. RP.L: patched at corner and unfinished behind socle.
5. RP.R (fig. 143): unfinished behind socle; best preserved under archangels.

C.   Projecting course of masonry crowning paneled bases (.20 meters across entire façade). Frontal floral patterns on the concave section and geometric motifs on the crowning fillet.

1. LP.L (fig. 144): frontal palmettes with drilled indentations above narrow bead-and-reel molding, capped by interlocking, indented T motifs forming a hesitant chevron pattern.
2. LP.R (fig. 65): similar to LP.L except pure chevron pattern on top molding and leaves in palmette patterns leaning to the right. (In both LP.L and LP.R, these blocks are undecorated behind the inner, smaller columns.)
3. CP.L (under Matthew—fig. 17): same as LP.R with some variation in leaves serving as fillers.
4. CP.R (under unidentified apostles—fig. 26): T pattern like LP.R and frontal acanthus with accented drill holes.
5. RP.L: like CP.R (4 above).
6. RP.R (figs. 143, 145): similar to LP.R, but no bead-and-reel motif at bottom and acanthus leaves flatter. (In contrast to LP.L and LP.R, these blocks are ornamented behind the inner columns.)
7. CP.L (over Cain and Abel reliefs—fig. 146): chevron pattern, frontal palmettes, and bead-and-reel like LP.R, but more leaves in central acanthus motif with greater variety of undercutting against the cut-away ground.
8. CP.R
   a. Jamb no. 1 (over rondels—fig. 51): chevron pattern with greater horizontal emphasis than CP.L. Acanthus pattern with rolled-out leaves with more plasticity than the treatment of the same motif on any other area on façade.
   b. Jamb no. 2 (north face—fig. 147): flat fillet-folded ribbon with clusters of five drill holes animating the background; bottom molding floral horseshoes; concave area decorated with an undulating vine with floral fillers (the front part of this block is nineteenth-century).
   c. Jamb no. 2 (south face—fig. 70): double-ax pattern above palmettes like 8, above. Bottom molding continuous beads (not bead-and-reel).

D.   Two courses of masonry directly below apostles and angels (LP.L and LP.R, under the eight apostles on the front face of the façade, and RP.L and RP.R—see figs. 2, 3, 7, 17).

1. Bottom piece: torus, scotia, torus framed by flat fillets.
2. Top of upper piece: bead-and-reel and egg-and-dart. (Dimensions vary slightly but are approximately .17 meters high for lower piece, and .45 for upper piece). The surface of these blocks is pitted. The total height of these two blocks equals the height of the lion socles under John, Peter, James, and Paul of the central portal and the dimensions of the double socles on the projecting pedestals.

E. Pilasters between and flanking apostles and angels and channeled jambs (all approximately 2 meters unless described differently).

1. LP.L (figs. 44, 3): left of Michael (one indented channel extending the height of statue); right of Michael and continuing around corner (two short blocks— with paneling left undecorated behind inner column); doorjambs (deeply undercut channels).
2. LP.R (fig. 148): same as LP.L (the corner two blocks to the left of Matthew have no projecting base just like the parallel sections on the LP.R).
3. CP.L (figs. 17, 21): framing Matthew, Bartholomew, Thomas, and James the Less (the three fluted pilasters framing and separating Bartholomew and Thomas have bases and capitals, while the ones to the left of Matthew and to the right of James the Less have no bases and no capitals). CP.L doorjamb similar to doorjambs of left portal. The deep channeling on the west face is covered up by the lion socle which was inserted under Peter.
4. CP.R (figs. 26, 27, 150, 151): doorjamb similar to opposite splay. Three pilasters framing and separating the unidentified apostles 4 and 5 have bases and capitals, while the pilaster to the left of CP.R 3 and to the right of CP.R 6 have no bases and no capitals. This system is similar to the treatment of the side pilasters in the CP.L
5. RP.L (fig. 151): short corner pilaster between CP.R 6 apostle and left splay of right portal is undecorated. Doorjamb similar to left portal.
6. RP.R (fig. 7): doorjamb like opposite side of portal. Short corner pilaster with channels is one piece and has no base or capital. No channeling between arch-angels and south tower. (The unfinished or altered pilasters are always the corner ones which separate the front face of the façade from the splays of the portals.)

F. Acanthus panels over apostles and angels (about .45 meters wide).

1. LP.L (over Michael—fig. 44): Undulating vines forming ovals filled with frontal patterns of leaves and buds. Three ovals with leaves filling most voids. The left-hand head of the figured frieze overlaps the right edge.
2. CP.L (over Matthew and Bartholomew—fig. 152): one block extending from the citizens of Jerusalem to the joint over the pilaster separating Bartholomew from Thomas. Three and one-half ovals of vine and fillers with more voids than the LP.L.
3. CP.L (over Thomas and James the Less—fig. 153): one block containing four and one-half ovals with floral fillers.

4. CP.L (over John and Peter—figs. 9, 154): same motif as 3 above, but vine thicker and undercutting more marked. Re-entrant over head of John with frontal acanthus pattern. Two ovals with thick rolled leaves and bird as filler on right side.

5. CP.R (over James and Paul—fig. 155): two ovals with plastic fillers. Small, squatting man in left corner. Thick vines continue around over the vertical acanthus panel.

6. CP.R (over unidentified apostles 3, 4—fig. 156): three loosely spaced ovals with floral fillers with acanthus leaves filling each end.

7. CP.R (over unidentified apostles 5, 6—fig. 157): the left-hand part is unfinished (fig. 158), while the right side of the block includes the left figure of the Emmaus scene of the frieze (fig. 159). The carving is cruder than the panels just described.

8. RP.R (over archangels—fig. 45): three tightly rolled ovals with floral fillers.

9. Conclusion: differences in these acanthus panels seem to be qualitative, with the finest ornament over the splays of the central portal. The least sensitive block is the one over the CP.R 5, 6 apostles.

G. Vertical acanthus panels flanking central portal.

1. CP.L (figs. 163, 164): panel of four ovals made by secondary stems from undulating vine. Intricately carved floral fillers with birds and animals occupying the voids tangent to the carved border. The left-hand side of the block is uncarved. The right-hand border abuts somewhat awkwardly the folded-ribbon pattern on the west edge of the block from which the John was carved.

2. CP.R (fig. 165): very similar to the above. Unfinished on the right side.

II. *Acanthus Panels on Underside of Lintels*

A. LP (fig. 160): Eight ovals, formed by secondary vines growing from undulating vines, are filled with floral fillers of varying patterns. Extra leaves or rosettes fill the voids between the ovals and the indented border.

B. CP (fig. 161): Three crudely carved ovals. Unfinished or altered on the side.

C. RP (fig. 162): Six ovals with thin stems and vines. More linear than LP and greater emphasis on voids.

D. Conclusion: pronounced differences in quality, with the LP panel the finest, the RP less sensitive and more linear and stretched out, and the central panel quite crude. The LP panel is similar to the acanthus frieze over the unidentified apostles CP.R 3, 4, while the RP panel is similar to the frieze over the unidentified apostles CP.R 5, 6.

III. *Ornament Framing Figured Friezes*

A. Left portal (fig. 78).

1. Left side.

a. Lower cornice: freely arranged, palmette leaves capped by a geometric fillet (ornament similar to that crowning CP.R pedestal—see fig. 147).

b. Upper cornice: uniform frontal acanthus motifs with bead-and-reel below and bead-and-reel and egg-and-dart moldings above. (This cornice extends across top of the lintel.)

    2. Right side (fig. 88).

a. Lower cornice: frontal palmettes alternating with projecting bear heads. Leaves form into folded-band pattern with raised nodes in voids.

b. Upper cornice: same as left side and same as cornice over lintel.

  B. Central portal.

    1. Upper cornice over Matthew, Bartholomew, Thomas, and James (fig. 111): (left to right) serpent, cow, two mastiffs, bearded head in profile, and two mastiffs.

    2. CP.L cornice over John and Peter (fig. 113): palmette crowned by chevron pattern.

    3. CP.L top cornice: undecorated—restoration.

    4. CP. cornice over lintel: egg-and-dart motif.

    5. Upper cornice over James and Paul (fig. 13): same as design over John and Peter.

    6. Upper cornice over four unidentified apostles (fig. 112): (left to right) two four-legged animals, frontal head, snake, two four-legged animals, and female profile head at corner.

  C. Right portal.

    1. Left side (fig. 104).

a. Lower cornice: frontal palmettes alternating with animal masks crowned by folded bands. Same design as LP.R, lower cornice, but carving less sensitive.

b. Upper cornice: acanthus pattern with elaborate moldings similar to top cornice across left portal and sides of CP.R.

    2. Right side (fig. 96).

a. Lower cornice: palmette and folded band.

b. Upper cornice: same as LP and CP.R.

c. Upper cornice over archangels: (left to right) profile female head facing north (balancing the head across the portal) and a four-legged animal.

IV. *Capitals: Inner Capitals in Jambs of Left and Right Portals and Large Capitals on Colossal Columns on the Front Face of the Façade*

  A. Left portal.

    1. Left side (fig. 3): inner capital is composite with three tiers of rolled acanthus leaves, tangent scrolls at corners, and rosette in middle of each face; outer capital, which is Roman, also composite with more detailed carving of acanthus leaves.

  B. Central portal.

    1. Left side (capital supporting sculptured frieze above Bartholomew and Thomas—fig. 166): two tiers of acanthus with frontal eagles with wings spread and joining at corners.

2. Left (over double columns—fig. 9): pair of Corinthian capitals, which do not appear on print of 1833. Damaged condition of inner ones suggests that it might be original.

3. Right (over double columns—fig. 13): pair of Corinthian capitals. Again inner one appears original. Neither one depicted in 1833 print.

4. Right (capital supporting sculptured frieze above CP.R 4 and 5 apostles—fig. 167): frontal half-figures with arms raised like caryatids emerging from acanthus leaves. Hands and cloak falling from arms to reinforce the corners.

C. Right portal.

1. Left side: inner capital of two staggered tiers of acanthus leaves (simpler than inner capitals on LP); outer large Roman composite capital with detailed acanthus leaves in lower half and corner volutes and central rosettes.

2. Right side (fig. 7): inner capital of two tiers of acanthus (similar to left capital); outer large capital, which is Roman, similar to opposite one, only damaged.

V. *Corbels Supporting Cornice above Upper Frieze of Central Portal*

A. Left side (fig. 111): angel, human, ram, and frontal eagle (left to right)—all weathered and surmounted by acanthus cornice.

B. Right side (fig. 112): bear, bull, caryatid, and acanthus (left to right).

W. Horn's Reaction to Ornament

W. Horn (1937), on the evidence of the incomplete border between two acanthus panels over the unidentified apostles 3, 4, and 5, 6 (fig. 158), of the style of the rest of the acanthus frieze, and of the integral connection between the ornamental panel over CP.R 6 and the figured frieze, reasoned that there was an evolution in the ornament which proved that the south portal was carved first and that the north developed from it.[2] He thus concluded that the acanthus panels over the archangel (RP.R) and next over the CP.R 5, 6 apostles (fig. 157) was carved first. Then work jumped to the panel over Michael (LP.L) and continued from left to right (north to south) over the left apostles, central portal, and met the first panel over the pilaster separating CP.R 4 and 5 apostles (fig. 158). This difference between the acanthus over CP.R 3, 4 and CP.R 5, 6 apostles (figs. 156, 157) indicated to Horn that the south-portal sculpture, including the figured frieze as well as the acanthus architrave, was earlier than the north portal. It would seem as though this one block over CP.R 5, 6 (fig. 157), with its unfinished edge and slightly lower-relief style, is insufficient evidence from which to draw such conclusions. The differences of the acanthus panels can be explained with equal validity by seeing degrees of quality. The best panels from the point of view of quality are found over the apostles of the central portal and over the CP.L 3, 4 (Thomas, James the Less) and over CP.R 3, 4. The less subtle panels are on the side portals. The differences between these acanthus panels are so slight that it is questionable whether Horn's conclusions are correct.

---

2. W. Horn, *Die Fassade von St. Gilles* (Hamburg: Paul Evert, 1937), 39–40.

CHAPTER 6

Dating the Façade

O N the basis of comparisons with dated Romanesque monuments in France and Italy, about which more will be said later, it is impossible to argue that any part of the façade was completed before 1116, the date of the inscription on the buttress of the crypt, or that any part was carved after 1209. The disturbed history of the monastery and town during the next sixteen years after 1116, until the Rule of Cluny was accepted, would seem to preclude a campaign of the magnitude of the façade. Furthermore, the pilgrims' guide to Santiago de Compostela, written toward 1139, included a detailed description of the tomb of Saint Gilles in the crypt and of the portals of Santiago, but no mention was made of the façade of Saint-Gilles.[1] The presence of two epitaphs dated 1142 on the west wall of the crypt and others of earlier date prove that the foundations for the façade could have been completed in the 1130's and certainly were by the early 1140's. Since the difficulties after 1179 up to 1209, or indeed up to 1226, would not seem to be conducive for artistic activity, it follows that the five decades, 1130's through 1170's, are the only possible period for the creation of the Saint-Gilles façade.

The influence of Saint-Gilles on sculpture in Provence and its bordering regions and the subsequent impact of both Saint-Gilles and its progeny on dated monuments

---

1. J. Vielliard, *Le Guide du pèlerin de Saint-Jacques de Compostelle* (Mâcon: Protat Frères, 1963), 41–47, 97–103.

in Northern Italy would seem to point to the 1140's into the early 1150's as the most logical date for the façade of Saint-Gilles. Evidence in the history of the abbey, in the architecture of the crypt, in the epitaphs on the west wall of the crypt, and in the iconography of the portals all helps confirm this date. (See Notes on Chapter 6 for conclusions of previous writers on the dating of Saint-Gilles.)

In neither the history of the town nor that of the abbey are there any dated documents, dedications, epitaphs, miraculous cures, or catastrophic events which would unequivocally establish the specific time in which the façade of Saint-Gilles was erected (see plan of town—fig. 170). Further, what few documents do exist are open to widely divergent interpretations. A summary of the legendary history of Saint Gilles and the history of the abbey which bears his name is included in the Notes to this chapter. A list of major events, which concern the Romanesque abbey, follows:[2]

1096: Urban II consecrated the altar of a new basilica (Goiffon, XVII, 35).

1105: Count Bertrand, in spite of the threat of excommunication by Pope Pascal II, invaded the town, fortified the abbey, and auctioned off the offerings (Goiffon, XX to XXIII, 38–41).

1107: Bertrand excommunicated (Goiffon, XXVII, 46).

1108: Bertrand, relieved of excommunication, again harassed the abbey (Goiffon, XXX, 48).

1109: Bertrand left on crusade.

1116: Inscription on pier of crypt stating that a new basilica was begun by Abbot Hugh.

1117: Bertrand, Count of Béziers, seized the abbey, built a chateau, and expelled Abbot Hugh (Goiffon, XXXIV, 51).

1118: Abbot Hugh free and received the Pope.

1119: Pope Calixtus II sojourned at Saint-Gilles; major part of treasury gone.

1120: Calixtus II threatened three Counts with excommunication unless they stopped robbing the monastery (Goiffon, XXXIX, 58).

1121: Alfonus Jourdanus, Count of Toulouse and brother of Bertrand, occupied the town, robbed the monastery, and built a chateau (Goiffon, XLI, XLII, 56–61).

1121: Pope protested in vain (Goiffon, XLI to XLV); Abbot Hugh held captive in chateau at Beaucaire and then sent to Cluny.

1122: Alfonus Jourdanus excommunicated (Goiffon, XLVI to XLVIII, 65–67).

---

2. L'Abbé Goiffon, *Bullaire de l'abbaye de Saint-Gilles* (Nîmes: 1882). Goiffon included all the papal bulls or communiqués related to Saint-Gilles. Goiffon's numbers of these documents are listed in the text by bull and page. The most complete discussion of the legends surrounding Saint Gilles and the history of the town and abbey is J. Charles-Roux, *Saint-Gilles. Sa légende—son abbaye—ses coutumes* (Paris: A. Lemerre, 1910).

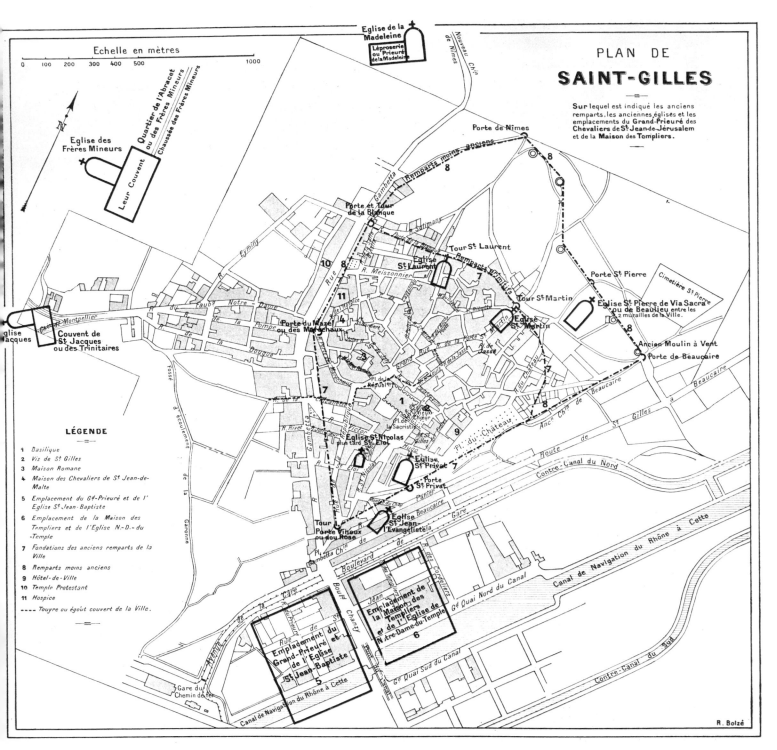

170. Plan of the town of Saint-Gilles.

1122: Galtier, Bishop of Maguelonne, and papal legate, tried to heal discords (Goiffon, XLVII, 66).

1125: Saint-Gilles given to the Order of Cluny for reform (Goiffon, L, 69).

1132: Rule of Cluny accepted (Bull of Innocent II: all future abbots of Saint-Gilles could come from their own ranks, but if outside monks were elected, they must be from the Abbey of Cluny (Goiffon, LII, 72).

1142: Two dated epitaphs on the west wall of the crypt.

1148: Visit of Louis VII on his return from the Second Crusade.

1151: Raymond V ceded all rights to the Abbey of Saint-Gilles in the presence of the Bishop of Nîmes.

1154: Raymond married Constance, sister of Louis VII.

1163: Abbey under royal protection after spices and letter sent to the King at Étampes (1162).

1165: Saint-Gilles sided with the Pisans in Genoese-Pisan War.[3]

1170–1172: Rabbi Benjamin of Toledo described crowds pressing against the tomb of Saint Gilles.

1171: Petrus Brunus signed peace treaty between Saint-Gilles and Genoa.[4]

1179: Trouble between Raymond V of Toulouse and the King of Aragon allied with the Bishop of Nîmes and the Viscount of Béziers over the jurisdiction of Saint-Gilles.

1179: Papal bull declared that Nîmes has no episcopal authority over Saint-Gilles (Goiffon, LXXI, 93). Disturbances caused fortification of abbey to connect it with chateau.

1186: Brunus signed an act with the Cathedral of Nîmes and was designated as "Petrus Brunus artifix in opera ligneo et lapideo."[5]

1196: Count of Toulouse ordered by Pope to repair damages and destroy chateau he had built (Goiffon, LXXIII, 96).

1198: Raymond VI, Count of Toulouse, to be absolved if he corrected all his excesses against Saint-Gilles (Goiffon, LXXIV, 99).

1199: Threat of new excommunication of Count Raymond unless fortress demolished (Goiffon, LXXV, 100).

1208: Pierre de Castelnau, a papal legate, was murdered at Saint-Gilles by the Albigensian friends of Raymond VI.

---

3. Basing his findings on analysis of documents discovered in Nîmes, Marcel Gouron, in "Dates des sculptures du portail de l'église de Saint-Gilles," *Bulletin de la Société d'histoire et d'archéologie de Nîmes et du Gard* (1933–1934), 45–47, analyzed the political relationships between the town of Saint-Gilles and Pisa and Genoa in the 1160's, 1170's, and into the thirteenth century.

4. *Ibid.,* 47–56.

5. *Ibid.,* 45–50.

1209: Raymond VI forced to make amends (in the nude) in front of the abbey as well as in front of the grave of Pierre de Castelnau in the crypt.

1212: Raymond VI admonished by the Pope for having demolished buildings belonging to the abbey (Goiffon, LXXXII).

1216: Raymond VI excommunicated (Goiffon, LXXXIII, 114).

1226: The town of Saint-Gilles submitted to the monarchy.

The bull of Honorius II of 2 April 1125, announcing to the monks of Cluny that Saint-Gilles had been given to Abbot Peter the Venerable to reform, and the bull of Innocent II of 14 November 1132, confirming the final Cluniac takeover and stating the rules of succession of abbots, would seem to be the earliest date (1132) for the beginning of such a large church with choir, ambulatory, and radiating chapels and the huge façade.[6]

The documents of 1171 and 1186 in which one of the signers was Petrus Brunus do not prove that the portals were begun in the 1170's.[7] The inscription to the left of Matthew's head reads *Brunus me fecit*, not *Petrus Brunus me fecit*. Peters Brunus of the documents could either be the Brunus of Saint-Gilles later in his life, or the son of the Brunus of Saint-Gilles, or another Brunus altogether.

The dating of the west wall and the western projection of the Saint-Gilles crypt, on which the façade rests, is obviously of paramount importance for the establishment of the approximate beginning of the west portals (figs. 171–173). The fact that the majority of the bays of the crypt are vaulted with ribbed vaults has led many scholars, who insist on the primacy of the Île-de-France in the formation of Gothic, to place the superstructure of the crypt in the late twelfth century.

In 1116 Abbot Hugh began the construction of a new basilica. This event is documented by an inscription (fig. 174) located near the bottom of the second wall buttress from the west on the south flank of the crypt. The plan of the crypt (fig. 171) indicates three types of vaulting: groin vaults over the fourth central bay from the west (no. 1) and three bays in south aisle, barrel vault in south aisle, and the rest ribbed vaults.[8] The fourth bay, originally containing the relics of Saint Gilles, is groin-vaulted. It is dated late eleventh-century by Lasteyrie, but not related to the altar consecrated by Pope Urban II in 1096.[9] This same bay is dated before 1116 by

---

6. Goiffon, *op. cit.*, 69–71.

7. Gouron, *op. cit.*, 45–56.

8. On the plan (fig. 171) the bays are numbered in numerals and in numerals in parenthesis. The plain numbers follow the order of construction established by Lasteyrie from 1 to 14. The numbers in parenthesis give the sequence of construction worked out by Horn from (1) to (8).

9. R. de Lasteyrie, "Études sur la sculpture française au moyen-âge," Académie des inscriptions et belles-lettres, Fondation Piot, *Monuments et mémoires*, VIII (1902), 86.

L. H. Labande, after 1116 by A. Fliche, and thought to be Carolingian by L'Abbé Nicholas and R. Hamann.[10] The walls of this bay appear to have been transformed to support groin vaults in place of the original wooden roof. Any vaults which existed prior to 1116 seem to have been demolished to prepare for Abbot Hugh's new church.

The *Liber Miraculorum*, written between 1121 and 1124 by the librarian of Saint-Gilles, and dedicated to Abbot Hugh, who died in 1124, includes a description, by a man standing on the walls of the crypt, of the destruction of this church and two others to make way for the new basilica. Further, the miraculous saving of workers who fell from walls, by the intercession of Saint Gilles, plus the story of two other men being saved proves that all vaulting of the crypt must be part of the campaign which began in 1116.[11]

The inscription of 1116, because of its location on an exterior wall buttress, proves that the crypt walls were in existence at that date. At the level of the sills of the crypt windows there is a marked break in the masonry and a change in the color of the stone. The yellow-orange stone of the lower section is limestone with a small amount of limonite, iron rust of the fraction of 1 percent, while from the sills upward the stones are gray limestone without limonite. This shift in the nature of limestone does not necessarily mean a long lapse in time, since stone from a different bed in the same quarry could have no limonite. The stone of the upper part of the walls of the crypt, which extend upward to form the exterior of the nave, could, however, be from a different quarry. This change in the nature of the stone can be seen in the fragments of the choir which are still standing.

Lasteyrie argued that the crypt was mostly finished by 1140. In his opinion the 1116 plus campaign involved only groin vaults (plan, 3, 4, 5—fig. 171). Then in the second quarter of the century, moving from east to west, the bays marked 6, 7, 8, 9, 10, 11 (fig. 171) were converted to support ribbed vaults. Only the western bay (no. 12) and the north-aisle bays (13, 14) were planned from the start to receive ribbed vaults. Since these vaults spring from the west wall of the crypt with its two inscriptions dated 1142, Lasteyrie concluded that the western part of the crypt was completed in the 1140's and the portals begun in the 1150's.[12]

---

10. L. H. Labande, "L'Église de Saint-Gilles," *Congrès archéologique de France*, I (1909), 170; A. Fliche, *Aigues-Mortes et Saint-Gilles*, Petites monographies des grands édifices de la France (Paris: Laurens, 1925), 76; C. Nicholas, "Construction et réparations de l'église de Saint-Gilles," *Mémoires de l'Académie de Nîmes*, XXIII (1900), 95–100; R. Hamann, *Die Abteikirche von St. Gilles und ihre künstlerische Nachfolge* (Berlin: Akademie-Verlag, 1955), 25.

11. W. Horn, *Die Fassade von St. Gilles* (Hamburg: Paul Evert, 1937), 12; Hamann, *op. cit.*, 71–72.

12. De Lasteyrie, *op. cit.*, 89–91.

L. H. Labande placed the ribbed vaults in the late twelfth century.[13] A. Fliche believed that the pillars and walls of the crypt were built between 1116 and 1129, the groin vaults after 1142, the western part of the crypt by 1179, and the ribbed vaults after 1179.[14] M. Gouron concluded that the campaign following 1116 included only the groin vaults, while the ribbed vaults were constructed much later.[15]

W. Horn, on the other hand, argued that the walls of the crypt up to the sills of the windows, the central bay with different superstructure (no. 1), and the barrel-vaulted bay (no. 2) were constructed before 1116, while the upper parts of the walls, including the ribbed vaults, were erected during the new construction designated by the inscription of 1116. Further, Horn refuted Lasteyrie's order of the construction of the ribbed vaults and made a strong case, based on the study of moldings and the nature of the keystones of the ribs, for a sequence from west to east (see numbers in parenthesis for Horn's order—fig. 171). According to Horn, the oldest rib-vaulted bay is the westernmost (bay 3).[16]

In his study of the crypt, which is even more detailed than Horn's, Hamann, for the most part, substantiated Horn's west-to-east sequence for the construction of the ribbed vaults. He reasoned that the vaulting proceeded gradually after 1116, that the façade was begun after 1096, and that the change in the sculptural program took place after 1116.[17]

The conclusions of Horn and Hamann seem valid. It is clear from a study of the crypt piers that work proceeded from west to east. The westernmost piers are square in plan with the diagonal ribs springing awkwardly from the corners (fig. 172), whereas the next pair of piers (to the east) are articulated with chamfered corners which are integrated with the diagonal ribs (figs. 172, 173). The treatment of the keystones certainly suggests a west-to-east evolution, especially in the western part of the crypt. Work began on the superstructure of the western bays of the crypt after 1116, but the turbulent history of the abbey from 1116 to 1125 or to 1132 suggests either that there was a delay in commencing the new campaign or that work progressed very slowly. The break in masonry at the sills of the crypt with more regular masonry above and the change in the color of the limestone seem to imply a lag in building activity. If this interruption transpired, as seems likely, one can conclude

---

13. Labande, *op. cit.*, 175.

14. Fliche, *op. cit.*, 76.

15. M. Gouron, "Saint-Gilles-du-Gard," *Congrès archéologique de France*, CVIII (1951), 107.

16. Horn, *op. cit.*, 13–15.

17. Hamann, *op. cit.*, 21–53. Even though Hamann's discussion of the architecture of the crypt and choir is detailed and scholarly, a monograph on Saint-Gilles, the building, both as monument and in relation to other Provençal buildings, is badly needed.

that the crypt was finished in the 1130's or at the latest by the early 1140's. Since the crypt with its projections serves as the substructure for the façade, it follows that the portals could have been started in the late 1130's or the early 1140's.

In spite of the fact that dating of epigraphy by stylistic analysis is difficult and often debatable, inscriptions on the west wall and west projection of the crypt must be considered, since their date helps establish the earliest possible time for the beginning of the façade. M. Schapiro studied three inscriptions, not mentioned by R. de Lasteyrie (figs. 175–177).[18] The names on these epitaphs appear in the necrology of a manuscript of the Rule of Saint Benedict in the British Museum (Add. ms. 16979). This manuscript can be dated by a colophon in the year 1129; so the epitaphs must be before that year. Since these inscriptions were not commemorative, they could not have been placed in the wall at a later date. Thus the west wall (see plan—fig. 171) must have been completed before 1129, and work on the façade, according to Schapiro, could have begun in the 1120's.

In a detailed analysis of these three epitaphs (figs. 175–177) and comparisons with the 1116 inscription (fig. 174) and with the two epitaphs dated 1142 (figs. 178, 179), Schapiro argued that the three epitaphs are closer stylistically and palaeographically to the 1116 inscription than to the 1142 epitaphs. The year, a nonreligious intrusion, is not included in the three epitaphs before 1129, but is in the 1142 ones as well as in the majority of epitaphs in the second third of the twelfth century. The 1116 inscription (fig. 174) has letters tangent to the ruled lines, which extend beyond the inscription, and exhibits a variety of spacing and shape of the letters. In the three epitaphs, before 1129 (figs. 175–177), the incised lines merely mark the zones for the inscription, although the letters still show different shapes. The 1142 epitaphs (figs. 178, 179) substitute a formal frame for the ruled lines, while the letters are more regular.[19]

Seven epitaphs of canons in the cloister of Saint-Paul-de-Mausole at Saint-Rémy-de-Provence, which can be dated 1104–1117, 1127–1134, 1134–1145, 1151–1153, 1163–1177, 1199–1206, 1231, help corroborate Schapiro's conclusions.[20] A study of photographs, taken by the author, reveals a relationship in epigraphic style between the first three of Saint-Paul-de-Mausole and the inscription of 1116 and three epitaphs before 1129, although all those in Saint-Paul are contained within frames. The fourth one of Saint-Paul, dated between 1151 and 1153, appears to be close in style to the two epitaphs of Saint-Gilles, dated 1142.

---

18. M. Schapiro, "New Documents on St.-Gilles," *Art Bulletin*, XVII (1935), 416–425.

19. *Ibid.*, 419–424.

20. E. Leroy, *Cartulaire de Saint-Paul-de-Mausole à Saint-Rémy-de-Provence* (Saint-Rémy-de-Provence: 1961), 11–17 (not illustrated).

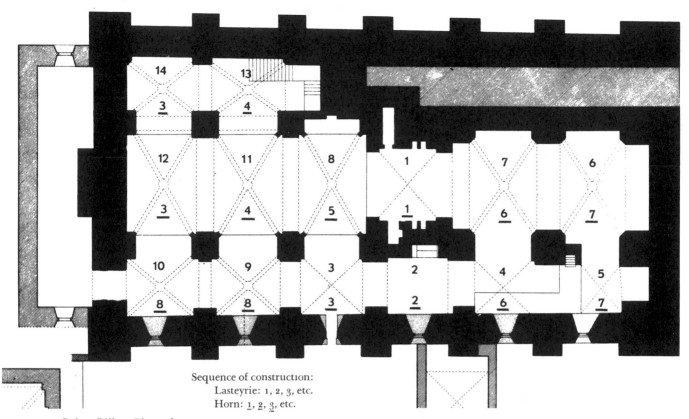

Sequence of construction:
Lasteyrie: 1, 2, 3, etc.
Horn: 1, 2, 3, etc.

171. Saint-Gilles. Plan of crypt.

172. Crypt, west wall, three western bays.

173. Crypt, to the east.

174. Saint-Gilles. Inscription, 1116.

175. Epitaph of Petrus de Brozet, before 1129.

176. Epitaph of Hubilotus, before 1129.

177. Epitaph of Frotardus, before 1129.

178. Epitaph of Gilius, 1142.

179. Epitaph of Causitus, 1142.

180. Detail, Bartholomew.

181. Detail, John.

182. Detail, James Major.

The location of the epitaphs of Saint-Gilles on the exterior west wall of the crypt is important, since their placement proves that the west wall, as well as the projection under the central portal, was finished by 1129. The epitaphs of Frotardus (fig. 177) and Hubilotus (fig. 176) are situated to the north and south, respectively, of the south door leading from the crypt to the area under the nineteenth-century vault which supports the staircase of the façade. The third epitaph of 1129 (Petrus de Brozet—fig. 175) is on the south side of the projection of the crypt. The Gilius epitaph, dated 1142 (fig. 178), is located on the west side of the projection, while the other of 1142, Causitus (fig. 179), is just to the south of the south door on the west wall of the crypt. Since the courses of masonry continue evenly across the entire west wall and since one epitaph of 1129 and one of 1142 are situated on the projection, it follows that the west wall and projection of the crypt were part of the same campaign and can be dated around 1129.

M. Schapiro argued that the sporadic difficulties which the town and abbey suffered during the period 1117 to 1125 would have only interrupted the work for several months[21] On the other hand, W. Horn claimed the incessant disorder caused a delay in building until 1125. As already stated, the break in the masonry at the bottom of the sills of the windows of the crypt with a change from yellow to gray limestone and a more regular system of laying up the stone was interpreted by Horn as a discontinuation of building during the hectic times between 1116 and 1125.[22]

The inscriptions on the apostles, Bartholomew, John, James Major (figs. 180–182), together with the inscriptions on Matthew and Paul, exhibit a consistently vertical axis to the letters and an even spacing of the letters. In these respects the inscriptions on the façade are closest in style to the epitaphs dated 1142 on the west wall of the crypt. If this comparison is valid, Brunus could have started work on the facade in the 1140's.

Using manuscripts to help date Romanesque sculpture and murals is a dangerous procedure. Manuscripts were illuminated by monks in monastic scriptoria, while portals were, in all probability, carved by lay sculptors under clerical supervision. On the other hand, there are sufficient stylistic similarities between the illuminations in Romanesque manuscripts and monumental sculpture in such areas as Burgundy and southwestern France to warrant a tentative discussion of possible relationships in Provence.

In Burgundy, the great library of Cluny was destroyed, but surviving manuscripts and fragments of others substantiate the contemporaneity of manuscript, mural painting, and monumental sculpture. The "Pentacost" from the Lectionary

---

21. Schapiro, *op. cit.*, 424–425.
22. Horn, *op. cit.*, 17–19.

from Cluny (Bibliothèque nationale, Ms. Nouv. acq. lat. 2246, fol. 79v) exhibits remarkable similarities with the frescoes of the chapel of the Cluniac grange of Berzé-la-Ville.[23] Gestures, facial types, treatment of drapery, and figures against a blue ground—all appear in illuminations and murals. Further, the general style of manuscripts and the monumental painting, more specifically, of Berzé-la-Ville have many parallels in the sculpture of Autun, as W. Sauerländer has clearly indicated.[24] In spite of the stylistic debt to Byzantium, a unique Burgundian style emerges. Another page from a Cluniac Bible further reinforces these interconnections of style and date.[25]

In Provence there seems to be a great deal of variety of styles in various scriptoria. Saint Luke from the Gospel of Saint-Sauveur of Aix, second half of the eleventh century (Aix-Méjanes, 7, fol. 169), with quiet pose and accented contours is vastly different from the elongated, agitated Isaiah from a Lectionary for usage at Montmajour, late eleventh century (Bibliothèque nationale, Lat. 886, fol. 6). The circular folds over thighs and shoulder of the Isaiah and the treatment of drapery over the feet recall the apostles by the Hard Master. In his article discussing the epitaphs on the west wall of the crypt of Saint-Gilles and comparing Provençal manuscripts with the sculpture of Saint-Gilles, M. Schapiro emphasized the stylistic connections between manuscripts of the 1120's and earlier from Provence and the façade sculpture of Saint-Gilles, concluding that the portals were begun as early as 1129.[26]

A manuscript of the Rule of Saint Benedict, now in the British Museum (Add. ms. 16979), can be dated 1129 by a colophon. As already stated, this manuscript contains a necrology of Saint-Gilles, which includes three names appearing in epitaphs

---

23. W. Stoddard, *Monastery and Cathedral in France* (Middletown: Wesleyan University Press, 1966), 80–85, fig. 115. W. Koehler, "Byzantium Art in the West," *Dumbarton Oaks Papers*, No. 1 (1941), 68–71. M. Schapiro, *The Parma Ildefonsus, A Romanesque Illuminated Manuscript from Cluny and Related Works*, Monographs of Archaeology and Fine Arts, XI (New York: 1964) 43–48, figs. 37–39.

24. W. Sauerländer, "Gislebertus von Autun, Ein Beitrag zur Entstehung seines künzstlerischen Stils," *Studien zur Geschichte der Europäischen Plastik; Festschrift Theodor Müller zum 19 April 1965* (Munich: Hirmer, 1965), 17–29. C. R. Dodwell, *Painting in Europe: 800–1200* (The Pelican History of Art, Penguin Books, 1971), 173–176, ill. 200–202, dated the Berzé-la-Ville paintings 1100–1140(?) on the basis of stylistic connections with the frescoes of the chapel of Saint Sebastian in the Lateran Palace, which have been attributed on stylistic grounds to the first three decades of the twelfth century. If the Berzé-la-Ville murals and the Lectionary from Cluny are compared to Burgundian sculpture, there seems to be no reason to date these paintings later than 1120 and more evidence to have them completed before the death of Abbot Hugh in 1109.

25. Miniature of Saint Luke from a Cluniac Bible owned by Mr. and Mrs. L. V. Randall, Montreal. See W. D. Wixom, *Treasures from Medieval France* (Cleveland: The Cleveland Museum of Art, 1967), 34, II, 7.

26. Schapiro, "New Documents on St.-Gilles," 426–430.

on the west wall of the crypt, supporting, in turn, the façade. One illumination from this manuscript, Saint Benedict giving the Rules to Three Monks (fol. 21v—fig. 183), was compared by Schapiro with the Payment of Judas in the upper left corner of the central frieze (fig. 136). As Schapiro stated, the illumination appears earlier than the upper frieze, which he dated from the 1130's or 1140's; yet the articulation of legs beneath drapery, the use of hooked folds on both legs of Benedict and on the right leg of the left-hand monk, and treatment of the sleeves of all the figures can be found in the monumental sculpture of Saint-Gilles, especially the apostles Matthew and Bartholomew and Paul (fig. 187) by Brunus.

The most convincing evidence for the possibility of the early dating of the Saint-Gilles sculpture in Provençal manuscripts is contained in manuscript no. 36 in the Nîmes Library, written at the monastery of La Grasse near Saint-Gilles (figs. 184, 185).[27] This Commentary on Paul's Epistles was written and illuminated in the abbacy of Rodbertus, between 1086 and 1108. Although the latest date of 1108 is over twenty years earlier than the possible start of the Saint-Gilles façade, many stylistic parallels between manuscript and the earliest sculpture of Saint-Gilles can be seen. In the Saint Paul (fol. 5v—fig. 184), the figure set in front of a pilaster and the marked articulation of his right leg and multiple folds above and adjacent to his left foot are related to the monumental apostles, especially Bartholomew, John, and Paul (figs. 186, 187). The second Paul (fol. 7v—fig. 185) appears to be even closer to Brunus' Paul (fig. 187). The stocky proportions and pronounced articulation of both illuminations and statues recall the Roman and Early Christian tradition which underlies Provençal Romanesque.

These stylistic relationships between manuscripts and the sculpture of Saint-Gilles are, however, insufficient proof to date the beginning of the façade of Saint-Gilles as early as the 1120's or 1129; but considered together with the history of the abbey, especially the acceptance of the authority of Cluny in 1132, the architecture of the crypt, and the inscriptions on the west wall of the crypt, these manuscript-sculpture connections reinforce the date of the late 1130's or more probably the 1140's as the time in which work started on the façade of Saint-Gilles.

Several critics have discussed the iconography of the façade of Saint-Gilles,[28] but only W. Horn, A. Katzenellenbogen, H. Kraus, and A. Borg have suggested a

---

27. *Manuscrits de la Bibliothèque de Nîmes.* Extrait du catalogue des manuscrits des bibliothèques des départments, VII (Paris: Imprimerie Nationale, 1884), 17–19. Schapiro, "New Documents on St.-Gilles," 426–429, fig. 20. Stoddard, *op. cit.,* 77–78, fig. 104—here compared with the Saint Peter of the western pier of the north gallery of the Arles Cloister.

28. The most detailed study of the subject matter on the façade can be found in Hamann's *Die Abteikirche von St. Gilles,* 79–100.

connection between the heresy of Peter of Bruys and the Saint-Gilles sculptural program.[29] R. Hamann, however, by-passed Petrobrusianism because he dated the façade before the burning of Peter. M. Colish, in an article published in 1972, has proved conclusively that indeed the façade of Saint-Gilles is a dramatic, anti-heretical statement.[30] Further, on the basis of the unquestionable date of 1137 to 1138 for the *Contra Petrobrusianos hereticos* by Peter the Venerable, Abbot of Cluny, which described Peter's death and his heretical doctrine in detail,[31] Colish reasoned that the incineration of Peter of Bruys, which had been variously dated 1132–33, 1137–40, 1139–43, and 1143, took place in all probability in 1135 or 1136.[32] Since this heresy persisted after Peter's death, the 1140's into the early 1150's would seem to be the most logical period for the erection of the Saint-Gilles façade.

Details of the lives of Peter of Bruys and his disciple, Henry of Lausanne, who joined him in southern France, need not be outlined here, but the recreation of the orthodox church to this movement, however, must be included. In 1119 at the Council of Toulouse the antisacramental doctrines, related to the heresies of Peter and Henry, were condemned. These condemnations were repeated in the Second Lateran Council of 1139. Theologians such as Peter Abelard and Saint Bernard joined in attacking these heretical beliefs. As proof of the virulence of this heresy, Saint Bernard carried out an extensive preaching campaign in southern France in the mid-1140's, which climaxed in 1147. Finally two canons of the Council of Reims of 1148 attacked heresy and more specifically the heresy in southern France.[33]

Peter the Venerable, Abbot of Cluny, with ecclesiastical control over Saint-Gilles, wrote the most complete account of the Petrobrusian doctrine in 1137–38. As Colish states:

> The Abbot of Cluny enumerates five heresies as taught by Peter of Bruys: that children prior to the age of reason cannot be saved by baptism; that it is unnecessary to build

---

29. Horn, *op. cit.*, 53–58, basing his conclusions on lectures of Erwin Panofsky, pointed out that Peter's heresy, his burning of the Saint-Gilles crosses, and immediate fiery demise may have caused a change in program of the portals of Saint-Gilles. A. Katzenellenbogen, *The Sculptural Programs of Chartres Cathedral: Christ, Mary, Ecclesia* (Baltimore: The Johns Hopkins Press, 1959), 22–23. H. Kraus, *The Living Theatre of Medieval Art* (Bloomington and London; Indiana University Press, 1967), 128, 134. A. Borg has also linked the heresy of Peter with Saint-Gilles in his doctoral dissertation for the Courtauld Institute of the University of London, *Architectural Decoration of the Romanesque Period in Provence*, (1969,) 353–356.

30. M. L. Colish, "Peter of Bruys, Henry of Lausanne, and the Façade of St.-Gilles," *Traditio*, XXVIII (1972), 451–460.

31. G. Constable, ed., *Peter the Venerable, Letters*, Harvard Historical Studies, 78 (Cambridge: 1967), II, 285–288.

32. Colish, *op. cit.*, 455–456 and fns. 22 to 32.

33. *Ibid.*, 456–457.

183. Saint Benedict giving Rule to three monks, dated 1129 (London, British Museum, Add. ms. 16979, fol. 21v).

184. Commentary on Paul's Epistles, 1086–1108 (Bibliothèque Municipale, Nîmes, Ms. 36, fol. 5v).

185. Commentary on Paul's Epistles, 1086–1108 (Nîmes, Ms. 36, fol. 7v).

186. Saint-Gilles. John.

187. Saint-Gilles. Paul.

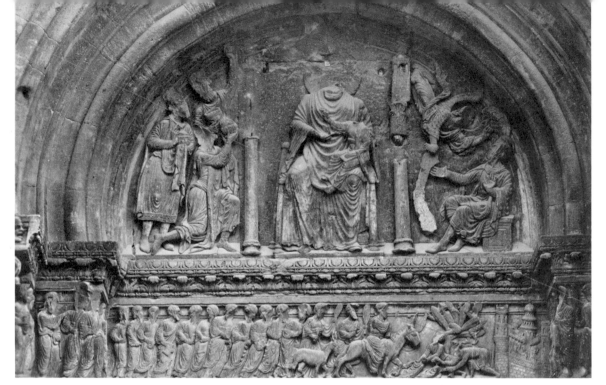

188. Saint-Gilles. Adoration of Magi, Entry into Jerusalem (LP).

189. Crucifixion (RP). Holy Women buying Perfume, Holy Women at Sepulchre.

churches, since Christians can worship just as well in a stable or a tavern as in a building especially consecrated for prayer; that crucifixes should be cut down and burned, not venerated, in order to blot out the shameful memory of the cruel death suffered by Christ; that Christ's body and blood are not really present in the Eucharist; and that prayer, sacrifices, and alms offered by the living for the dead are of no benefit to the souls of the departed. He adds that some say that Peter rejects the authority of the Bible.[34]

By concentrating on the tympana and lintels of the three portals, Colish reveals how this structure stresses orthodox doctrines and strongly attacks the heresy of Peter of Bruys and Henry of Lausanne. The most obvious answer to Peter's act of cutting down and burning the crucifixes of Saint-Gilles is the crucifixion tympanum of the right portal (fig. 189). As stated before, the Crucified Christ is rarely depicted in Romanesque tympana (Saint-Pons, Condrieu, and Champagne, the latter two reflections of Saint-Gilles), but what makes this tympanum unique is the accompanying figures and their gestures and actions. Colish writes:

> The emphasis placed by the sculptor on the soldiers and Ecclesia in the act of venerating the Crucified Christ, and on the Angel striking down Synagoga for her refusal to do so, suggest a strong desire on his part to stress the importance and sanctity of the Crucifixion, in sharp opposition to Peter's rejection of the crucifix on the grounds that Christ's death had been a shameful event. Furthermore, by including the figures of Ecclesia and Synagoga in the Crucifixion scene, he suggests the idea that the visible, institutional church is a corollary and an extension of Christ's saving mission on earth. He also strikes the note that this visible Church while excluding the blind Synagoga, embraces the true Synagoga, the *ecclesia ex circumcisionis*, symbolized by the Virgin and Saint John, and also the *ecclesia ex gentibus*, symbolized by the Roman soldiers. Thus, the sculptor of the south tympanum of St.-Gilles symbolically depicts the cosmos, heaven, and the new Christian communion of mankind bearing witness to the holiness of Christ's salvific death, and relates the meaning of that death in no uncertain terms to the Resurrection in the lintel below it.[35]

Further, the two scenes on the lintel of the right portal depicting the Holy Women buying Perfume and the Holy Women at the Sepulchre of the resurrected Christ, which may also reflect liturgical dramas connected with Easter, join the Crucifixion with the Resurrection. As Colish states:

> In any event, by associating the Crucifixion with the Resurrection, the whole sculptural ensemble of the south doorway stresses the principle that the suffering of Christ on the Cross was a theological necessity, that the Crucifixion was not a disgrace, but a triumph over sin and death and a token of the believer's rebirth in the Christian life and his

---

34. *Ibid.*, 455.
35. *Ibid.*, 459.

eventual glorification in eternity, a belief confirmed by Heaven in the person of the Angel as well as by the Church in the person of the three Maries.[36]

In the left portal, the Passion is linked to the Incarnation by the juxtaposition of the Entry into Jerusalem on the frieze and lintel and the Virgin and Child, Magi, and Joseph's Dream in the tympanum (fig. 188). The combination of Magi, Virgin and Child, and Joseph in the tympanum can be found only in the portal of Montfrin (Gard) in a provincial reflection of Saint-Gilles via the lost tympanum of Beaucaire. Colish writes as follows:

> The Magi may be taken to represent the *ecclesia ex gentibus* while Saint Joseph stands for the *ecclesia ex circumcisionis*. In the north tympanum the reverence done to Christ is linked to his persecution and suffering to come; in the south tympanum the reverence done to Christ is linked to His suffering consummated and transfigured. The Angel in the north tympanum, like the Angel in the south tympanum, reflects the idea that these focal events in the life of Christ have been decreed and approved by Heaven. The similarities between the north and south tympanum—hieratic, even iconic central figures of Christ flanked by figures and attitudes of veneration representing Heaven and Earth, the circumcised and the Gentiles—emphasize the theological connection between the Incarnation and the Passion, the sacred and divinely ordained character of Christ's entire life and death, and the idea of a visible, historical community of believers offering worship and honor to the Savior. In thematic sequence the visitor's eye is directed first toward the Incarnation and Passion and then toward the Crucifixion and Resurrection, and finally toward the central doorway, where the Last Supper depicted on the lintel gives the doctrine of the Eucharist equal centrality with the apocalyptic Christ in majesty.[37]

Thus in all three portals the Incarnation, Passion, and Resurrection and the church sacraments are interrelated in a coherent totality of subject composition and content to combat efficiently and dramatically the heresies of Peter of Bruys and Henry of Lausanne.

Other scenes of the Passion of Christ on the upper frieze of the central portal are not discussed by Colish, but corroborate her conclusions. Besides augmenting the Passion cycle and supplying the necessary transitions from the Incarnation on the left portal to the Crucifixion and Resurrection on the right portal, several scenes which are rarely found in Romanesque sculpture dramatize Christ's strength, His miraculous powers, and His suffering. The Purging of the Temple (fig. 122), unique in portal sculpture, emphasizes Christ's ability to punish evil physically, while the Raising of Lazarus prefigures perhaps Christ's own resurrection. On the right side of the central portal, Christ's suffering is dramatically depicted, as He is pulled and

---

36. *Ibid.*, 458.
37. *Ibid.*, 459–460.

pushed toward Pilate and bound to a pillar and struck by two flagellants. The cross weighing heavily on Simon points directly to the Crucifixion on the right tympanum.

In the right-hand portal the side figures as well as the lintel and tympanum are compositionally balanced. In the re-entrant angles the splays of the frieze, the number and placement of figures, and their poses and gestures are mirror images, but carved by different sculptors. One panel on the left side depicts Christ being anointed by Mary in a house in Bethany (fig. 190). The Saint-Gilles sculptor seems to have followed quite literally the description in the Gospel according to John (xii, 1–8):

> Six days before the Passover, Jesus came to Bethany, where Lazarus was, whom Jesus had raised from the dead. There they made him a supper; Martha served, but Lazarus was one of those at table with him. Mary took a pound of costly ointment of pure nard and anointed the feet of Jesus and wiped his feet with her hair; and the house was filled with the fragrance of the ointment. But Judas Iscariot, one of the disciples (he who was to betray Him) said, "Why was this ointment not sold for 300 denarii and given to the poor?" This he said, not that he cared for the poor but because he was a thief, and as he had the money box he used to take what was put in it. Jesus said, "Let her alone, let her keep it for the day of my burial. The poor you always have with you, but you do not always have me."

Judas on the left is pointing to Christ with his right hand, while Jesus points to Mary and to himself. As stated earlier, this scene is out of order in the chronology of the Gospels; it should follow the Raising of Lazarus, which is located on the left side of the central portal and, incidentally, is found only in the Gospel of John. It is quite possible that this scene was placed intentionally out of order to dramatize the connection between the Betrayal on the right side of the central portal, through Christ's suffering on the upper right-hand frieze, to Christ's Cruxifixion and Resurrection on the right-hand tympanum and lintel. Judas is pointing to Christ and to the Crucified Christ.

The selection of scenes to illustrate the Passion would seem to indicate a convergence of antiheretical doctrine and local legend. Emphasis on the Marys (Mary Magdalene appears five times) and the depiction of the Raising of Lazarus could conceivably reflect the Provençal legend of the arrival of Mary Salome, mother of the apostles James and John, Mary Jacobus, sister of the Virgin, Lazarus and his sisters, Martha and Mary Magdalene, and the black servant Sarah at Les-Saintes-Maries-de-la-Mer. Furthermore, many episodes which are located only at Saint-Gilles and on monuments influenced by the sculpture of Saint-Gilles seem to be derived from representations on Early Christian sarcophagi, which were originally in Les Alyscamps at Arles.

Recently H. Kraus interpreted much of the Saint-Gilles sculpture in terms of the Jewish-Christian debate. He pointed to the Synagogue as an example of the

190. Saint-Gilles. Christ in the House in Bethany (R.P.L).

191. Condrieu. Crucifixion and Last Supper.

anti-Semitic cast of the façade.[38] On the other hand, B. Blumenkranz noted that the crown being knocked off the Synagogue by the angel is two stages of a tower capped by a cupola. A similar structure rises above the walls of Jerusalem on the lintel of the left portal. Blumenkranz reasoned that the Synagogue losing the crown-tower symbolized the loss for the Jews of their country, city, and temple and served as a reminder during the Crusades that Christianity must reconquer it.[39] As N. Golb has proved in his analysis of a manuscript preserved in the University Library, Cambridge, a disastrous pogrom occurred in the town of Monieux in the Vaucluse (Provence) as Crusaders set out across the Alps under the command of Raymond of Saint-Gilles in the summer of 1096.[40] However, there is no documentary proof of any persecutions before the Second Crusade of 1147. The interpretation of the Synagogue by Blumenkranz might point to the late 1140's for the date of the tympana of Saint-Gilles.[41]

Evidence for dating Saint-Gilles by comparisons with monuments in France and in Northern Italy also points to the 1140's into the 1150's as the period in which the façade was created. Attempts by scholars to date Saint-Gilles, the north gallery of the Arles cloister, and the portal at Arles on the basis of their influence on or the influence from the Early Gothic of the Île-de-France make little sense, since there is no stylistic connection between the Royal Domain and Provence. Suger's façade of Saint-Denis, certainly begun by 1137, is an extraordinary amalgam of new ideas with influences probably from Burgundy, western France, and the Meuse Valley. The Royal Portals of Chartres, completed by 1150 or earlier, exhibit three distinct personalities: a Saint-Denis Master, the Étampes Master, and a Headmaster.[42] The origin of the latter is still being debated. However, the sculpture by these three Chartres sculptors and their assistants is entirely different from any sculpture on the façade of Saint-Gilles. Furthermore, Chartres was probably completed before Saint-Gilles.

The Thomas Master of Saint-Gilles, who carved the pedestal reliefs on the central portal, the two socles on the right portal, and the apostles Thomas, James the Less, and Peter (figs. 21, 28, 50), has been connected with sculpture on the façade at Angoulême in southwestern France (figs. 22, 23, 56, 57). The Cathedral of Angoulême

---

38. Kraus, *op. cit.*, 150–155.

39. B. Blumenkranz, "La polémique antijuive dans l'art chrétien du moyen-âge," *Bullettino dell'Istituto storico italiano per il medio evo e Archivio Muratoriano*, LXXVII (1965), 41–42; and B. Blumenkranz, *Le juif médiéval au miroir de l'art chrétien* (Paris: Études Augustiennes, 1966), 66.

40. N. Golb "New Light on the Persecution of French Jews at the Time of the First Crusade," *Proceedings of the Academy for Jewish Research*, XXXIV (1966), 1–63.

41. For a detailed study of the Church and Synagogue see W. Seiferth, *Synagoge und Kirche im Mittelalter* (Munich: Kosel-Verlag, 1964).

42. W. Stoddard, *The West Portals of Saint-Denis and Chartres* (Cambridge: Harvard University Press, 1952), 20–22.

was begun in 1100, constructed from west to east, and dedicated in 1128. There is, however, no proof that the façade was completed by 1128. The monogram in the right-hand upper spandrel seems to contain a "G" for Bishop Girard, who died in 1136, and an "I" for Iteus Archembaldi, a canon, who was the main donor of the cathedral and who died in 1125.[43] Porter argued that the façade was completed for the consecration of 1128 or very soon thereafter and that the Thomas Master, his Angoulême Master, came to Saint-Gilles in the 1140's.[44] If the date of 1128 is correct or if the façade was finished in the 1130's, which seems more probable, one could assume that the Thomas Master, either coming from the workshop of Angoulême or being influenced by Angoulême, could have started work at Saint-Gilles in the late 1130's or 1140's. The head of the Apostle Thomas seems closer to the Prophet Isaiah at Souillac (fig. 25) and to other monuments in southwest France which date from the 1130's or early 1140's. It therefore can be argued that the Thomas Master's activity at Saint-Gilles commenced in the 1140's.

The sculpture in Toulouse, which seems to exhibit stylistic parallels with Saint-Gilles, especially with the developed Brunus style of John and Paul, is the apostles from Saint-Étienne, originally inside the chapter house and now in the Musée des Augustins.[45] This sculpture has been dated as early as 1120 and as late as the 1150's.[46]

---

43. C. Daras, *La cathédrale d'Angoulême:* (Angoulême: Corignan et Lachanand, 1948), 148–149.

44. A. K. Porter, *Romanesque Sculpture of the Pilgrimage Roads* (Boston: Marshall Jones, 1923), vol. 1, 307–310.

45. L. Seidel, "A Romantic Forgery: The Romanesque 'Portal' of Saint-Étienne in Toulouse," *Art Bulletin*, L, 1 (1968), 33–42. Seidel proved that apostles originally supported the transverse arches of the barrel vault of the chapter house like the paired apostles in the Cámara Santa in Oviedo. She dated the sculpture about 1125.

46. The dating of the sculpture from the chapter house of Saint-Étienne of Toulouse has never been firmly established. See P. Mesplé, *Toulouse. Musée des Augustins. Les sculptures romanes.* Inventaire des collections publiques françaises, 5 (Paris: Éditions des Musées Nationaux, 1961), Ill. 1, 5, 8, 11, 15, 19, 22, 24. R. Rey placed the Saint-Étienne sculpture around 1120 in *La sculpture romane langue-docienne* (Toulouse: Edouard Privat, 1936), 190–202. M. Lafargue dated this sculpture between 1125 and 1134 after the second series of capitals from La Daurade in *Les chapiteaux du cloître de Notre-Dame la Daurade* (Paris: 1940), 86–87. W. Sauerländer related the apostles of Saint-Étienne to the porch of Moissac (1125–1130) and claimed that the commencement of the façade of Saint-Denis around 1137 was the *terminus ante quem* for their carving, in "Chefs d'oeuvre romans des musées de province," *Kunstchronik*, II (1958), 35 and 51ff. A. K. Porter reasoned that the Saint-Étienne apostles are later than the sculpture of the west portals of Saint-Denis (1140) and contemporary with the Chartres portals (1140's) (Porter, *op. cit.*, 159–160). This author argued that the Saint-Étienne apostles were later than the Saint-Denis portals and had more stylistic characteristics in common with the portals growing out of the Chartres Royal Portals, in *West Portals of Saint-Denis and Chartres*, 44–46. It is probably wrong to place these statues as late as the 1150's and 1160's; yet it is difficult to date them before the 1140's. A detailed study of the evolution of the Romanesque sculpture of Languedoc is badly needed.

In placing the Saint-Étienne apostles in the stylistic evolution of southwestern French sculpture, these figures would seem to be later than the Moissac porch (1125–1130) and later than Souillac, and therefore carved in the late 1130's or more probably the 1140's.

The Saint-Gilles style extended up the Rhône Valley and can be seen in the fragments preserved in the Cathedral of Valence and in the paired apostles of the portal of Saint-Bernard at Romans (see Part II, Chapter 11). The sculpture in three monuments in Vienne reveals a homogeneous, regional style which seems to have grown out of influences from Burgundy to the north and Provence, especially the capitals of the cloister of Notre-Dame-des-Doms at Avignon. However, the chronological relationship between Provence and Vienne is still uncertain. J. Vallery-Radot dated the capitals in the Romanesque nave arcade of the Cathedral of Saint-Maurice of Vienne between 1107 and 1140.[47] Clearly the capitals of Saint-André-le-Bas of Vienne evolved from those of the cathedral. The inscription of 1152 on the base of the nave pier, signed by Wilhelmus Martini, proves that the capitals of Saint-André-le-Bas were carved in the 1150's.[48]

Other statues, formerly on a portal but now located inside the north porch of Saint-Maurice, and the Saint Peter in Saint-Pierre of Vienne have stocky, massive proportions, sandaled feet, and accented ridge folds—characteristics which are vaguely related to the Saint-Gilles apostles, but more specifically connected to the Avignon capitals. These figures possess less of the late Burgundian influence than the capitals of Saint-André-le-Bas.

The same regional, hybrid style of the middle Rhône Valley, only on a reduced scale, appears in the capital, Christ meeting two Apostles on the Road to Emmaus, beside the south door of the Cathedral of Vienne. These three figures are extremely close stylistically to the tympanum of the church of Condrieu (fig. 191), which is only six miles southwest of Vienne.[49] The Condrieu tympanum, now set in a Gothic portal with the Last Supper from a larger portal serving as lintel, depicts the Holy Women at the Sepulchre, the Crucifixion, and Christ carrying the Cross, three scenes appearing at Saint-Gilles. As A. K. Porter pointed out, the structure behind the Holy

---

47. J. Vallery-Radot, "L'ancienne cathédrale Saint-Maurice de Vienne des origines à la consécration de 1251. Chronologie et décor des parties romanes," *Bulletin monumental*, CX (1952), 297–362.

48. J. Vallery-Radot, "L'église Saint-André le-Bas de Vienne et ses rapports avec Saint-Paul de Lyon, Notre-Dame d'Andance et Notre-Dame de Die," *Bulletin monumental*, XCVII (1938), 145–172. See also E. Albrand, *L'église et le cloître de Saint-André-le-Bas à Vienne* (Vienne: 1951).

49. For the best analysis of the Vienne style or middle Rhône Valley style, see W. Sauerländer, "Eine trauernde Maria des 12. Jahrhunderts aus dem Mittleren Rhonetal," *Berliner Museen*. Berichte aus den Staatlichen Museen der Stiftung Preussischer Kulturbesitz Neue Floge (1964), 2–8. Sauerländer perhaps tends, in following Vallery-Radot, to date the Vienne sculpture too early.

Women reflects the tomb in the Church of the Holy Sepulchre built for the Crusaders. Further, Porter believed that the architecture behind Christ carrying the Cross consisted of the bell tower of the Holy Sepulchre, the dome of the Anastasis, and the column of the Flagellation (from right to left). Thus, he concluded that the Condrieu sculptor must have been to Jerusalem, seen the tower completed by 1154, and been familiar with the central portal of Saint-Gilles of the 1140's.[50] Since the Condrieu tympanum reflects Saint-Gilles in terms of subject and has vague stylistic connections with Provence and can be dated in the 1150's, it follows that the superstructure of the Saint-Gilles façade was completed in the early 1150's.

The connections between Saint-Gilles and Provençal sculpture and the art of Northern Italy have been discussed in detail by many scholars. It is obvious that the Genesis reliefs on the façade of the Cathedral of Modena (fig. 53) are earlier than the façade of Saint-Gilles, whether one follows the early dating of Porter (1106) or Jullian (1117 or about 1120). Further, the Prophets of Cremona, which survived the earthquake of 1117, must predate Saint-Gilles. Both Modena and Cremona manifest an archaic character, reminiscent, in their stage of evolution, of the ambulatory reliefs of Saint-Sernin at Toulouse (1095) and reliefs from the cloister of Moissac (1100). In contrast to these early twelfth-century Italian monuments, the pontile of the Cathedral of Modena (fig. 192), which was carved around 1170, reveals a marked stylistic departure.[51] The Modena sculptor must have seen the Saint-Gilles façade and the frieze of Beaucaire, since the iconography follows Saint-Gilles from the lintel of the central portal through the right-hand upper frieze with the same sequence of scenes: Christ washing the Feet, Last Supper, Betrayal, Christ before Pilate combined with the Flagellation, and Simon carrying the Cross. In the spandrels beneath the choir screen are depicted Christ's Prophecy of Peter's Denial and the Payment to Judas, which are located on the left frieze of the central portal of Saint-Gilles and also appear on the frieze of Beaucaire. In spite of the iconographic and compositional dependence on Saint-Gilles and Beaucaire, the Modena pontile exhibits stylistic relationships with the sculpture at Saint-Trophîme at Arles. In turn, the Arles sculpture, to be discussed in Part II, is strongly influenced by Saint-Gilles.

50. A. K. Porter, "Condrieu, Jerusalem, and Saint-Gilles," *Art in America*, XIII (1924-1925), 117-129.

51. The most recent studies, including analysis of the pontile of Modena, are in general agreement on its date. R. Jullian, in *L'éveil de la sculpture italienne. La sculpture romane dans l'Italie du Nord* (Paris: 1945, 1949), 186-187, placed the Modena pontile at the end of the third quarter of the twelfth century. G. de Francovich, in *Benedetto Antelami. Architetto e scultore e l'arte del suo tempo* (Milan and Florence: 1952), 56-57, argued that the pontile was begun between 1160 and 1165 and finished between 1170 and 1175. A. C. Quintavalle, in *La cattedrale di Modena* (Modena: 1964-1965), 251-252, followed the conclusions of Francovich.

192. Modena, Cathedral. The Pontile.

193. Parma, Cathedral. The Deposition by Benedetto Antelami (1178).

The *terminus ante quem* for the façade of Saint-Gilles is the Deposition relief in the Cathedral of Parma, signed by Benedetto Antelami, and dated 1178 (fig. 193). This Deposition combines scenes from the lintel and tympanum of the right portal of Saint-Gilles (fig. 189) with a figured style more closely reflecting the late work at Arles (east cloister and portal). By working backward in time from the date of 1178 of the Parma Deposition, it is possible to date the choir screen of Modena around 1170 and the Arles north gallery, east gallery and portal in the 1150's to early 1170's. This procedure would then place the Saint-Gilles façade generally in the 1140's into the early 1150's. Connections between Provence and Italy will be elaborated in the chapters on Beaucaire and Arles.

NOTES—CHAPTER 6
Dating the Façade

(1) *Conclusions of Critics* (1830's to 1950's)
    French scholars tend to date the Saint-Gilles façade in the second half of the twelfth and early decades of the thirteenth centuries, while Germans and Americans place the portals toward the mid-twelfth century. Nineteenth-century writers typify the variety of dating. Prosper Mérimée argued that the crypt was completed by 1150, followed by the façade soon thereafter.[52] E. Viollet-le-Duc, concentrating on architecture, dated Saint-Gilles and all the sculpture of Saint-Trophîme of Arles in the late twelfth century.[53] On the other hand, H. Revoil placed the portals around 1140 before the Arles portal, which, he argued, was completed in 1152.[54] The establishment of two rival schools of dating occurred in 1894 with the publication of W. Vöge's book.[55] Analyzing the monumental art of the Middle Ages in general and especially the origins of Gothic, Vöge placed Saint-Gilles around 1150 after the cloister and portal of Arles. Vöge saw a strong influence of Arles, especially the façade, on the Royal Portals of Chartres and thereby started the whole debate concerning the priority of Provençal or Île-de-France sculpture. Two French writers, A. Marignan and L'Abbé Nicholas, represent extremes in dating—about 1200-1250 by the former and after 1116 by the latter.[56]
    R. de Lasteyrie, writing in 1902, was the first critic to challenge the conclusions of W. Vöge.[57] Basing his findings on a study of the architecture of the crypt, choir, and nave,

52. P. Mérimée, *Notes d'un voyage dans le Midi de la France* (Paris: Librairie de Fournier, 1835), 336–345.

53. E. Viollet-le-Duc, *Dictionnaire raisonné de l'architecture française du XIe au XVIe siècle*, 10 vols. (Paris: Bance, 1854–1868), VII, 417.

54. H. Revoil, *L'architecture romane du Midi de la France*, 3 vols. (Paris: Morel, 1873),II, 47–66.

55. W. Vöge, *Die Anfänge des monumentalen Stiles im Mittelalter* (Strassburg: 1894), 47ff., 101ff.

56. A. Marignan, "L'école du sculpture en Provence du XIIe et XIIIe siècle," *Moyen-âge*, III (1899), 1–64. C. Nicholas, "Construction et réparations de l'église de Saint-Gilles," *Mémoires de l'Académie de Nîmes*, XXIII (1900), 95–149.

57. R. de Lasteyrie, *op. cit.*, 80–115.

and claiming the strong influence of the Île-de-France on Provençal sculpture, Lasteyrie dated the Saint-Gilles portals in the second half of the twelfth century. Lasteyrie argued that the monumental apostles and angels were carved after 1150, the side portals and the left-hand frieze of the central portal were completed by about 1180, and the rest of the super-structure of the central portal was finished by the end of the twelfth century. L. H. Labande accepted Lasteyrie's conclusions, but pushed the start of the sculptural work later.[58] J. Charles-Roux also agreed with Lasteyrie that the apostles could be dated in the middle of the twelfth century; yet he tended to push their completion toward the middle of the third quarter of the century. He included in his first campaign (third quarter of the twelfth century) the fourteen monumental statues and the frieze of the central portal extending from the left (Payment of Judas) to Christ before Pilate. His second campaign, which he dated in the thirteenth century, consisted of the tympana and friezes of the side portals and the right section of the central frieze (Christ before Pilate through the Carrying of the Cross).[59] Like Labande, A. Fliche argued for a later dating of the crypt and façade and divided the sculpture into three periods: 1180–1190; before 1209; and 1209–1240.[60]

A. K. Porter was the first twentieth-century scholar to date the first program of sculpture as early as 1135–1142.[61] His argument was based on the early dating of the ribbed vaults of the crypt and the stylistic connections between Saint-Gilles and dated monuments in France and Italy. Porter dated the statues of the angels and the tympana and friezes of the side portals considerably later. M. Aubert continued Lasteyrie's line of reasoning—the strong impact of Île-de-France on Provençal sculpture in the late twelfth century—but he has the Saint-Gilles sculpture begun in 1160.[62]

R. Hamann concluded that the inscription of 1116, on the buttress of the south wall, divided his two campaigns on the façade. Thus his first campaign, which included only the apostles, was begun after the consecration of an altar by Pope Urban II in 1096, and the second campaign followed the year 1116.[63] M. Gouron, in an article of 1933–1934 which was reiterated by Aubert in 1934, discovered that a Petrus Brunus was one of the signators of a treaty of alliance between Saint-Gilles and Genoa in 1171. This same Brunus signed an act with the Cathedral of Nîmes in 1186 and was designated as "Petrus Brunus artifex in opera ligneo et lapideo." Since the name "Brunus" appears to the left of the apostle Matthew and originally on Bartholomew, Gouron associated the Petrus Brunus with the Brunus inscription on the Saint-Gilles statues. Gouron used these documents plus other historical events to date the apostles in the 1180's plus, and the rest of the façade around 1209.[64]

---

58. L. H. Labande, *op. cit.*, 168–181.

59. J. Charles-Roux, *op. cit.*, 120–122.

60. A. Fliche, *op. cit.*, 71–102.

61. A. K. Porter, *op. cit.*, vol. 1, 273–297.

62. M. Aubert, *French Sculpture at the Beginning of the Gothic Period* (New York: Harcourt, Brace, 1929). 56–58.

63. R. Hamann, "The Façade of Saint-Gilles: A Reconstruction," *Burlington Magazine*, LXIV (January 1934), 19–29.

64. M. Gouron, "Dates des sculptures du portail de l'église de Saint-Gilles," *op. cit.*, 44–56. 1171: Leonard, Catalogue no. 57, note 1. 1186: Archives du Gard: G353. M. Aubert, "Petrus Brunus, sculpteur à Saint-Gilles-du-Gard," *Bulletin de la Société nationale des antiquaires de France* (1934), 138–139.

M. Schapiro in 1935, without any knowledge of Gouron's discovery, discussed three inscriptions on the west wall of the crypt and dated them 1129, since they appear in a necrology of Saint-Gilles in a manuscript of that date in the British Museum (Add. ms. 16979).[65] This evidence, plus comparisons with early twelfth-century manuscripts, led to his conclusion that work on the façade could have been begun as early as the 1120's. In a note of 1937, Schapiro attacked Gouron's conclusions as being purely conjectural. According to Schapiro, the Petrus Brunus might be the son of the Brunus who signed the Matthew, but he argued that no evidence exists for the dating of the Saint-Gilles portals in the second half of the century.[66] He added two other documents, which, although not explicit, help defend the conclusions of his previous article. The first document, written 1141 or 1142 and describing the visit of Bishop Adelbert of Mainz to Saint-Gilles in 1137 on his way to study natural sciences at Montpellier, mentioned altars. Schapiro interpreted this to mean that the upper church was in use by 1137. The second, a letter written in the 1160's, praised the splendors of the abbey and indicated, according to Schapiro, that work was far advanced.

M. Aubert attacked the early dating of Saint-Gilles by R. H. C. Hamann, which appeared in his article on the Lazarus Tomb in Autun. He reiterated the late dating and added the further evidence of the documents discovered by Gouron.[67]

W. Horn's book is the first thorough study of Saint-Gilles.[68] Horn combined an interpretation of existing documents and the history of Saint-Gilles with a careful, scholarly examination of masonry, moldings, and sculpture. He dated the portals between 1125 and 1145, or, for sure, between 1116 and 1152.

M. Gouron, in 1951, added further historical references to his previous findings to date a first campaign in the 1180's with other sections completed around 1209.[69] Finally, with the publication of R. Hamann's extensive study of Saint-Gilles (1955) we find an expansion of his ideas first stated in 1934.[70] More evidence, both internal and external, is brought to bear to establish the date of 1096 for the beginning of the first sculptural program and 1116 as the year of the change in plan.

We thus see an extraordinary variety of dates. Each writer either followed an older tradition of dating or introduced new documents or different interpretations of older ones.

A summary of the dating of the portals follows:

Mérimée (1835): after 1150

Viollet-le-Duc (1854–1868): late twelfth century

Revoil (1873): about 1140

Vöge (1894): about 1150 after Arles

Marignan (1899): 1200–1250

Nicholas (1900): after 1116

---

65. M. Schapiro, "New Documents . . ." *op. cit.*, 415–431.

66. M. Schapiro, "Further Documents on Saint-Gilles," Notes in *Art Bulletin*, XIX (1937), 111–112.

67. M. Aubert, "Les dates de la façade de Saint-Gilles. À propos d'un livre récent" (R.H.L. Hamann, "Das Lazarus-Grap in Autun," *Kunstgeschichtliches Seminar*, *Marburg* (1935), *Bulletin monumental* (1936), 369–372.

68. W. Horn, *op. cit.*, 11–24.

69. M. Gouron, "Saint-Gilles-du-Gard," *op. cit.*, 104–119.

70. R. Hamann, *op. cit.*

Lasteyrie (1902): Part I: Apostles after 1150
　　　　　　　　　Part II: Side portals and left-hand central frieze by 1180
　　　　　　　　　Part III: rest of central portal by end of the twelfth century
Labande (1909): 1175–1200
Charles-Roux (1910): Part I: third quarter of twelfth century
　　　　　　　　　　Part II: thirteenth century
Porter (1923): First Campaign: 1135–1142
　　　　　　　　Second Campaign: about 1180
Fliche (1925): Atelier I: 1180–1190
　　　　　　　Atelier II: before 1209
　　　　　　　Atelier III: before 1240
Aubert (1929): 1160–1170
　　　　　　　Side portals late twelfth century
Hamann (1934): Plan I: 1096
　　　　　　　　Plan II: after 1116
Gouron (1933–1934): after 1185
Schapiro (1935): first style in 1120's
Aubert (1936): 1160–1170
Schapiro (1937): same as 1935
Horn (1937): 1125–1145
Gouron (1951): 1180's plus; completed after 1209
Hamann (1955): Plan I: after 1096
　　　　　　　　Plan II: after 1116

(2) *History of the Abbey of Saint-Gilles-du-Gard*

Saint-Gilles-du-Gard had a tortuous history of depredations, conflagrations, demolitions, and restorations. Founded supposedly in the late sixth century by the hermit Saint Gilles, the abbey became the center of a large town and important port on the river Rhône. Since the town is located on the west bank of the west branch of the Rhône, it was part of Medieval Languedoc under the suzerainty of the Counts of Toulouse and became its administrative center. In an attempt to assure the future existence of the abbey, Saint Gilles went to Rome, according to legend, and offered the abbey to the Papacy. However, the protection of the Papacy did not prevent the Counts of Toulouse from stealing the offerings and committing other acts against the monks. The papal letters reveal how the clergy of Saint-Gilles struggled against the Counts of Toulouse as well as against the Bishops of Nîmes, who wished to add Saint-Gilles to their diocese. The destruction of the sixteenth and the restorations of the seventeenth and nineteenth centuries must be added to these invasions of the rights of the clergy of Saint-Gilles during the Middle Ages.

Legends, which accumulated primarily in the tenth and eleventh centuries around the life of and miracles performed by Saint Gilles, are more important than facts. Pilgrims came from all over Europe and Scandinavia to worship at the grave of Saint Gilles and often continued on to the Holy Land, where two churches were dedicated to this hermit saint.[71]

---

71. Charles-Roux, *op. cit.*, 1–5.

The port of Saint-Gilles was one of the main embarkation points for the Holy Land until it was replaced by Aigues-Mortes in the thirteenth century.

According to legend, Saint Gilles was born in Greece of royal lineage. After giving away his worldly possessions to the poor and sick and curing many by simple prayers, Saint Gilles set out for Rome. Upon arrival at the sea, he was taken from Greece to Marseille by sailors whose vessel he had saved. He left Marseille for Arles, attracted by the fame of Bishop Caesarius. After curing a woman who had been paralyzed for years, he was invited to live with the Bishop. (Since the Bishop died in 543, the legend is obviously inaccurate.) After twelve years in the Bishop's house, during which he performed many cures, Saint Gilles retreated to the desert. He spent twelve years of prayer and meditation with a hermit named Veredemius. Four men, carrying a sick friend, located Saint Gilles, and the Saint cured the ailing man. Saint Gilles then retreated to a grotto where a doe regularly visited him and slept in a hut constructed by the Saint. Following the legend, King Florentius, having heard about the doe and about the hermit living in the woods, went hunting with the Bishop of Nîmes, wounded the doe, and followed it to Saint Gilles' grotto. The King often visited the hermit, who finally inveigled the King into founding a monastery. The King insisted that Saint Gilles be the Abbot.[72]

The fame of the hermit Saint and the abbey he founded spread rapidly. Many churches were dedicated to him all over Europe, while fifteen communes in France were named after him. Major events in his life were depicted in stained-glass windows and on portals. Saint Gilles giving his mantle to a poor man, King Florentius as he approaches the grotto, and Saint Gilles and his doe—all can be seen on the archivolts of the portal of the Confessors on the south transept of Chartres Cathedral. Saint Gilles built two churches, the larger dedicated to Saint Peter. These two were probably destroyed by the Saracens about 719. By the early thirteenth century a large fortified town and port with seven dependent parish churches grew up around the abbey.[73]

The early history of the Abbey of Saint-Gilles is obscure. By a pontifical act, dated 879, John VIII recalled the founding of the monastery by Saint Gilles and reaffirmed the papal jurisdiction over Saint Gilles.[74] During the eleventh century, Saint-Gilles became involved in a controversy with local Counts and with the Bishop of Nîmes. Around 1077 Pope Gregory VII asked the Abbot of Cluny to reform Saint-Gilles.[75] In 1090, at the Council of Toulouse, Raymond IV made amends for having stolen the offerings from the abbey. Urban II's acts of 1095 gave restitution to the Count, and between 15 and 21 July 1096 Urban consecrated an altar for the new basilica.[76] Work certainly stopped in 1105 when Count Bernard, son of Raymond IV, invaded the town, fortified the monastery, and robbed the treasury.[77] In 1107 Bertrand was excommunicated, and in 1109 he left Saint-Gilles with four thousand troops for the Holy Land.[78]

---

72. *Ibid.*, 4–18.
73. *Ibid.*, 19–30.
74. Goiffon, *op. cit.*, III, 5.
75. *Ibid.*, XII, 26.
76. *Ibid.*, XV, XVI, XVII, 30–35.
77. *Ibid.*, XXII, 40.
78. *Ibid.*, XXVII, 46.

Documents dealing with the present structure commence with the inscription on the exterior crypt wall which states that a new basilica was begun in 1116. Two documents can be cited, which would seem to indicate that none of the superstructure of the crypt existed in 1116. The *Liber Miraculorum*, written by the librarian of Saint-Gilles between 1121 and 1124 and dedicated to Abbot Hugh, describes the destruction of two or more churches to make way for the one mentioned in the inscription of 1116.[79]

In 1117 Bertrand, Viscount of Béziers, expelled the Abbot and erected a chateau against the monastery. After Pope Pascal II had placed Bertrand under interdict, the Viscount capitulated, and in the following year Abbot Hugh of Saint-Gilles received the Pope, Gelasius II. The monastery, however, was still in trouble because Pope Calixtus II wrote on 28 June 1119 from Maguelonne prohibiting the monks from selling the treasures of Saint-Gilles except under certain conditions such as a famine or redemption of captives.[80] Again in 1120 and 1121 the Pope informed seigneurs that he would excommunicate them unless they respected the territorial rights of the abbey. Alphonus Jourdanus, Count of Toulouse, and Bertrand's brother, occupied the town, built a chateau, and robbed the monastery in 1121. The Pope asked the neighboring archbishop to force Alphonus to repent, while he further ordered the Count to cease his usurpation of town and monastery and destroy the chateau he had constructed. In spite of the papal protest Alphonus incarcerated Abbot Hugh and forced him to swear he would never return to Saint-Gilles. Threats against Alphonus proved futile, and he was finally excommunicated on 22 April 1122. There are no records of events between 1122 and 1125. On the second of April 1125 Saint-Gilles was placed under the Order of Cluny for reform; yet internal disorders did not end in 1125. The monks refused to be administered by Cluny, and the final accord did not transpire until 1132.[81]

In the mid-1130's Peter of Bruys, a leader of a heretical sect, destroyed the crucifixes of Saint-Gilles in front of the abbey and was himself promptly burned on the same spot. This event is clearly reflected in the antiheretical iconography of the façade.[82]

Epitaphs on the west wall of the crypt and its projection should be cited, since these sections of the crypt support the façade. Two inscriptions are dated 1142, while several others can be placed around 1129 on epigraphic grounds.[83] No other specific documents exist for the 1140's. The bull of Pope Adrian IV (1154–1159) granted forty days of indulgence to the faithful who visited Saint-Gilles.[84] Descriptions of crowds pressing against the tomb of Saint Gilles, written between 1157 and 1178, point up the importance of the pilgrimage to Saint-Gilles. In 1154 Louis VII's sister Constance married Count Raymond of Toulouse, and Saint-Gilles came under royal protection in 1163.

In 1165 the town of Saint-Gilles sided with Pisa during the Genoese-Pisan War, which took place outside the walls of Saint-Gilles. By 1169 the *entente* with Pisa had waned. In 1171

---

79. Horn, *op. cit.*, 11–12; Charles-Roux, *op. cit.*, 4.
80. Goiffon, *op. cit.*, XXXIV, 51; XXVI, 53.
81. *Ibid.*, XXXIX–LII, 58–71.
82. M. L. Colish, *op. cit.*, 451–460.
83. Schapiro, "New Documents . . ." *op. cit.*, 415–431.
84. Goiffon, *op. cit.*, LVII, 78.

a treaty of alliance for twenty-nine years was signed with Genoa, and one of the signators was Petrus Brunus.[85]

In 1179 Saint-Gilles was caught in the struggle for power between Raymond V of Toulouse and the King of Aragon, whose allies were the Viscount of Béziers and the Bishop of Nîmes. Churches in the town were burned, and the monastery was fortified and connected with a chateau. In 1196 Pope Calixtus III ordered the Count of Toulouse to demolish the chateau he had built and repair the wrongs he had caused the monastery. Threats of excommunication appeared in both 1198 and 1199.[86]

The final chapter of the medieval history of Saint-Gilles is concerned with the Albigensians. Although not a member of this heretical sect, Rayond VI of Toulouse protected them. Pope Innocent III intervened, and peace was maintained until 1207, when Raymond VI again aided the heretics. On 15 January 1208, Pierre de Castelnau, a papal legate, was assassinated by an Albigensian, who escaped to Beaucaire. The legate's body was transferred by order of Innocent III to the crypt of Saint-Gilles. On 12 June 1209 Raymond was forced to humiliate himself before the façade and before the tomb and finally was given absolution. Raymond was then forced to take up the sword against his own subjects in the bloody Albigensian crusades. In 1212, Raymond VI was admonished by the Pope for having destroyed buildings belonging to the abbey, and four years later his excommunication was confirmed.[87]

In 1226 Saint-Gilles submitted to the monarchy and enjoyed great prosperity under Saint Louis, who visited Saint-Gilles in 1254 and 1270. The abbey was, however, not completed by 2 November 1265, when Clement IV, deploring its unfinished state, declared one hundred days of indulgences.[88] Early in the fourteenth century the nave and choir were joined, but work was not entirely finished by 1417. In 1506 Julius II, formerly Abbot of Saint-Gilles, granted indulgences for those who visited Saint-Gilles or contributed to the repair of the abbey. Paul III secularized the abbey in 1538.[89]

In 1562 the Protestants attacked the town, burned the monastery, archives, and library, and threw the Catholics into the Rhone. The abbey was transformed into a fortress and repulsed an attack in 1574. The Duc de Rohan ordered the abbey razed in July 1622, so that it would not fall into the hands of the Catholics. The royal troops, however, arrived before this planned demolition took place. Money was raised, and new vaults for the nave and choir were constructed between 1650 and 1665. Restorations of the façade were begun in 1650. These acts involve the closing up of the side portals and the construction of an oval central staircase. These changes appear in a lithograph dated 1833. During the French Revolution the choir was demolished and damage done to the portals. The paired columns on the pedestals, extending in front of the central portal, and the large single column to the right of the north portal were destroyed.[90]

---

85. Gouron, "Dates des sculptures," 45–50.
86. Goiffon, *op. cit.*, LXXIII, LXXIV, LXXV, 96–100.
87. *Ibid.*, LXXXII, LXXXIII, 113–114.
88. *Ibid.*, CIII, 135.
89. *Ibid.*, CLXXIV, 236; CLXXX, 254–291.
90. Charles-Roux, *op. cit.*, 128–136.

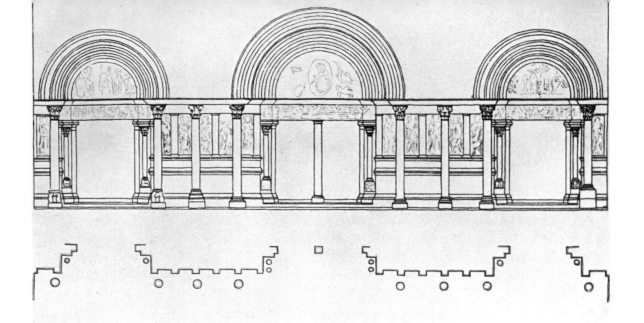

194. Saint-Gilles. R. Hamann: Reconstruction of original design of the façade.

195. R. Hamann: Reconstruction of original design of the façade.

196. Façade. (Revoil).

CHAPTER 7

The First Campaign

R. DE LASTEYRIE was the first to point out the lack of harmony in the façade and to suggest the distinct campaigns: no. 1—1150 plus—the apostles; no. 2—about 1180—CP.L frieze and side portals; no. 3—CP.R frieze and archivolts of the central portal at the end of the twelfth century.[1] A. K. Porter split the campaigns as follows: no. 1—central portal—just before 1142; no. 2—side portals—about 1180.[2] Since work on the façade proceeded in a continuous campaign with three sculptors, who each carved two figures, responsible for almost all the sculpture on the super-structure, it follows that the reasoning of Lasteyrie and Porter for distinct campaigns, separated by long intervals of time, is incorrect. Since the 1930's three attempts have been made to divide the sculpture of the façade into two separate campaigns and to reconstruct its original format.

(1) R. HAMANN'S FIRST CAMPAIGN (1934)

In 1934, R. Hamann published two different reconstructions of an original design of the façade, one with and one without tympana and lintels (figs. 194,

---

1. R. de Lasteyrie, "Études sur la sculpture française au moyen-âge," Académie des inscriptions et belles-lettres, Fondation Piot, *Monuments et mémoires*, VIII (1902), 102, 107.

2. A. K. Porter, *Romanesque Sculpture of the Pilgrimage Roads* (Boston: Marshall Jones, 1923), vol. 1, 292–297.

195).[3] To solve the present ambiguity of paired columns, Hamann removed the entire pedestal of the central portal with its double socles and paired columns and substituted one large column in the same plane in space as the other large columns (see plan—fig. 194). This alteration allowed room for ten apostles between the six large columns on the central portal (fig. 194). According to Hamann, the paired columns were originally in the splays of the central portal and were put in their present location when the apostles John, Peter, James, and Paul were moved to the splays of the central portal during the second campaign. The central portal thus corresponded to the side portals, but was deeper by one column. Originally, Peter and Paul flanked the central portal on the front face of the façade, and James and John were at the extremities of the façade in the niches now occupied by the angels.

His argument was based primarily on a detailed analysis of the socles supporting the paired columns (figs. 73, 74). According to Hamann, the double socles were carved only on their western and inner sides (inner toward the center of the façade). Later, during the second campaign and after the change in plan, they became freestanding and were carved on their outer sides. Acanthus panels replaced Peter and Paul, and angels were located in the outer niches which formerly contained James and John.

Of his two reconstructions, Hamann favored the second, which reminded him of Poitevin façades and Roman triumphal arches. In the second reconstruction only the twelve apostles belonged to the first campaign, and the angels, all three tympana, lintels, and frieze in its entirety to the second. Toulousian plus Roman influence was stressed for the first campaign and Burgundian for the second.

The greatest weakness of Hamann's reconstruction is his failure to base his conclusions on actual measurements and careful study of construction. The overlapping blocks and courses of masonry of the central portal (figs. 9, 10) correspond to the system found on the side portals (figs. 5, 6). Hamann disregarded any function for the projection of the crypt. In our study of the construction, we saw that this crypt projection acts as the substructure for the projecting pedestals, which now support the double columns (fig. 9). It would seem strange, indeed, if the splays of the entire central portal were enlarged in a second campaign to cover a substructure already existing. Finally, it would seem even stranger to add the projecting pedestals to support paired columns, which, in turn, held up nothing.

Further, Hamann's arbitrary placement of John, Peter, James, and Paul on the front face of the façade overlooks the fact that they were designed for their present position (figs. 28, 29). John and Peter (fig. 28) are conceived as a pair with heads

---

3. R. Hamann, "The Façade of St. Gilles: A Reconstruction," *Burlington Magazine*, LXIV (January 1934), 19–29.

turned toward each other. On the right splay, James Major and Paul portray the same relationship, especially in the placement of the feet and treatment of drapery over the ankles. Paul's mantle projects across the vertical line which separates the two blocks containing the two apostles (see detail, fig. 43). It is therefore impossible to argue that the Paul once stood in a niche between two pilasters. The outer or western sides of John on the left side and Paul on the right correspond to each other and, at the same time, reinforce the edge of the jamb in a truly Romanesque manner. These four apostles were carved for their present location.

Although Hamann laid great stress on the differences between the sides of the outer double socles, the Angel appearing to David versus the David and Goliath (figs. 68, 70) and the lion and two men versus the camel and two apes (figs. 73, 71), it is impossible to see these differences, when the sides are compared. The worn, north face of the left socle (fig. 71) seems somewhat cruder than the south face. In any event, the role of the projecting crypt and systematic construction of the bays of the splays of the central portal, and their continuity with the projecting pedestals, would preclude this violent transformation of the central portal with a change in the program.

Another criticism of Hamann's reconstructions (figs. 194, 195) is his arbitrary changing of the side portals so that the top of the heads of the figures in niches flanking the portals coincide with the horizontal ornamented abacus supported by the door-jamb, the inner columns, and the matrix of the façade. He accomplishes this by elongating the inner columns and thus making the inner parts higher to coincide with the figures in niches. There is no evidence that would allow for this complete change in the proportions of the side portals. This coordination of the height of apostles and angels and the disposition of the splay can be partially accomplished by the removal of the four blocks and the resulting lowering of the façade as already described.

(2) W. HORN'S FIRST CAMPAIGN (1937)

W. Horn's reconstruction of the first campaign (fig. 197) is quite different from Hamann's. It consists of a single portal with portico supported by double socles and paired columns and with the twelve apostles, four on the splays and eight on the front plane. Brunus, Matthew, Thomas, and James the Less were carved for this screen portal. The right-hand four unidentified apostles, which he thought represented a stylistic fracture with the figures by Brunus, were carved only after a new program with tympana, lintels, and friezes was envisaged. The relationship of these unidentified apostles to the superstructure of the right portal proved to

Horn that they were not finished until the expanded program began. To substantiate these conclusions, he reasoned that the oldest moldings and decorative forms frame the Brunus statue on the left. He further argued that this sequence of carving was echoed in the order in which the acanthus frieze was carved: first, the right portal; then the left; third, from the left portal across the central portal meeting above the apostles, CP.R 5 (see fig. 158).[4]

Since Hamann failed to notice the gradual transformation of the façade, Horn argued that his reconstruction was incorrect. Horn reasoned that the bases or pedestals, double socles, and paired columns were part of the first campaign, since the bases were connected with the façade masonry. The double socle with columns could not have been placed originally in the splays of the portal because the large bases with the Cain and Abel reliefs were already *in situ* in the first campaign. Horn further argued that these bases in front of the central portal were related to the projection of the crypt, which, in turn, was homogeneous with the south wall of the crypt bearing the 1116 inscription.[5]

Horn also disagreed with Hamann's analysis of the double socles. Horn saw an iconographical unity in the north and south side of the left outer socle. One side depicts a lion and men fighting, and the other two, apes and a camel. According to his interpretation, these animals represented basic instincts: the lion, evil; the camel, wrath; and the apes, evil. Differences in carving were attributed to weathering.[6]

Finally, since there was good iconographical precedent for the present location of the four apostles (John, Peter, Paul, and James Major), Horn saw no reason to place them on the front face of the façade flanking the central portal and in the niches where the angels now reside. Horn also described Hamann's method as speculative without close observation of construction. In his opinion the crypt projection must have supported something, and the projecting double socles with their paired columns were planned for their present position in the first design, but were carved after the second campaign had started.[7]

Horn's reconstruction of the first campaign (fig. 197) included the planning for the twelve apostles and the projecting portico. This project remained unfinished. His second project included the side portals, the superstructure of the central portal, and the large columns in front of the façade which were an integral part of the side portals. Horn suggested that this interruption during the first campaign and the

---

4. W. Horn, *Die Fassade von St. Gilles* (Hamburg: Paul Evert, 1937), 26–32.
5. *Ibid.*, 35–49.
6. *Ibid.*, 49–51.
7. *Ibid.*, 52–54.

resulting changes of plan were caused by the heresy of Peter of Bruys, which he dated in 1137 or 1138. This heretical movement was quickly suppressed, and the church celebrated its victory by the expanded sculptural program, including the frieze with the Last Supper and the right-portal tympanum depicting the Crucifixion. Horn, following Panofsky's conclusions, believed that 1137 or 1138 was the *terminus post quem* for the change in plan.[8] The first project was thus a unified façade with one portal under a portico, while the second, related to the Roman arch of Orange, consisted of the present façade.

There are certain parts of Horn's reconstruction (fig. 197) with which it is impossible to agree. Since the side portals are continuous structurally with the corner buttresses, the outer walls of upper crypt, and aisles, they must have been part of the first design. The nature of the courses of the bases, their structural organization, and the style of ornament are similar in all three portals. The finest ornament appears on the right outer base of the central portal (fig. 147); yet sculpture of almost equal quality decorates the first horizontal course above the capital of the inner column in LP.L (fig. 78). Any differences in ornament between central and side portals appear to be the result of degrees of quality. The original design must have included all three portals. Horn's design seems too abrupt. It is not integrated with the façade as a whole. At Arles the portal was attached to an earlier façade, while at Saint-Gilles it was contemporary with the construction of the church.

If the side portals were part of the original concept, as seems likely, it follows that the six freestanding Roman columns were also included in the first campaign. A study of the side portals reveals the fact that these large columns are essential as supports for the outer archivolts of side portals (figs. 3, 7). Thus it seems logical to place both the side portals and the freestanding columns in the first concept of the façade as a whole.

With the exception of these questions, Horn's reconstruction has more validity than Hamann's.

(3) M. GOURON'S RECONSTRUCTION (1951)

A third attempt at reconstructing the first design of the façade of Saint-Gilles was made by M. Gouron in 1951.[9] According to M. Gouron, the apogee of the pilgrimage to Saint-Gilles was between 1157 and 1178; yet sculptural work on

8. *Ibid.*, 55–64.
9. M. Gouron, "Saint-Gilles-du-Gard," *Congrès archéologique de France*, CVIII (1951), 110–113.

the façade did not commence until after 1185, when a peace was signed between Raymond and the King of Aragon. Gouron explained that the masonry projection of the crypt had the double function of supporting a fortified porch and containing a wooden staircase. Gouron's first campaign (between 1185 and 1195) included the twelve apostles in niches, Last Supper, Prophecy of Christ, and the Betrayal on the central portal. The top frieze to the left of the central portal was older and originally located elsewhere, while the frieze to the right of the central doorway was carved later. Most of the side portals were after 1209, although some older, dismantled pieces were used.

Gouron's reconstruction of the first campaign shows six apostles on each side of the central portal. His single-portal project resembles Horn's but has twelve apostles on the front face of the façade instead of eight. During the Albigensian heresy, John and Peter, which were in the niches nearest the portals, were destroyed. Afterward they were remade and placed on the left splays of the central portal. Paul and James were moved to the right splays of the central portal, and the acanthus panels filled the areas they previously occupied. The lion socles, directly beneath these four apostles, originally supported large columns framing two portals.

Because of the cut-off edges of the reliefs in medallions in the right bases of the central portal (fig. 51), Gouron believed that they belonged to two separate splays, possibly on the transept portals. He dated them, along with the Cain and Abel reliefs, in the early thirteenth century. The top frieze of the central portal was originally under the highest cornice of the pediment, as on the Cathedral at Nîmes. Further, Gouron went on to describe in detail the repairs caused by religious wars. He believed that the Arrest of Christ was carved in 1655 and that parts of the frieze with undecorated cornices have been remade. The documents signed by Brunus in 1171 and 1186, which Gouron discovered, correspond to his late dating of the sculpture.[10]

It is difficult to separate out sections of the frieze for transept portals and frieze under the pediment, since the friezes and lintels of the side portals plus the upper frieze of the central portal portray an iconographical unity in their present location. It is impossible to eliminate the side portals and colossal columns from the original campaign. Further, the relationship in dimension between the western projection of the crypt and the central portal with deep pedestals cannot be ignored. The interpenetration of the masonry of these pedestals, plus the stylistic connection between the reliefs and the apostle Thomas, which was carved at the beginning of the project, indicate that this lower part of the central portal has not been altered and existed from the outset. The use of this projection of the crypt for a wooden stairway sur-

---

10. *Ibid.*, 114–117.

rounded by a fortified porch, if such ever existed, does not preclude its original use as the substructure for the present central portal.

Gouron places six apostles and seven pilasters on each side of the central portal. The left side of the central portal measures 5.19 meters, while the six statues and seven pilasters are 6.09 in width. The cut-off edges of the reliefs of the right base, far from suggesting that they were pieces used elsewhere, form a unified composition (fig. 51). The carved border of the hunter rondel is preserved and proves that it was not cut off. The fragment from the left base (fig. 54), preserved in the Museum, echoes the composition of the offerings of Cain and Abel (fig. 52). These reliefs must have always been in their present emplacement.

(4) R. HAMANN'S FIRST CAMPAIGN (1955)

In his book published in 1955, R. Hamann reproduced the same two reconstructions of the first plan of the façade (figs. 194, 195) which appeared in his article of 1934.[11] He recapitulated and augmented the evidence for his design. The major change in his argument was his shift, following Horn, to an evolving sequence of activity with only a small number of statues completed before his change in plan of 1116. Of the apostle figures, only Thomas and James the Less (CP.L 4, 3) and James Major (CP.R 1) were finished when work was interrupted and the present, more elaborate program begun. James Major was carved for a niche on the front face of the façade, while the other three (Paul, Peter, and John) were made for their present position on the splays of the central portal. He argued that his first reconstruction (fig. 194) with lintels and tympana in all three portals solved the unharmonious relationship between the figure frieze on the side portals and acanthus frieze over the apostles; yet he preferred the second design (fig. 195) on iconographical grounds and because of its connection with western French façades and Roman triumphal arches. He considered the master of the second plan, who also designed the choir, as an artist excelling in utilizing existing conditions to the best advantage.

Hamann felt that the Roman arch at Orange (fig. 200) inspired the first design, while Nîmes and Modena (fig. 201), with their horizontal friezes, grew out of Saint-Gilles. The projection of the crypt, according to Hamann, was constructed for a ramp in front of the central portal to strengthen it for the crowds of pilgrims. Since the projection was already built, it was possible to utilize it for the paired columns with double socles and large bases after the change of plan resulted in their trans-

---

11. R. Hamann, *Die Abteikirche von St. Gilles und ihre künstlerische Nachfolge* (Berlin: Akademie-Verlag, 1955), 3–15.

ference from the inner splays to their present location. Hamann reasoned that this projection did not necessarily mean that the first design involved only one portal. The change in plan was probably caused by the desire to place the apostles in the central doorway and thereby make it deeper and more integrated with the interior. This transformation allowed space for the angel statues.[12]

Horn's reconstruction of the first design (fig. 197) came under strong attack. Hamann was opposed to the separation of central portal and the apostles by the double columns. In his opinion, Horn's design appeared abrupt and pasted on like the portal of Arles. He considered his triple-portal plan with large columns supporting an entablature more unified than Horn's. Finally, Hamann explained away Horn's reasoning that the construction of the splays and projecting bases of the central portal were continuous with the bases for the apostles by stating that the inner bases received their final form later when the paired columns had been moved.[13]

Hamann also disagreed with M. Gouron's reconstruction of a single portal flanked on each side by six apostles. Gouron's evidence that the projection supported stairs to the central portal seemed insufficient to Hamann. Hamann interpreted the lithograph of 1833 (fig. 202), which shows an arc-shaped staircase in front of the central portal, as being a baroque transformation along with the walling up of the side portals and not a basis for Gouron's scheme. In spite of the valuable historical background published by Gouron, Hamann stated that the historical account must be coordinated with the history of the construction of Saint-Gilles.[14]

Even though Hamann's book expands the reasons behind his reconstruction first stated in his article, the same criticisms are valid. He was not successful in refuting Horn's major criticisms of his reconstruction of the first campaign. He failed to interpret the purpose of the projection of the crypt and to substantiate the different dates for the inner and back sides of the socles. He did not justify his arbitrary changes in the elevation of the side portals, so that the flanking large figures are a harmonious part of the portal design. His conclusions with regard to the sculpture completed before 1116 and his date for the change in plan are also open to question. In his opinion, the Master of the James Major was the designer of the first campaign. His classic-imitative style was the reason for the classical façade based on Roman architecture, especially triumphal arches like Orange. This master carved the James (fig. 29) and the Angel appearing to David on the right socle (fig. 68). The only other artist whose work can be placed in the first campaign is the Master of the Thomas or Hamann's archaic-Toulouse Master. This sculptor carved the Thomas and the

---

12. *Ibid.*, 15–18.
13. *Ibid.*, 18–19.
14. *Ibid.*, 19–20.

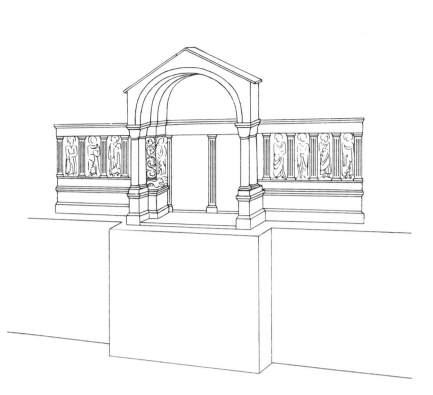

197. Saint-Gilles. W. Horn: Reconstruction of the first design.

198. Façade (detail).

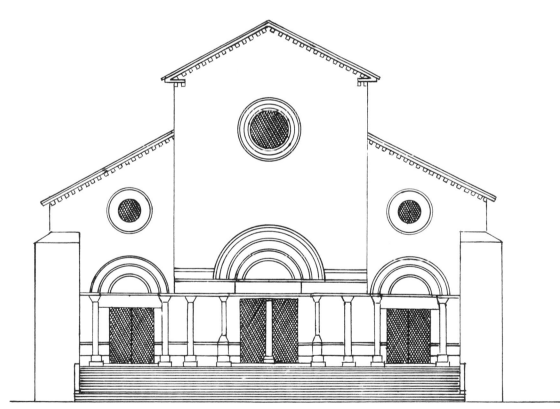

199. Saint-Gilles. V. Lassalle: Reconstruction of the façade.

socles of the right portal before 1116. By making the James Major statue the pivotal point in the proto-Renaissance of Saint-Gilles and placing it before the plan change, Hamann justifies the classical character of his reconstruction. The style of James Major, on the other hand, suggests that it is the Brunus formula at a more developed state than the Matthew and Bartholomew. If the James Major was created after the beginning of the program, which seems much more likely, the double socles were also carved later, and Hamann's reconstruction becomes untenable. Further, his dating of the Cain and Abel reliefs and the rondels of the bases of the central portal early in his second campaign fits in with his transformation of the whole central portal during the expansion of the sculptural program, but it cannot be justified on structural or stylistic grounds. Finally, the Michael Master, according to Hamann, is the designer of the second campaign and leads the way to Chartres by deepening the portal and placing the four apostles in the splays. This interpretation is also questionable, since the four apostles were planned for their present location at the outset of work on the façade. A study of the projection of crypt, construction of portal, and style of reliefs indicates that the pedestals with the sculptural reliefs were, like the four apostles, planned and carved during the earliest stages of work. Finally, it seems highly questionable, to say the least, to have the Michael Master coming from Burgundy, designing the second campaign, and then becoming the Headmaster of Chartres.

(5) V. LASSALLE'S RECONSTRUCTION OF THE FAÇADE (1966)

In an article of 1966 V. Lassalle published a reconstruction of the entire façade of Saint-Gilles (fig. 199).[15] Since the present towers are nineteenth-century (figs. 1, 2) and the north side of the left one and the south side of the right one are aligned with the wall buttresses along the flanks of the church, Lassalle interpreted them as corner-enveloping wall buttresses, following a format often employed in Provençal churches. The corner buttresses on the transepts of Saint-Trophîme at Arles, which contain staircases, perhaps served as model. His reconstruction, concerned only with the superstructure, gives meaning to the break in the plane of the superstructure, articulates the interior disposition of nave and aisles, and, at the same time, proves that three portals must have been conceived from the outset of work on the façade.

---

15. V. Lassalle, "La façade de l'Abbatiale de Saint-Gilles. Essai de Restitution," *Bulletin de l'École antique de Nîmes* (1966), 79–89.

(6) SUMMARY

Since all reconstructions, Hamann's (figs. 194, 195), Horn's (fig. 197), and Gouron's, contain features which make their acceptance debatable, it can perhaps be argued that a fourth reconstruction is possible. Certainly, changes were made in the elevation of the side portal as work progressed, and the central portal underwent a marked transformation which its present unfinished state manifests (fig. 198). If a first design, separate and distinct from the present one, ever existed, what would it include? Or to put the question differently, what parts of the present three portals can be removed to help establish a first campaign? The study of the masonry of the façade, the ornamental sculpture, and the integral connection between the walls of the corner buttresses and the façade indicates that the original design included all three portals. Thus, in this aspect Hamann's reconstructions (figs. 194, 195) are more nearly correct than those of Horn (fig. 197) and Gouron. Since the monumental columns which flank the side portals and divide the apostles on the front face of the central portal are essentially for the support of the entire superstructure of the façade, it is inconceivable that they were not part of the original plan. To reason that the façade was first designed as a screen portal without massive supports for the cornice and upper frieze, following Horn and Gouron, is to ignore the entire plastic conception of the three portals (fig. 198). Here, again, Hamann's reconstructions (figs. 194, 195) seem closer to the first design. Thus the side portals and the monumental Roman columns cannot be eliminated from the original design.

The function of the projection of the crypt as a support for a deep, monumental central portal cannot be overlooked, as it was by Hamann, nor misinterpreted, as by Gouron. Horn's evidence for the connection between this projection and the deep pedestals of the portals, augmented by evidence already described, would seem to prove that these projecting pedestals or base were part of the original concept of the central portal and therefore cannot be arbitrarily removed. The elaborate borders on the western edges of John and Paul (figs. 9, 13) and the pose of the paired apostles within the splays of the central portal indicate that they were planned for their present locations. Accordingly, Horn's reconstruction (fig. 197) appears to be more accurate. It therefore follows that the angels must have been conceived for their places on the extremities of the façade from the beginning. Neither Horn nor Gouron includes these two figures, since their reconstructions of the original design consisted of a single portal. On the other hand, Hamann, with no evidence at his disposal, rearranged the locations of the apostles and reasoned that the front faces of the central portal contained ten apostles and the outer sides of the side portals were planned for the remaining two. During Hamann's second campaign the four apostles were placed on, and incidentally three of the four carved for, the splays of the central portal. Thus from the point of view of the design, Hamann did not include the two angels in his first project. It would seem to be impossible to preclude the Michael and Archangels from the original program. Furthermore, the style of the angels is related to the apostles, as the comparison of the heads of Michael and CP.R 3 apostle reveals (figs. 46,47).

The twelve apostles and two angels appear to be the work of five sculptors. Brunus carved five; Matthew, Bartholomew, Paul, James Major, and John. The Thomas Master carved the low reliefs on the pedestal of the central portal, the socles of the right portal, and three apostles: Thomas, James the Less, and Peter. Furthermore, the Thomas Master was not involved in the superstructure of any of the three portals. At the same time or probably slightly later, three sculptors, the Soft Master, the Hard Master, and the Michael Master, each created two monumental figures and then proceeded to divide up the work of the side portals and the frieze and the lintel of the central portal. While Brunus was carving his last three apostles and the Thomas Master was completing his work, the other three sculptors were working on the side portals. The latest phase of the work was the completion of the central portal by the three responsible for the side portals. Thus the whole façade seems to have been carved by five sculptors without any interruption.

What were the changes in design as work progressed on the façade? R. Hamann, W. Horn, and M. Gouron argued that the sculpture on the superstructure was part of an expanded program, although Gouron included some relief sculpture along the frieze under the pediment of the central pavilion in his first design. Since the three tympana, lintels, and entire frieze represent an iconographical unity of extraordinary completeness, this sculpture must either be part of an enlarged program or have been conceived at the very outset. The fact that the entire sculptural program of the superstructure directly reflects the position of the church against the heresy of Peter of Bruys, considered together with the present anachronism of the central portal, with paired columns supporting nothing, points to the conclusion that the tympana, lintels, and friezes belong to a second and distinct campaign.

The method of procedure may have been as follows: A triple-portaled façade, tied in with the corner buttresses and supported by Roman columns, was projected at the outset. The central portal with its deep pedestal was to be enframed by a portico and probably had a wooden staircase in front of it. This first project therefore combined the plasticity of Hamann's second reconstruction (fig. 195) and the projecting portico of Horn's reconstruction (fig. 197). The influence of Roman triumphal arches, such as Orange (fig. 200), and features from the façade of Modena, such as a portico (fig. 201), coalesced. Two sculptors, Brunus and the Thomas Master,

200. Orange, Roman triumphal arch.

201. Modena, Cathedral. Façade.

202. Saint-Gilles. Lithograph of façade (1833).

started work on this program either in the late 1130's or more probably in the 1140's. The absence of any mention of the façade in the pilgrim's guide to Santiago de Compostela, dated about 1139, points to the 1140's as the most propitious period for the start of the façade. The foundations of the façade, the west wall of the crypt, and its projection were certainly finished by the late 1130's. The Brunus and Thomas Master were soon joined by three other sculptors, the Soft Master, Hard Master, and Michael Master. The reason for this marked increase in the size of the *chantier* was the decision to augment dramatically the sculptural program by the addition of tympana, lintels, and friezes. The heresy of Peter of Bruys and Henry of Lausanne had not terminated with Peter's violent death. Rather, as already outlined, the virulence of the heresy had necessitated drastic measures, such as Saint Bernard's preachings in southern France in the mid-1140's with his most extensive traveling in 1147. The decision of the clergy to state in stone the official position of the church against this heresy resulted in the abandonment of the simple triumphal arch façade, modified by the projecting central portico. In order to make the new sculpture of the superstructure more dramatic, the entire façade was raised, as already described, and the horizontal frieze of the central portal resulted in the abandonment of the central portico upheld by paired columns. The fact that the double socles, supporting the paired columns of the central portal, are related stylistically to sculpture in the superstructure suggests that they were among the last parts carved. The projecting pedestals of the central portal had to support something, now that their original function of supporting a portico was given up to allow the continuous Passion cycle to extend uninterruptedly across the entire façade.

If the decision to augment the program by the creation of the dramatic Passion cycle took place toward the middle of the 1140's, which seems probable, the façade was probably completed by the early 1150's.

PART II
*The Influence of the Sculpture of Saint-Gilles
on French Monuments*

PILGRIMS flocked to worship at the grave of Saint Gilles, while others gathered at Saint-Gilles to embark down the Rhône for the Holy Land or to set out on foot across southern France to Santiago de Compostela in northwestern Spain, the burial place of Saint James Major. The local impact of the sculpture of Saint-Gilles can be seen in the cloister and portal at Saint-Trophîme at Arles, twelve miles away on the east branch of the Rhône. The remains of the portal of Beaucaire, eleven miles up the Rhône from Arles, reflect directly the Saint-Gilles façade. Nearby churches with portals and cloisters (Bouches-du-Rhône and Vaucluse) exhibit the continuation of the proto-Renaissance style; yet the fame of Saint Gilles and of the crypt and church which crown his tomb transcended local Provence. The portal at Thines (Ardèche), reliefs in the Cathedral of Valence (Drôme), the portal of the church of Saint-Barnard at Romans-sur-Isère (Drôme), and the sculpture in Vienne and nearby Condrieu (Isère, 150 miles north of Arles)—all are reflections in varying degrees of the façade of Saint-Gilles.

The impact of the sculpture of Saint-Gilles and Arles on Italian sculpture has already been mentioned. It is clear that Benedetto Antelami had seen Saint-Gilles, Beaucaire, and Arles. Many other Italian monuments show a Provençal influence in both style and iconography.

Although the major influence of Provençal Romanesque sculpture can be located up the Rhône Valley and in Northern Italy, there are important isolated monuments in southern central France which exhibit strong connections with Saint-Gilles. The foremost monument of this category is Saint-Guilhem-le-Désert (Hérault).

In Part II no attempt will be made to include a discussion of all the monuments which exhibit the direct influence of the façade of Saint-Gilles or of Saint-Gilles together with the sculpture at Arles. Rather, four monuments which reveal different connections with Saint-Gilles will be analyzed. The cloister and the portal at Saint-Trophîme at Arles exhibit strong stylistic influences from Saint-Gilles, but it would appear that no sculptor from Saint-Gilles worked at Arles. The fragments of the portal and frieze of Beaucaire are a provincial reflection of Saint-Gilles, with some influence from Arles, while the figures on the portal at Romans could conceivably have been carved by a sculptor from Saint-Gilles. The sculpture of Saint-Guilhem-le-Désert, which is now located in The Cloisters of The Metropolitan Museum of Art in New York City, in Montpellier, in Saint-Guilhem-le-Désert, and in other nearby towns was probably carved by several Saint-Gilles sculptors. These four monuments thus represent different relationships between the façade of Saint-Gilles, the source of the proto-Renaissance style, and its progeny.

CHAPTER 8

The Frieze of Notre-Dame-des-Pommiers at Beaucaire

DIRECTLY across the Rhône from Tarascon lies the town of Beaucaire (Gard). When the church of Notre-Dame-des-Pommiers at Beaucaire was reconstructed, the remains of the Romanesque frieze were built into the new transept, 15 meters above the ground (figs. 203–205). The Virgin and Child on the stairs of the vicarage is the only remaining part of the tympanum with the Three Magi and the Angel appearing to Joseph in a Dream, which is the same composition as the left portal of Saint-Gilles.[1] Both iconographically and stylistically the Beaucaire sculpture proclaims strong affinities with the portals of Saint-Gilles, although the quality of the sculpture is definitely inferior.

The Beaucaire frieze consists of eighteen blocks making up ten scenes of the Passion of Christ (figs. 203–205). The sequence of subjects has been confused in two instances in their move from the façade to the south transept. Starting from the left,

---

1. Aubin-Louis Millin, *Voyages dans les départements du Midi de la France*, 5 vols. (1808), vol. III, 434–435, described the tympanum as follows: "Le portail est orné de figures relatives à la naissance du Christ; au milieu est la Vierge, qui tient entre ses bras le divin Rédempteur; on lit au-dessous en caractères gothiques: *in gremio matris residet sapientia dei*.

"A droite, l'ange prescrit à S. Joseph d'emmemer la Vierge et son enfant en Égypte; on lit encore: *ducit in Aegyptum Joseph cum virgine Christum*.

"Enfin, sous l'adoration des mages, qui est à gauche, on a écrit: *Nostro divino dant tres tria munera trino*."

the first two blocks contain Christ's Prophecy of the Denial of Peter, while the next block shows Christ washing Peter's Feet (fig. 203). The Last Supper (four blocks) has five disciples behind the table on each side of the enlarged Christ and one disciple seated on a stool on the end at the extremities of the scene (fig. 204). Adjoining the Last Supper is the episode of Peter cutting off the ear of Malchus (fig. 204), a scene which originally preceded the Betrayal (scene No. 6). The next scene, one block, shows Judas receiving the Silver from the High Priest Caiphas (fig. 204). This event is the earliest in the whole chronology of the Passion as seen at Saint-Gilles. The block containing three soldiers, two with scourges, one with a sword, is part of the Betrayal scene in the next block (fig. 204). The episode of Christ being led before Pilate (figs. 204, 205), which consists of two blocks, includes Christ being pulled toward Pilate, who, in turn, is enthroned between two soldiers. Next appears Christ bound to the Column (one block—fig. 205). The three soldiers to Christ's right (another block) probably belonged to the right side of the Betrayal scene. In the next block (fig. 205) two soldiers, holding large nails and a hammer, follow Simon carrying the Cross (a different block). The last two scenes are reversed in order (fig. 205). The first portrays the Angel appearing to the Holy Women at the Sepulchre, the second the Holy Women buying Perfume from two Merchants. Thus if the order of the episodes were revised and the blocks placed in the correct sequence, the scenes would run as follows: Judas receiving the Silver, Christ's Prophecy of Peter's Denial, Christ washing Peter's Feet, the Last Supper, Betrayal (two episodes), Christ before Pilate, Flagellation, Carrying the Cross, Buying Perfume, and the Women at the Sepulchre. The connection between these episodes in the upper frieze at Saint-Gilles, starting with the central portal and proceeding across the right portal, is obviously very close.

As already stated, the Virgin and Child (fig. 237) in the rectory was originally the central part of a tympanum flanked on the left by the Magi and on the right by the Angel appearing to Joseph in a Dream. Here again we see further evidence of the connection with Saint-Gilles, in this case the tympanum of the left portal. Thus all ten scenes of the remaining frieze of Beaucaire, as well as the Virgin and Child Enthroned, exist on the façade of Saint-Gilles.

The sculptor of the major reliefs of the Pontile of Modena (fig. 192) was familiar with both Saint-Gilles-du-Gard and Beaucaire. From left to right, the Modena pontile contains five scenes: Christ washing Peter's Feet, the Last Supper, the Betrayal, Christ before Pilate combined with the Flagellation, and Simon carrying the Cross. Since the stylistic relationships between the Beaucaire frieze and the Modena reliefs is closer than that between Saint-Gilles and Modena, comparisons between the same subjects of all three monuments will be included to help establish their chronology.

203. Beaucaire, Notre-Dame-des-Pommiers. Frieze, Peter's Denial, Christ washing Peter's Feet.

204. Frieze, Last Supper, Betrayal, Christ before Pilate.

205. Frieze, Flagellation, Simon carrying the Cross, Holy Women at Sepulchre, Holy Women buying Perfume.

206. Beaucaire. Christ's Prophecy of Peter's Denial.

207. Saint-Gilles. Christ's Prophecy of Peter's Denial,
seven Disciples.

208. Saint-Gilles. Christ's Prophecy of
Peter's Denial, Peter, the cock, Christ.

Christ's Prophecy of Peter's Denial at Beaucaire (fig. 206) contains only three apostles and Christ, as opposed to eight and Christ at Saint-Gilles (figs. 207, 208). The four low-relief heads in profile behind the three apostles on the left block at Saint-Gilles give a sense of spatial depth which is totally absent at Beaucaire. The stiffness of pose and drapery at Beaucaire finds no parallel in the graceful rhythms which animate the Saint-Gilles figures. Awkward anatomy, especially the feet under the crossed legs of the left two apostles at Beaucaire, can be contrasted with the clearly articulated legs, ankles, and feet of the Saint-Gilles apostles. Besides spatial and anatomical differences, none of the transfixed nature of Beaucaire has any counterpart at Saint-Gilles. The sinuous flow and undulation of drapery, the variety and meaningfulness of gestures, are completely different from the congealed character of the Beaucaire relief. The treatment of drapery and the poses of the three Beaucaire apostles are practically identical, while Christ is the same pose in reverse. By contrast, all five seated figures of Saint-Gilles are individualized. It would seem as though the Beaucaire sculptor grasped externals of the Saint-Gilles composition, eliminated figures and spatial illusion, and at the same time, was unable to achieve the subtlety of the Saint-Gilles relief, especially the consistent treatment of the folds over the ankles. A related scene appears on a spandrel of the pontile of Modena.

In comparing the scenes of Christ washing Peter's Feet (figs. 209–212), the Saint-Gilles relief exhibits a freedom of pose and gesture and a curvilinear treatment of drapery which are in marked contrast to the frozen linearism of Beaucaire. The Beaucaire sculptor (fig. 210) copied from the Saint-Gilles relief the arrangement of Christ's mantle, knotted around his waist and falling in a truncated fold, but he failed to capture the fluid expressiveness of the model. The Modena relief (fig. 212), which lost its column when the pulpit was added, is composed vertically with two additional disciples behind Christ. The pose of Christ approximates that of the Christ of Saint-Gilles; yet details of drapery, especially the wattled sleeves, resemble the Christ of Beaucaire. It seems clear that the Modena sculptor knew both Saint-Gilles and Beaucaire.

Disciples of the Last Supper of Saint-Gilles (fig. 214) are reacting positively to Christ's words, as opposed to the mechanical gestures and transfixed countenances of the disciples at Beaucaire (fig. 213). The Beaucaire sculptor borrowed the composition of Saint-Gilles, including seated disciples on each end of the table, Christ giving the sop to Judas, and the swooning John, but he eliminated Judas' pointing, left hand (fig. 214). In the Modena relief (fig. 215), the sculptor repeated exactly the poses, gestures, and drapery arrangement of Judas, John, and Christ of Beaucaire. Indeed, the four left-hand apostles of the relief of Beaucaire and Modena have

209. Beaucaire. Christ washing Peter's Feet, the Last Supper.

210. Beaucaire. Christ washing Peter's Feet.

211. Saint-Gilles. Christ washing Peter's Feet.

212. Modena. Pontile, Christ washing Peter's Feet.

213. Beaucaire. Last Supper.

214. Saint-Gilles. Last Supper.

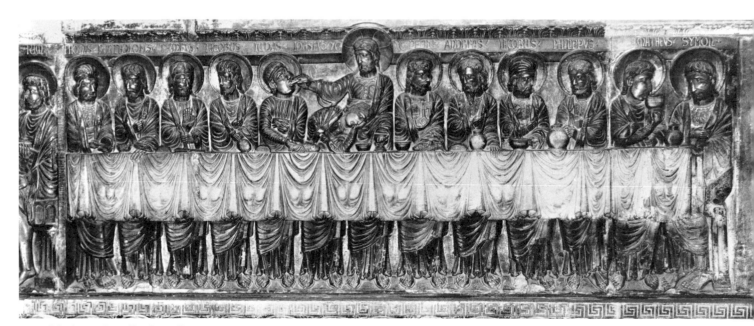

215. Modena. Pontile, Last Supper.

216. Beaucaire. Betrayal, Soldiers and Kiss of Judas.

217. Beaucaire. Betrayal, Peter cutting off the Ear of Malchus.

218. Beaucaire. Betrayal, Soldiers.

identical gestures, with the same tableware. The Modena artist elongated the figures to such an extent that they seem to be standing behind a suspended table. Because of the similarity of both pose and drapery, it is abundantly evident that the Modena Last Supper is based on the frieze of Beaucaire.

These first three scenes of Beaucaire were carved by one artist who copied essentially the scenes from Saint-Gilles, which, in turn, were created by two sculptors, Christ's Prophecy of Peter's Denial by the Soft Master and the two scenes on the lintel of the central portal by the Hard Master.

The scene of the Betrayal at Beaucaire (figs. 216–218), consisting of four separate blocks, which include the episode of Peter cutting off the Ear of Malchus, the three soldiers moving to the right, the scene of the Kiss of Judas, and the three soldiers to the right of Christ bound to the Column, is a stretched-out version of the frieze on the right side of the central portal of Saint-Gilles (fig. 219). Costumes of soldiers are similar in both reliefs, and the composition of Judas, Christ, and the flanking soldiers is identical. The two layers of figures in Saint-Gilles create an illusion of space which is absent in Beaucaire. Again, the expressive gestures of the reliefs of Saint-Gilles are transfixed at Beaucaire, and the figures become puppets suspended in a narrow space. The more mechanical treatment of the drapery is vastly different from the subtle undulations in the Saint-Gilles relief. A third sculptor, the Michael Master, is responsible for the Saint-Gilles double scene, while it appears as though the same Beaucaire artist who did the previous scenes is responsible for the Betrayal. Because of the constricted nature of the pontile, the Modena sculptor condensed the two major scenes into one almost square panel (fig. 220). Malchus, rather than a soldier, is pushing Christ toward Judas. Costumes of soldiers with their belts resemble those of Beaucaire, although the overlapping of figures creates a sense of depth which is not existent in the frieze of Beaucaire, but always present at Saint-Gilles. Christ holds a book in both the Beaucaire and Modena reliefs, but not in the Saint-Gilles. However, the drapery style of Christ and Judas and the wattled stockings of the soldiers of Modena closely resemble the Saint-Gilles Betrayal. Thus, the Modena sculptor seems to have borrowed iconographical ideas from Beaucaire and stylistic features from Saint-Gilles. This dependence of Modena on both Saint-Gilles and Beaucaire suggests that the sequence in time is Saint-Gilles, Beaucaire and Modena.

Christ being led before Pilate at Beaucaire (fig. 221) has lost the psychological expressiveness of the Saint-Gilles relief of the same subject (fig. 222). Little of the rhythmic forcefulness of the juxtaposition of the humble Christ and haughty Pilate is manifested at Beaucaire. In the Modena relief the composition is obviously simplified, since the panel includes the Flagellation (fig. 223). The Modena artist eliminated the extra soldiers flanking Pilate at Beaucaire and pushed the soldier pulling

Christ in behind Pilate. Although the costumes of the Pilates of Beaucaire and Modena are almost identical, the treatment of drapery and gouged-out folds and the elongation of the figures of Modena are entirely different. These gouged-out folds recall the treatment of the drapery in the Peter of the north gallery of Arles (fig. 249), with which the Modena sculptor surely was acquainted.

Although clearly based on the Saint-Gilles scene (fig. 227), the figure of Christ attached to the column (figs. 224, 225) has none of the sense of pain and suffering which is so apparent in the Flagellation scene of Saint-Gilles. Instead of a sagging Christ with accented rib cage and clearly articulated arms and hands, the Beaucaire Christ is wooden and suspended in space. Since the Flagellation is compressed into the right side of the Christ before Pilate panel at Modena (fig. 223), the position of Christ is reversed. The pose and costume of the Modena figure, however, repeat the format of Beaucaire. The Flagellation of the Puerta de las Platerias at Santiago de Compostela (fig. 226) bears only superficial relationship to the Beaucaire relief in pose and costume, but at Santiago the Christ is being tied to the column. It is apparent that the Beaucaire figure is derived from Saint-Gilles.

The awkward, expressionless figure of Simon carrying the Cross (figs. 228, 229) is in marked contrast to the dramatic intensity still evident in the damaged relief of Saint-Gilles (fig. 230). In the Modena relief (fig. 231) the costumes of the soldier and Simon follow the arrangement of the same figures at Beaucaire, but the sense of the weight of the cross on Simon, which is so dramatically portrayed at Saint-Gilles, is totally absent at Beaucaire and partially revived in the Modena relief. In all these juxtapositions of Saint-Gilles, Beaucaire, and Modena, the vast difference in quality between Saint-Gilles and Beaucaire is ever present, while the Modena sculptor, always dependent on the composition and costumes of Beaucaire, transforms his models into a more original and meaningful artistic statement.

The Holy Women buying Perfume from two Merchants and the Angel appearing to the Holy Women at the Sepulchre (fig. 232) are related in composition to the lintel of the right portal of Saint-Gilles (fig. 233) and to two capitals in the Museo Civico in Modena (figs. 235, 236). In comparison with Saint-Gilles, the scene with the two merchants is similarly organized, except that the left-hand merchant is seated behind the end of the counter at Saint-Gilles. The position of the measuring scales and the gestures of the merchants and the Holy Women are very similar in the two reliefs. The extensive modeling of the three Marys before the merchants is different from the previous Beaucaire reliefs and indeed is different from the flatter carving of the Saint-Gilles lintel. It would appear that this relief was carved by a different sculptor, who must have known the relief of the Holy Women on the northwest pier of the Arles cloister (fig. 234). Thus this Beaucaire sculpture relied on the Saint-Gilles

219. Saint-Gilles. Betrayal.

220. Modena. Pontile, Betrayal.

221. Beaucaire. Christ before Pilate.

222. Saint-Gilles. Christ before Pilate.

223. Modena. Pontile, Christ before Pilate, Flagellation.

224. Beaucaire, Flagellation.

225. Beaucaire, Flagellation.

226. Santiago de Compostela. Puerta de las Platerias. Christ being bound to a Column.

227. Saint-Gilles. Flagellation.

228. Beaucaire. Simon carrying the Cross.

229. Simon carrying the Cross.

230. Saint-Gilles. Simon carrying the Cross.

231. Modena. Pontile, Simon carrying the Cross.

compositions, but seems to have been influenced stylistically by the Arles sculpture in the cloister. The Modena capitals (figs. 235, 236) repeat the Beaucaire compositions. The Sepulchre of Beaucaire, with inset circles and draped shroud, is a heightened version of the sepulchre on the Saint-Gilles lintel. This motif is repeated in the Modena capital.

In each instance when Beaucaire and Saint-Gilles are compared, the Beaucaire sculpture appears more provincial. It is impossible to argue that the extraordinary subtlety of carving and expressiveness of the Saint-Gilles relief could have grown out of these frozen interpretations at Beaucaire. The fact that the last two scenes, involving the Holy Women and revealing a knowledge of both Arles and Saint-Gilles, places Beaucaire after the façade of Saint-Gilles and the north gallery of the Arles cloister.

The Madonna and Child of Beaucaire in the vicarage of Beaucaire is the central part of a tympanum (figs. 237, 239). The head and hands of Christ and the right hand and head of the Virgin are restorations. The pose of the Virgin and Child and the general arrangement of drapery are similar to the Madonna and Christ Enthroned in the left tympanum of Saint-Gilles (figs. 238, 240). The enframement of the Beaucaire statues suggests the original state of the Saint-Gilles throne. The closest connections between these two reliefs are the arrangement of the mantle between the Virgin's legs and the flaring fold descending from her wrists. The relief is lower in the Saint-Gilles Madonna, while the actual projection of individual folds seems to be closer to the Christ of Saint-Gilles now in the Museum (fig. 139). If the differences in scale, yet stylistic parallels, between the Beaucaire Virgin and Child and the Holy Women in the two scenes in the Beaucaire frieze are taken into consideration, it is possible that the second Beaucaire sculptor carved all three.

In spite of the few stylistic affinities between the Holy Women in the two scenes at Beaucaire and the Arles cloister, Beaucaire remains a provincial and derivative reflection of Saint-Gilles. The Beaucaire sculptors, whose artistic sensibility is far below that of the sculptors of Saint-Gilles, grasped at the externals of the Saint-Gilles scenes. Figures become transfixed in a shallow space far different from the illusionistic space of Saint-Gilles, derived from Early Christian sarcophagi. None of the subtleties of gesture, freedom of pose, subtle treatment of drapery, and psychological expressiveness carry over into the Beaucaire sculpture. It is impossible to argue that this new idea of a running frieze originated in the town of Beaucaire, which is much less important than Saint-Gilles, a pilgrimage center. Further, the obvious dependence of the pontile of Modena on the Beaucaire frieze for sequence of subjects, compositions, costumes, and gestures is further proof of the sequence: Saint-Gilles, Beaucaire, Modena.

232. Beaucaire. Holy Women at Sepulchre and Holy Women buying Perfume.

233. Saint-Gilles. Holy Women buying Perfume and Holy Women at Sepulchre.

234. Arles. Northwest pier of cloister, Holy Women buying Perfume.

235. Modena, Museo Civico. Capital, Holy Women at Sepulchre.

236. Modena, Museo Civico. Capital, Holy Women at Sepulchre.

237. Beaucaire. Virgin and Child enthroned.

238. Saint-Gilles. Virgin and Child, detail of LP tympanum.

239. Beaucaire. Virgin and Child enthroned, detail.

240. Saint-Gilles. Virgin and Child, detail.

The only reason to question the chronological sequence of Saint-Gilles to Beaucaire to Modena is the relatively low quality of the Beaucaire sculpture as the major source of the more sophisticated pontile of Modena. However, the sculptor of the reliefs of the Modena pontile seems to have been inspired by more than one monument in southeastern France. Clearly, the major source for compositions, details of drapery, and gestures is the Beaucaire frieze, but he knew Saint-Gilles, as evidenced in his introduction of some of the dramatic forcefulness of the Saint-Gilles frieze (compare Betrayal scene—fig. 216, 219). Furthermore, the Modena sculptor of the reliefs was influenced by the north gallery of Arles in the method of creating undercut, gouged folds (see Peter—fig. 249). The pontile of Modena, which is markedly different stylistically from earlier sculpture in North Italy and therefore manifests its dependence on outside influences, would thus seem to be inspired by several Provençal monuments. Finally, every detail of Beaucaire was derived directly from Saint-Gilles or the north gallery of the Arles cloister. For these reasons it is evident that the sequence Saint-Gilles to Beaucaire to Modena is valid.

If the Saint-Gilles façade is dated in the 1140's with work finished in the early 1150's, and if the north gallery of the cloister of Arles can be placed in the 1150's, it follows that all the Beaucaire sculpture can be dated around 1160, before the Modena pontile of 1165–1175.[2]

---

2. The literature on Beaucaire seems about evenly divided between dating the frieze before and after Saint-Gilles-du-Gard. M. le chanoine Durand, "La frise du XIme siècle à Notre-Dame de Beaucaire," *Bulletin du Comité de l'art chrétien du diocèse de Nîmes*, VII (1902), 209–214, dated the frieze in 1095 when the church was restored.

R. de Lasteyrie, "Études sur la sculpture française au moyen-âge," Académie des inscriptions et belles-lettres, Fondation Piot, *Monuments et mémoires*, VIII (1902), 118–122, placed Beaucaire between the frieze of the Cathedral of Nîmes (about 1150) and the Saint-Gilles frieze (about 1180), but he believed Beaucaire is nearer Nîmes.

P. Deschamps, *French Sculpture of the Romanesque Period* . . . (1930), 85, considered the Beaucaire frieze earlier than Saint-Gilles. He dated the frieze around mid-twelfth century, but the Virgin and Child not before the 1160's or 1170's because of the inscription.

M. Aubert, *French Sculpture at the Beginning of the Gothic Period* (New York: Harcourt Brace, 1929), 57 and 65, followed Lasteyrie in dating all Provençal Romanesque in the second half of the twelfth century. Aubert described the Nîmes frieze as the beginning with Beaucaire and Saint-Guilhem-le-Désert leading to the culmination with the frieze of Saint-Gilles. Aubert also thought that the Virgin and Child of Beaucaire was twenty years later than the frieze.

A. K. Porter, *Romanesque Sculpture of the Pilgrimage Roads* (Boston: Marshall Jones, 1923), vol. 1, 238, 246, 271–274, 280–282, also believed Beaucaire to be earlier than Saint-Gilles. However, Porter's reasoning was quite different from that of Lasteyrie, Deschamps, and Aubert. Stylistically Porter derived the Beaucaire frieze from sculpture at Santiago de Compostela. Since he dated the sculpture at Santiago de Compostela about 1120, it followed that he should date all the Beaucaire sculpture around 1135. He thus derived much of the Saint-Gilles frieze as well as Virgin and Child of the left portal from

Beaucaire. With the exception of the superficial similarities in the Flagellation scene, I find it impossible to see any connection between Santiago de Compostela and Beaucaire. Evidence derived from a detailed comparison of Saint-Gilles and Beaucaire would seem to indicate that Beaucaire is a provincial reflection of Saint-Gilles.

M. Schapiro, "New Documents on St.-Gilles," *Art Bulletin*, XVII (1935), 430, fn. 43, argued that Beaucaire was a schematization of Saint-Gilles. He dated the Virgin and Child later, in the second half of the twelfth century.

W. Horn, *Die Fassade von St. Gilles* (Hamburg; Paul Evert, 1937), 65–68, considered Beaucaire later than Saint-Gilles with strong influence coming both from Saint-Gilles and Arles.

R. Hamann, *Die Abteikirche von St. Gilles und ihre künstlerische Nachfolge* (Berlin: Akademie-Verlag, 1955), 185–190, contrasted Saint-Gilles and Beaucaire and concluded that Beaucaire is later in date.

G. de Francovich, *Benedetto Antelami. Architetto e scultore e l'arte del suo tempo* (Milan and Florence: 1952), 63–68, emphasized the dependence of the Modena pontile on the frieze of Beaucaire as well as on the portal of Arles.

241. Arles, Saint-Trophîme. Cloister, north and east galleries.

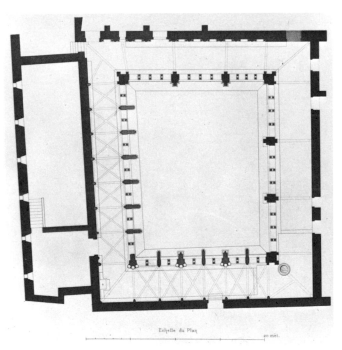

242. Plan of cloister (Revoil).

243. Exterior of north gallery.

CHAPTER 9

The Cloister of Saint-Trophîme at Arles

(1) THE NORTH GALLERY

ALTHOUGH Arles is only twelve miles from Saint-Gilles, none of the five major sculptors of the Saint-Gilles façade worked in the north gallery of the cloister of Saint-Trophîme. But it is clear that at least one Arles sculptor knew Saint-Gilles intimately, yet absorbed this influence creatively. The major source of inspiration was the developed Brunus style of the apostles John and Paul on the central portal. In spite of stylistic connections between the two monuments, the relationship between sculpture and architecture is quite different. At Saint-Gilles the monumental figures are either sunk between pilasters on the face of the façade or conceived in pairs on splays perpendicular to the front plane of the façade, while at Arles the figures are integrated with transverse or diagonal arches which, in turn, reinforce the barrel vault of the cloister walk.

The cloister of Saint-Trophîme at Arles is the oldest and the most impressive of a series of unusual vaulted cloisters in Provence. The north and east galleries (figs. 241, 242) are Romanesque, while the west and south galleries are Gothic. Articulated piers divide the north gallery into five bays (figs. 242, 244). The thickness of the compound piers stabilizes the outward thrust of the barrel vault with its lower impost on the garden side of the cloister. On the interior of the north gallery the piers support four transverse arches, two diagonals in the northwest and northeast corners (figs. 246, 247) and the transverse arch at the northern end of both the west and east galleries (see plan—fig. 242). On the intermediate piers the blocks which contain the two figures of Christ (fig. 244) support the impost block from which the transverse arches spring, while the more complex corner piers, northwest and northeast, have three figures, each related to arches which strengthen the vault at its junction with the barrels of the east and west galleries (figs. 246, 247). The configuration of the barrel vault, with high impost on the north side and transverse arches supported by corbels (fig. 245), recalls the vaulting of the aisles of the church of Saint-Trophîme as well as the majority of Provençal monuments, including Cistercian abbeys such as Le Thoronet. The fact that each pier has a structural function as well as a decorative and didactic role affects the ponderation and forms of the figures. This difference between Saint-Gilles and Arles in architectural context helps explain the originality of the Arles sculpture in spite of the strong stylistic influence from Saint-Gilles.[1]

Monumental Sculpture of the North Gallery

On stylistic grounds, one of the two major masters of the north gallery of the Arles cloister, the Peter-Paul Master, was responsible for four apostles—Peter and John on the northwest pier, James on the eastern intermediate pier, and Paul on the northeast pier—and one other figure that will be discussed later. This sculptor must have been familiar with Saint-Gilles, especially the late work of Brunus on the central portal. If the Arles Peter (figs. 248, 249) is compared to John and Paul of Saint-Gilles (figs. 250, 251) the general organization of drapery over right shoulder, forearms, and legs, the articulation of knees, hems raised over ankles, and sandaled feet are similar in all three apostles. In spite of this dependence on the Saint-Gilles format, the nature of the carving is entirely different in the Peter. As details of the Arles Peter and Saint-Gilles Paul exhibit (figs. 254, 255), the individual folds of the Peter have flat or pointed profiles, while the ridge folds of Paul are rounded. Hooked and loop folds on the Paul and John of Saint-Gilles are multiple, rounded projections in contrast to the gouged-out indentations on Peter's right leg (fig. 254), reminiscent of the drilled technique of some Early Christian sarcophagi (see fig. 20). Folds appear

---

1. Before turning to an analysis of the sculpture of the north gallery of the Arles cloister, it is necessary to point out the repairs carried out in the nineteenth century. The majority of the restorations involved the drainage system of the cloister. The estimate of 1843 lists the following parts in need of repair: roof, gutters, down drains, exterior capitals, the cloister bench, door to refectory, and condition of columns and capitals of the north wall. This estimate further describes the necessity of patching the Ascension relief and of placing new cornices over Saint Paul and over the Christ of the Doubting Thomas; it includes the urgent need to restore the Flagellation pier of the east gallery and replace three columns in the south bay of the east walk. All these repairs were carried out in 1846 and are visible today. Arles, Église 1er Dossier (Bouches-du-Rhône, 197), Monuments historiques, 1842–1892. 1846: "Elles ont été exécuter avec intelligence et le soin."

244. Arles, Saint-Trophîme. North gallery to the west.

245. Arles, Saint-Trophîme. North wall of north gallery.

246. Northwest bay of north gallery.

247. Northeast bay of north gallery.

248. Arles, Saint-Trophîme. Peter, northwest pier. Peter-Paul Master.

249. Peter. Peter-Paul Master.

250. Saint-Gilles, John (CP.L 2). Brunus.

251. Saint-Gilles. Paul (CP.R 2). Brunus.

252. Arles, Saint-Trophîme. Peter, head.

253. Saint-Gilles. Paul, head.

254. Arles. Peter, detail.

255. Saint-Gilles. Paul, detail.

applied to the surface on Peter of Arles, but part of the total plastic conception on the Saint-Gilles figures. The essential starkness of the drapery style of Peter is reminiscent of the earlier work of Brunus, his Matthew and Bartholomew; yet the drapery motifs are derived from Brunus' later John and Paul. Peter's head (fig. 252) exhibits many characteristics related to Saint-Gilles heads, especially that of Paul (fig. 253). Hair pulled over ears, parted lips, deep eye sockets with drilled holes for irises and at corners—all are similar. The Arles head lacks the massive presence of the head of Paul of Saint-Gilles.

John, on the west face of the northwest pier (figs. 256, 257), balances the Peter on the north side. Bundles of folds with sharply defined profiles can be seen in both statues. The arrangement of the mantle across the chest and stomach is a frozen variant of that of the Saint-Gilles Paul (fig. 251). The drapery of the James on the angle of the eastern intermediate pier (figs. 258, 259) resembles that of the John, while the arrangement of James's bodice recalls that of Peter. The heads of all three figures have the same treatment of hair, eyes, and especially the ears. The major difference between James, on the one hand, and Peter and John, on the other, is determined by their architectural function. Peter and John present rectangular masses reflecting the imposts and arches they support, while James is square in plan and mass to articulate the corner of the pier, adjacent to the Christ from which spring the impost block and transverse arch.

The statue of Paul on the north face of the northeast pier (figs. 260–263) is closer stylistically to the Paul of Saint-Gilles than is the figure of Peter. Drapery over the chest and stomach, ornamented collar, folds falling from arms, and arrangement of hands on scrolls prove beyond any doubt that the Peter-Paul Master of Arles knew Saint-Gilles. The Paul of Arles is stiffer and more angular. Convex edges and flat, filletlike folds predominate, while the figure is less massive with squatter proportions. The heads of the two Pauls (figs. 253, 262) exhibit marked similarities in spite of axial differences. Certainly, the Peter-Paul Master has been profoundly affected by the Saint-Gilles sculpture; yet he emerges as a distinct artistic personality.

The second master, the Stephen Master, seems to have created six statues in the north gallery of the Arles cloister. At the outset, he was only slightly influenced by Saint-Gilles, but as he developed, his style became transformed either by contact with the Peter-Paul Master or by knowledge of the apostles of Saint-Gilles or, more probably, by both. His first statue, Stephen, on the corner of the northeast pier (figs. 264–268), is markedly different from Peter and Paul. The Stephen is only 1.29 meters high in contrast to Peter and Paul, which are 1.66 meters. Stephen, in a frontal, symmetrical pose, exhibits a decidedly lithic plasticity. Although small in size, it is monumental in scale. The heavy, straight-falling mantle with flat folds, animated with

256. Arles, Saint-Trophîme. John, northwest pier. Peter-Paul Master.

257. John, head.

258. James, eastern intermediate pier. Peter-Paul Master.

259. James, head.

260. Arles, Saint-Trophîme.
Paul, northeast pier. Peter-
Paul Master.

261. Paul.

262. Paul, head.

263. Paul, detail.

264. Arles, Saint-Trophîme. Northeast pier, unidentified Apostle, Stephen and Paul.

265. Arles, Saint-Trophîme. Stephen. Stephen Master.

266. Stephen, detail.

267. Stephen, head.

268. Stephen, head.

269. Toulouse, Saint-Sernin. Christ, ambulatory.

270. Toulouse, Saint-Sernin. Symbol of lion, Musée des Augustins.

271. Marseille. Tomb of Saint Isarne, Musée Borély.

272. Saint-Gilles. Head of Paul.

small ridge folds along the sides, imparts a massiveness which belies its size. The head appears transfixed (figs. 267, 268). Thick locks of hair are accented with drill holes, while eyes are deeply set with pronounced edges determining eyebrows and continuing to delineate the nose.

Because of the squat proportions, frontality, and congealed character, the Stephen recalls the ambulatory reliefs of Saint-Sernin at Toulouse of 1096 (fig. 269); yet the massive projection of Stephen is more reminiscent of later sculpture from Saint-Sernin, such as the Sign of the Lion and the Ram of about 1115 from the south transept, now in the Musée des Augustins at Toulouse (fig. 270). If the attenuated proportions and cross-legs are ignored, there are some stylistic common denominators between the Stephen and these figures. Fragments from the west façade of Saint-Sernin also exhibit some vague similarities in drapery style. However, if Stephen's head (figs. 267, 268) is compared with that of the Christ of the ambulatory of Toulouse (fig. 269), it is obvious that the source of the Stephen Master's style is not Languedoc. The massive blockiness of Stephen's head with eyes set in deep sockets framed by sharp edges has no stylistic counterpart in the Toulouse heads. Rather, Stephen's head manifests more connections in style with the Paul of Saint-Gilles by Brunus (fig. 272) and, at the same time, appears related to the head of Saint Isarne, who died in 1048 and whose tomb is now in the Chateau Borély in Marseille (fig. 271). Thus it would seem that the Stephen Master's style was developed in Provence. The Stephen, his earliest work in the Arles cloister, already reveals a debt to the proto-Renaissance style of the Saint-Gilles apostles.

The second statue by the Stephen Master is the Saint Trophîme on the corner of the northwest pier (figs. 273–277). Since Arles was originally dedicated to both Saints Stephen and Trophîme, the former the patron saint of Arles and the latter its first bishop, their location on the corners of the north-gallery piers is both appropriate and meaningful. Saint Trophîme is 1.66 meters high, as are the adjacent statues of Peter and John. The entire pier is completely homogeneous and coordinated with diagonal and transverse reinforcing arches of the vault. By contrast, the smaller size of Stephen and the necessity of inserting a block beneath it raises the possibility that the Stephen was carved for a less elaborate project. In style Trophîme resembles Stephen, especially in the lower sections (compare figs. 276 and 266). The contained rectangularity, the lack of any anatomical articulation, and the flat folds relate these two statues; yet the greater complexity of the mantle of Trophîme and the arrangement of folds over the abdomen recall the Peter-Paul Master, especially the apostles Peter and John. Trophîme's head (figs. 275, 277) combines features from both Stephen and those of the Peter-Paul Master. Thus we see the Stephen Master becoming more influenced by the Provençal proto-Renaissance style. The parallel phenomenon of this kind of transformation can be found on the façade of Saint-Gilles. The Thomas Master, perhaps coming from Angoulême and exposed to other monuments in western France, continued his heritage in the low reliefs and apostle Thomas of Saint-Gilles. However, in his later work at Saint-Gilles, such as the apostle James the Less, and especially in his Peter on the central portal, he was strongly influenced by the indigenous style of Brunus.

On the western intermediate pier, the blessing Christ, garbed as pilgrim, is flanked by pilgrims (figs. 278–281). Christ is 1.33 meters high, while the pilgrims are 1.45 meters. The double meaning of Christ meeting the two Disciples on the Road to Emmaus and Christ dressed as pilgrim, signifying the pilgrimage to Santiago de Compostela, is clearly expressed. The right-hand pilgrim (fig. 280) wears the cockle-shell, symbol of James Major, on his hat. Gesture and treatment of drapery and feet of the Christ are close to that of Saint Trophîme, but the multiplicity of folds, the organization of folds across the waist, the triangular arrangement of the sleeve, and the implied articulation of the knee manifest the increasing influence of the Peter-Paul Master. Christ's head is a slightly attenuated version of that of Trophîme. The heads of the two pilgrims, especially the handling of hair, eyes, and ears, are practically identical in the head of Christ, and the general passivity of all three heads of the pier is in marked contrast to the psychological intensity of Peter and Paul. On the other hand, the emphasis on multiple folds with flat fillets and sharp edges seems to be related to figures by the Peter-Paul Master. Thus, if one can argue that work in the north gallery proceeded from west to east with the exception of the Stephen, which was carved before the Trophîme, it follows that the Stephen Master, with his distinct style as seen in the Stephen, gradually absorbed more and more of the point of view of the Peter-Paul Master.

On the eastern intermediate pier (fig. 282), James on the right, already discussed, is by the Peter-Paul Master (figs. 258, 259). The other two are Christ and the Doubting Thomas (figs. 282–285). Although Thomas, which, like James, is 1.45 meters high, resembles James in pose, it is clear from a comparison of surfaces that Thomas is by a different sculptor. Stiffness of gesture and style of drapery resemble the Christ and two Pilgrims on the adjacent pier by the Stephen Master. Thomas' head (fig. 284) is very similar to the heads of the three statues on the west intermediate pier and the head of Trophîme. Because of these stylistic relationships with other statues by the Stephen Master, it can be concluded that the Stephen Master carved the Thomas, but was forced to conform to the James by the Peter-Paul Master in pose and general arrangement of drapery.

273. Arles, Saint-Trophîme. Northeast pier, Peter, Trophîme, John.

274. Arles, Saint-Trophîme. Trophîme. Stephen Master.

275. Trophîme, head.

276. Trophîme, detail.

277. Trophîme, head.

278. Arles, Saint-Trophîme. Western intermediate pier. Christ and Pilgrim.

279. Christ and Pilgrims. Stephen Master.

280. Christ and Pilgrim.

281. Christ and Pilgrim, detail.

282. Arles, Saint-Trophîme. Eastern intermediate pier, Thomas, Christ, James.

283. Thomas, Christ, James, detail.

284. Thomas, head. Stephen Master.

285. Thomas, Christ. Peter-Paul Master.

The remaining figure of the north gallery is the Christ showing his Wounds to Thomas (figs. 282, 283). This Christ, which is only 1.15 meters high and the smallest of all the statues, is considerably shorter than Thomas and James. It seems strange to have Christ smaller than Thomas in a scene which combines the two. The figure rests on a large block and appears awkward in relation to the other statues. The pier as a whole is not unified, as are the other intermediate pier and the northwest pier. Christ's head is set against a flat halo, as opposed to the projecting cornice in the Christ with Pilgrims or the curved halos as in all the other figures except Stephen. If Saint Trophîme was carved by the Stephen Master after he had come under the spell of the Saint-Gilles style, either by direct contact or by influence from the Peter-Paul Master, and if the Stephen Master, after completing Trophîme, was responsible for the Christ and two Pilgrims and the Thomas, it follows that the Stephen Master could not have carved the Christ of the Doubting Thomas. Rather, there remains the strong possibility that this Christ is the earliest work by the Peter-Paul Master, and like Stephen was carved either for a smaller cloister or for a different location. In contrast to the Stephen, Trophîme, and Christ by the Stephen Master, in which the feet appear suspended from the body, the large feet of this Christ carry weight. The knee is defined and the legs revealed beneath the drapery. This sense of articulation is carried much further in statues by the Peter-Paul Master than in those by the Stephen Master.

When compared to statues by the Peter-Paul Master, especially the Peter (figs. 248, 249), the Christ figure exhibits many stylistic similarities. Feet and ponderation, arrangement and surface of undergarment above ankles, accentuation of knee, configuration of bottom hem of mantle, and narrowing of silhouette to feet—all are features of the Christ and Peter. Connection in style with Trophîme and the Christ with the Pilgrims can be explained by the influence of the Peter-Paul Master which gradually transformed the Stephen Master.

If the Christ of the Doubting Thomas (fig. 283) is compared with Paul by Brunus of Saint-Gilles (figs. 251, 255), many similar characteristics are revealed. The lower half of the Christ appears to be a primitive variant of the Paul. Wind-blown folds, which sweep out toward the James on the Saint-Gilles portal, become a frozen projection in the Christ. The impact of the Saint-Gilles sculpture is not digested in the Christ, whereas in the Peter of Arles, the same artist is emerging as a mature individual who has creatively transformed a borrowed style. Thus because of the discrepancy in size, the lack of unity in the pier as a whole, the stylistic connections with Peter, and because of the impossibility of placing this Christ in the evolving style of the Stephen Master, it seems plausible to argue that the Christ is the first work of the Peter-Paul Master, to be followed by Peter, John, James, and Paul, probably in that order. Thus the Peter-Paul Master was responsible for five statues in the north gallery, and the Stephen Master carved six: Stephen, Trophîme, Christ, two pilgrims, and Thomas.[2]

Reliefs on Piers of the North Gallery

Two reliefs on the northwest pier depict the empty tomb between Peter and Trophîme (figs. 286, 287) and the Holy Women buying Perfume from Merchants between Trophîme and John (figs. 288, 289). The scenes are balanced in format with smaller, lower registers containing two sleeping soldiers and two merchants. The sepulchre, flanked and surmounted by angels is reflected in the register containing the three Holy Women. The worn relief of the empty tomb is related stylistically to the adjacent apostle Peter. Groups of ridge folds reveal legs on both relief and figure. Undercut gouged folds appear on the shoulder and thighs of both angels and on Peter's right leg.

The three Holy Women above the two merchants, seated behind a table, recalls the same scene on the right portal of Saint-Gilles (fig. 99). This subject is treated on

---

2. H-A. von Stockhausen ("Die Romanische Kreuzgänge der Provence. Teil I: Die Architektur," *Marburger Jahrbuch für Kunstwissenschaft*, VII [1935], 135–190, and "Teil II: Die Plastik," VIII, IX [1936], 89–171; offprint, combining both articles published in 1932) concluded that the north gallery of Arles was profoundly influenced by the sculpture of Saint-Gilles. Von Stockhausen (1936, 91–92), following the unpublished findings of R. Hamann, divided the sculpture of the north gallery between two workshops: the Peter-Paul workshop and the Stephen-Trophîme workshop. The Peter-Paul workshop carved, besides Peter and Paul, John, James, all the reliefs, capitals, and corbels; the workshop of Stephen-Trophîme was responsible for the two Christs, two pilgrims, and Thomas. These conclusions do not probe into the evolution of the two artists, who seem to have carved all the figured sculpture, nor do they attribute the Christ of the Doubting Thomas pier to the Peter-Paul Master. Furthermore, as will be described later, not all the capitals were carved by the Peter-Paul Master or workshop.

R. Hamann, in *Die Abteikirche von St. Gilles und ihre künstlerische Nachfolge* (Berlin: Akademie-Verlag, 1955), 190–198, divided the sculpture of the north gallery of the Arles cloister between the Toulouse style of Saints Stephen and Trophîme and the classic-imitative style of Peter and Paul. The latter stemmed from the Saint-Gilles sculpture which he placed in his earliest campaign, namely the James Major and the slightly later Paul. According to his interpretation, the two apostles signed by Brunus (Matthew and Bartholomew) were carved later than the James and Paul, as were the Peter and Paul of Arles. He pointed out the connection between the Pauls of Saint-Gilles and Arles, but related the Peter of Arles to the Archangel and Lazarus relief of Saint-Gilles. Hamann explained the greater freedom and baroque character of Peter and Paul of Arles as representing a style pointing toward Chartres. Since he dated the James Major of Saint-Gilles before 1116 and the Paul soon afterward and since he related Stephen and Trophîme to the ambulatory reliefs of Saint-Sernin at Toulouse of 1096, it was possible to date all four statues around 1120. As already pointed out in Part I, this early dating cannot be substantiated. Furthermore, it is impossible to see an evolution toward Chartres when the greater, projecting bulk of the Arles Peter and Paul is part of a totally different architectural ambience.

the horizontal lintel of Saint-Gilles as a continuous narrative with the actual trans-action taking place, while at Arles the rectangular relief is divided into two zones. Stylistically, the Arles relief has no connection with the thick, sagging folds of the Saint-Gilles lintel by the Hard Master. Rather, the grouping of multiple ridge and loop folds relates the relief specifically to the adjacent statue of John as well as the other figures by the Peter-Paul Master. The heads of the Holy Women are practically identical to that of John (figs. 289, 257), while the heads of the merchants resemble those of the soldiers in the Resurrection relief and the head of Peter. The three Holy Women, with elaborately articulated mantles and with raised terminations (see left-hand Mary), are reminiscent of the apostles James, Paul, and John of Saint-Gilles by Brunus. Thus the impact of Saint-Gilles on the Peter-Paul Master is revealed in the five figures he carved as well as the two narrative reliefs on the northwest pier. This relief of the Holy Women influenced the sculptor who carved the same scene and the Holy Women at the Sepulchre on the Beaucaire frieze. The iconography of these scenes at Beaucaire was derived from the right-portal lintel of Saint-Gilles, but the style of the figures recalls the relief at Arles by the Peter-Paul Master.

The Ascension on the north face of the northeast pier, between Stephen and Paul (figs. 290, 291), contains seven disciples, Christ in a *mandorla*, and two angels. Over half of the left-hand frame is restored. The top of the *mandorla* is out of alignment, and the inner hands of the angels are modern. Proportions of figures and drapery in multiple ridge and hooked folds connect this relief with the scene of the Empty Tomb and with the style of the Peter-Paul Master. Indeed, the drapery of Christ in the Ascension and Christ's head are very close to the adjacent statue of Paul.

The Stoning of Stephen, the first Christian martyr, and Stephen's vision of Christ, on the east face of the northeast pier adjacent to the statue of Stephen (figs. 292, 293) does not balance compositionally the Ascension. Two-thirds of the relief show two figures stoning the kneeling, praying Stephen. The drapery over the left leg of Stephen is identical to that on the right-hand disciple of the Ascension (figs. 290, 291), while the garments of the executioners have counterparts in figures in the other three reliefs by the Peter-Paul Master. The Christ (fig. 293), however, reveals more stylistic connections with the Stephen Master, as seen in the shape of the head and in the rounded ridge folds with parallel concavities; yet the quality of this fragment is lower than that of the Stephen. Thus, it would seem that all four reliefs were carved by the Peter-Paul Master, with the exception of the Christ above the Stoning of Stephen.

Since the figures of Peter, John, and Paul overlap the reliefs of the Empty Tomb, the Holy Women bringing Perfume, and the Ascension, these reliefs must have been put in place before the apostles. This fact, together with the stylistic connections

286. Arles, Saint-Trophîme.
Empty Tomb, northwest
pier. Peter-Paul Master.

287. Empty Tomb, detail.

288. Holy Women buying Perfume, northwest pier. Peter-Paul
Master.

289. Holy Women, detail.

290. Arles, Saint-Trophîme. Ascension, northeast pier. Peter-Paul Master.

291. Ascension, detail.

292. Stoning of Stephen, northeast pier. Peter-Paul Master.

293. Vision of Stephen, northeast pier.

between apostles and reliefs, suggests that the reliefs were carved in the workshop either before the apostles or contemporaneously with them. Thus, the sequence of the Peter-Paul Master's work is as follows: The Christ of Doubting Thomas for a smaller cloister, the Empty Tomb relief, Peter, the Holy Women and Merchants, John, James, the Ascension, and Paul. The sequence of the Stephen Master's work appears to be: Stephen for a smaller project, Trophîme, Christ and the Two Pilgrims of the western intermediate pier, and the Thomas of the eastern intermediate pier. With the exception of the Christ of the Doubting Thomas and the Stephen, work proceeded from west to east. The northwest pier, with the exception of the Trophîme, is by the Peter-Paul Master. The western intermediate pier, Christ meeting Apostles on the Road to Emmaus, is entirely by the Stephen Master. The eastern intermediate pier, which is not harmoniously organized like the previous two, contains the Christ, the earliest work of the Peter-Paul Master, the James, a late work of the Peter-Paul Master, and the Thomas, the latest statue by the Stephen Master. This pier, both iconographically and compositionally, appears to be an assemblage. Thomas is considerably larger than the Christ, and the James has no connection with the Doubting Thomas scene.

The last relief of the campaign of the north gallery is Stoning and Vision of Saint Stephen on the east side of the northeast pier. Since the relief appears to be unfinished (see area immediately below the Christ) and the ornamental cornice breaks with the unified palmette design of the north side and over the Stephen, and the Apostle Andrew on the left has been inserted to relate to the east gallery of the cloister, it follows that the relief of Christ may have been begun by the Stephen Master, but certainly finished later by an assistant as work began on the east gallery.[3]

Capitals, Ornament, and Corbels

Of the eighteen capitals of the north gallery, six of the inner ones are historiated, while the remaining three inner ones and all nine on the outer or courtyard side are Corinthian in format. Starting from the west (nos. 1 to 9), the inner capitals contain the following (see fold-out plan of the cloister): First or western bay—Raising of Lazarus (no. 1—figs. 294, 295), Sacrifice of Abraham (no. 2—figs. 296, 297), and the Angel stopping Balaam (no. 3—figs. 298, 299); second or middle bay—Angel appearing to Abraham and Sarah (no. 4—figs. 300, 301), Paul before the Areopagites (no. 5—figs. 302, 303), and a Corinthian capital (no. 6—fig. 311); third or eastern bay—Moses receiving the Tablets of the Law (no. 7—figs. 304, 305), and two Corin-

---

3. Professor Alan Borg pointed out to me the unfinished nature of this relief.

294. Arles, Saint-Trophîme. North-gallery capital (1), Raising of Lazarus. Stephen Master.

295. North (1), Raising of Lazarus. Stephen Master.

296. North-gallery capital (2), Sacrifice of Abraham. Peter-Paul Master.

297. North (2), Sacrifice of Abraham. Peter-Paul Master.

298. Arles, Saint-Trophîme. North-gallery capital (3), Angel staying Bileam. Peter-Paul Master.

299. North (3), Angel staying Bileam.

300. North-gallery capital (4), Angel appearing to Abraham and Sarah. Peter-Paul Master.

301. North (4), Angel appearing to Abraham and Sarah.

thian capitals (nos. 8, 9—figs. 314, 316). The decrease in the number of historiated capitals on the inner colonnade from three in the western bay to two in the middle bay to one in the eastern bay suggests, perhaps, that the work proceeded from west to east. If this assumption is correct, it helps confirm the conclusions reached in the study of the figures and reliefs.

All the capitals are squat in proportion and are supported by round or octagonal shafts capped by torus moldings. Some of the round shafts appear to be Roman. The tops of the capitals, which are square in plan, have deep concavities on each face. The crowning section has two moldings: a flat section above a narrow frieze. The heads of the central figures break the concavity of the capitals and replace the rosettes of the Corinthian capital. Corners of the capitals are reinforced by tangent scrolls or heads.

The small size of the capitals, even when compared to the reliefs, makes it difficult to attribute them to specific hands. Furthermore, the distinct styles of the Peter-Paul Master and the Stephen Master, as seen in the Christ of the Doubting Thomas and the Stephen, tend to merge as work progressed in the north gallery. However, there are several characteristics, such as the treatment of the moldings of the capitals, the depth of the relief, and the articulation of the figures, which make it possible to assign two capitals to the Stephen Master and four to the Peter-Paul Master.

The westernmost capital, depicting the Raising of Lazarus (no. 1—figs. 294, 295), is the only scene from the New Testament. Found on the frieze of the central portal of Saint-Gilles, this scene reflects the importance of Lazarus, who purportedly landed with the Holy Women at Les-Saintes-Maries-de-la-Mer. In the Arles cloister, the Lazarus capital is adjacent to the pier containing the three Holy Women buying Perfume. The style of the Lazarus capital appears to be a narrative, small-scaled version of the figures by the Stephen Master, especially his Trophîme or the figures of Christ and the two pilgrims on the western intermediate pier. Moldings at the top and bottom of the capital are undecorated, and feet do not overlap the bottom molding. The general flatness of the figures, when viewed from the side, as well as the awkward, jerky articulation resembles the statues by the Stephen Master.

The adjoining capital, the Sacrifice of Abraham (no. 2—figs. 296, 297), reveals much more freedom of pose, greater articulation beneath the drapery, and a gracefulness which is not displayed in the Lazarus capital. The angel staying the sword of Abraham (fig. 296) is an animated version of the three Holy Women in the relief of the northwest pier (fig. 289) by the Peter-Paul Master. Both the top and bottom moldings are ornamented with frontal floral patterns, and several feet of the figures extend into the torus molding. The top of the capital is not as concave as the Lazarus capital. Thus, because of the different format of the capital and the relationship in style, both in articulation and treatment of drapery, with figures by the Peter-Paul Master, this capital can be assigned to the Peter-Paul Master.

The angel with sword stopping Balaam (no. 3—figs. 298, 299) resembles the Abraham capital in format (moldings decorated top and bottom) and in style. Although the lower part of the drapery of the angel does exhibit similarities to the adjacent Christ between pilgrims by the Stephen Master, there are, however, more stylistic connections between this capital and the reliefs by the Peter-Paul Master, especially the figures in the scene of the Empty Tomb (fig. 286).

The two historiated capitals of the middle bay of the north gallery (nos. 4, 5—figs. 300—303) are very close in style to the Balaam and Abraham capitals and thus seem to have been carved by the Peter-Paul Master. Both have floral moldings at the top and bottom. The Angel appearing to Abraham and Sarah (no. 4—figs. 300, 301) the westernmost capital, exhibits the same complexity of drapery, pronounced yet smooth articulation, and large heads which are seen on the other capitals by the Peter-Paul Master. The middle capital of the central bay, probably depicting Paul before the Areopagites (no. 5—figs. 302, 303), portrays the same marked articulation of thighs and legs and square heads as other capitals by the Peter-Paul Master.

The figure of Moses receiving the Tablets of the Law on the only figured capital of the eastern bay (no. 7—figs. 304, 305), is almost identical to those of the Lazarus capital (figs. 294, 295). Awkward articulation, flat profiles, undecorated moldings at top and bottom, and pronounced depth of the concavity of the capital—all are characteristics which can be found in the Lazarus capital. Thus it would seem that the Stephen Master carved two capitals, the westernmost (Lazarus) and the easternmost (Moses), while the Peter-Paul Master carved four, two in the western bay and two in the middle bay.

All nine outer capitals and three inner ones of the north gallery are Corinthian (figs. 306–317). They are composed of interlocking tiers of rolled acanthus leaves with rosettes or heads accenting the middle of each face and with scrolls reinforcing the corners. Although these capitals resemble the inner capitals of the side portals of Saint-Gilles in format (see figs. 3, 7, 148, 151), their proportions are squatter, and the frontal acanthus motifs, which have less details than those at Saint-Gilles, do not flare out from the bell of the capital. None of the complexity of the Roman capitals, surmounting the huge monolithic columns of the façade of Saint-Gilles, or their Romanesque variants in the nave and choir of Saint-Gilles can be found in these Arles cloister capitals. Varying degrees of quality suggest that some of these floral capitals and their ornamented abaci blocks, which stabilize the inner and outer arcades, were carved by an assistant. At the same time, the location of the most sensitive sculpture reveals fascinating insights into the procedures of the workshop.

302. Arles, Saint-Trophîme. North-gallery capital (5), Paul before the Areopagites. Peter-Paul Master.

303. North (5), Paul before Areopagites.

304. North-gallery capital (7), Moses receiving Tablets. Stephen Master.

305. North (7), Moses receiving Tablets.

306. Arles, Saint-Trophîme. North gallery, capital (1A).

307. North gallery, capital (2A).

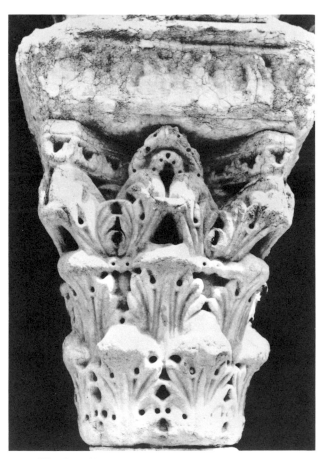

308. North gallery, capital (3A).

309. North gallery, capital (4A).

The westernmost capital (no. 1A—fig. 306) behind the Lazarus capital (no. 1—figs. 294, 295) is unique in format. Scrolls, which usually reinforce the corners, are replaced by two human and two eagle heads which, in turn, are connected by a convex, floral frieze. The masterly drill work in heads and acanthus leaves suggests that this capital was carved by the Stephen or the Peter-Paul Master. The abacus which crowns this and the Lazarus capital is decorated with undulating vines and complex floral fillers (see figs. 294, 295, 306). Subtle palmettes, located in the middle of each side, balance the ornamental composition. On the north face (fig. 294) two nudes grasping vines, a unique motif in the decoration of the abaci, flank the central palmette. The carving of leaves resembles the treatment of the acanthus tiers and ornamented cornice on the outer capital as well as the south face of the Lazarus capital. Since the Stephen Master was the author of the Lazarus capital, it can be surmised that he carved the Corinthian capital and the abacus which unites them. This pair of capitals, located adjacent to the western pier, served as one of the models for the rest of the arcade.

The second outer capital from the west (no. 2A—fig. 307) with three tiers of acanthus leaves, converging volutes at corners and at the center, and with an ornamented cornice presents a format entirely different from that of the westernmost capital of the Stephen Master. However, the style of carving, especially the extensive and consistent drill work and the subtle flare of the acanthus leaves, is very close to the capital just discussed. Although the ornamented cornice resembles that on the Sacrifice of Abraham capital by the Peter-Paul Master (no. 2—figs. 296, 297), with which it is paired, it would seem that this capital was also carved by the Stephen Master. The abacus joining this and the Abraham capital is a more plastic variant of the abacus crowning the first pair. Fillers of rosettes and leaves suggest more depth than in the first abacus. As will be discussed later, this abacus is almost identical to the ornamental frieze on the western pier. Both this abacus and the frieze of the western pier seem to have been carved by the Peter-Paul Master.

The easternmost capital of the western bay (no. 3A—fig. 308), consisting of two tiers of interlocking, acanthus patterns and large corner scrolls, is a simplified version of the middle capital (no. 2A—fig. 307). Although the drill work is less pronounced, the voids made by the drill have the same shapes. The palmettes of the abacus (see especially over Balaam—fig. 299) are identical to those on the faces of the Lazarus capital of Stephen. In this pair of capitals we have the Peter-Paul Master carving the historiated capital of Balaam, and the Stephen Master being responsible for the outer capital and the abacus.

In the central bay of the north gallery, the western capital (no. 4A—fig. 309) is so badly weathered that any conclusion concerning its authorship is difficult. However, in format and in the nature of the drill work it resembles closely the middle capital of the west bay (no. 2A—fig. 307). The abacus consists of simplified frontal leaves with accented midribs (see Angel appearing to Abraham and Sarah—no. 4, fig. 300). The middle Corinthian capital of the central bay (no. 5A—fig. 310), with frontal heads in the center and plain torus at base and undecorated top, is distinctly different from the four capitals just discussed. It is smaller in size and cruder in its surfaces and reveals drill work of long rounded voids. This capital is clearly the work of an assistant, but is based on the format of no. 3A (fig. 308). The abacus is plain except for masks at the four corners. Both the inner and outer capitals of the east side of the middle bay (nos. 6, 6A—figs. 311, 312) seem to have been carved by the assistant responsible for no. 5A (fig. 310). Like the westernmost floral capital by the Stephen Master (no. 1A—fig. 306), this inner capital has corners of human, goat, and eagle heads replacing the volutes. However, the quality of the carving is decidedly lower (contrast the eagle heads—figs. 306 and 311). The running vines with floral fillers of the abacus are connected in form with the westernmost two abaci, but the treatment of leaves and buds is coarser. Thus, for the first time, the assistant sculptor is responsible for a pair of capitals and their crowning abaci.

The east bay has only one historiated capital, Moses receiving the Law (no. 7—figs. 304, 305). The other five capitals (nos. 7A, 8, 8A, 9, 9A—figs. 313–317) appear to be the work of the assistant since their forms, the thickness and heaviness of the acanthus leaves, and the nature of the drill work with long, thin voids with rounded ends relate them to the other capitals by the assistant: nos. 5A, 6, 6A (figs. 310–312). The two inner capitals, nos. 8 and 9 (figs. 314, 316) are ornamented with heads on the center of each face. This elaboration of format, like the use of corner heads on capital no. 6 (fig. 311), makes these capitals slightly different from the outer range and more sympathetic to the historiated capitals. The palmette abacus of the Moses capital and no. 7A (figs. 304, 313) seems to be a harsh variant of the abacus of Balaam and no. 3A, while the undecorated abacus with corner masks over nos. 8 and 8A resembles that of nos. 5 and 5A. Finally, the undulating vine and floral fillers on the abacus over the easternmost capitals, nos. 9 and 9A (figs. 316, 317) is a mediocre reflection of the abaci over the two westernmost pairs of capitals, nos. 1 and 1A and 2 and 2A.

The two major sculptors seem to have organized the program for the sculpture of the double arcade as follows: the Stephen Master carved the entire westernmost pair of capitals and abaci to serve as model; the Peter-Paul Master carved the Sacrifice of Abraham capital, the Stephen Master was responsible for the Corinthian capital, and the Peter-Paul Master may be the author of the abacus; and a second model, involving collaboration, was established. In the third pair of capitals, Peter-Paul carved the Balaam scene, while Stephen seems to have done the abacus and the outer Corinthian capital. As work proceeded eastward more work was delegated to the

310. Arles, Saint-Trophîme. North gallery, capital (5A).

311. North gallery, capital (6).

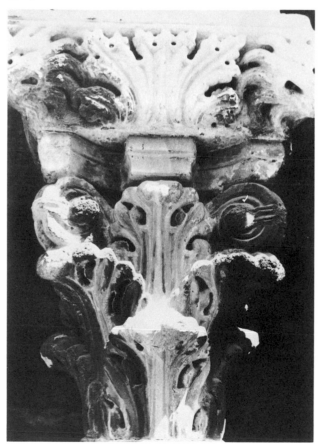

312. North gallery, capital (6A).

313. North gallery, capital (7A).

314. Arles, Saint-Trophîme. North gallery, capital (8).

315. North gallery, capital (8A).

316. North gallery, capital (9).

317. North gallery, capital (9A).

assistant. In the middle bay all four capitals except the two historiated ones, the Angel appearing to Abraham and Sarah and Paul before the Areopagites, both created by the Peter-Paul Master, were carved by the assistant. Finally, in the east bay five capitals and all the abaci were made by the assistant. Only the Moses capital was carved by Stephen. The increase in the work of the assistant from three in the middle bay to five capitals in the eastern bay certainly confirms the sequence of work from west to east in the north gallery. Other work by the assistant can be found in the marble choir capitals of Les-Saintes-Maries-de-le-Mer.

In contrast to the Saint-Gilles façade, in which ornament animates pedestals, friezes, lintels, and appears in two registers along the splays of the portals, the decorative sculpture of the Arles north gallery is confined to cornices uniting each pier, panels flanking the Stephen and Trophîme, and the abaci which join the nine pairs of capitals in the arcade. On the continuous frieze which crowns the three figures and two reliefs of the northwest pier (figs. 318, 319), an undulating vine with fillers of rolled leaves and rosettes above a bead-and-reel extends across the two reliefs and the Trophîme, while frontal palmettes appear above the Peter and James on the corners of the pier. As the detail exhibits (see fig. 277), the leaves with ridge ribs and drill holes and rosettes connected to secondary stems are plastically conceived in spite of the relatively low relief. Motifs, surfaces, and drill work are identical to the abacus over the middle capital of the west bay (see fig. 296). If indeed the Peter-Paul Master, who carved the Sacrifice of Abraham, also carved the abacus which surmounts it, it follows that the Peter-Paul Master was responsible for the entire northwest pier except the statue of Saint Trophîme. The closest stylistic parallel to the ornament of Saint-Gilles can be seen in the bottom of the lintels of the three portals (figs. 160–162) and the frieze over the apostles (figs. 152–157); yet at Saint-Gilles the much greater width of these panels allows for greater freedom of the fillers. The thin vertical panels of ornament which frame Trophîme (figs. 274, 275, 288) show an attenuated variant of the upper frieze with more complicated fillers, consisting of leaves and birds. Under the spell of Roman ornament, the vines and leaves are more three-dimensionally conceived than the abaci of the capitals of Moissac or the two series of capitals from La Daurade, now in the Musée des Augustins in Toulouse.

On the western intermediate pier (fig. 279) the palmettes resemble those on the abacus over the third capital by Stephen (no. 3A—fig. 308). Thus there is the distinct possibility that Stephen carved the entire pier: Christ, the two disciples, and the frieze. An undecorated modern block replaced the palmettes over the Christ of the eastern intermediate pier (fig. 282). The remaining palmettes over Thomas and James are very close in style to those on the west intermediate pier. This palmette motif is similar in format to the upper frieze on all three portals at Saint-Gilles.

On the northeast corner pier palmettes extend from Paul (a nineteenth-century replacement over Paul) across the Ascension relief and around the corner over Stephen (figs. 320, 321). The relative quality of the carving is higher than that of the abacus over the Moses capital by the assistant (no. 7—fig. 313), and this could conceivably have been carved by the Stephen Master. The panels flanking Stephen appear to be a simplified version of the ornament framing Trophîme. On the east face of this pier (fig. 321) there is a marked break in style in the re-entrant angle to the right of Christ. The palmette design ends abruptly, and an undulating vine with fillers replaces the palmettes. The stretched-out nature of this ornament with prominent voids is similar to that on the abaci of the two northernmost and adjacent capitals of the east gallery. Thus the northeast pier is not unified like the northwest pier, and the change in ornament reflects the interruption in the work on the monumental figures and the relief of the Stoning of Stephen.

Corbels, from which the six transverse arches spring across the north gallery, consist of frontal animal heads or atlantes with abaci of palmettes (figs. 245–247, 322, 323). The corner corbel (fig. 322), supporting the diagonal extending to Trophîme, consists of a splendid ram's head with horns functioning as volutes. The plastic abacus is reminiscent of the sculpture, both large figures, reliefs, and capitals, by the Peter-Paul Master. The remaining four corbels (from west to east) consist of an upside-down figure (fig. 245), a badly damaged bird, an ass with long ears, and a lion. Animated surfaces and marked articulation recall the style of the Peter-Paul Master. All these corbels are more complex and more freely composed than those supporting the top cornice of the central portal of Saint-Gilles.

The north gallery of the Arles cloister would thus seem to be the work of two sculptors, the Stephen and Peter-Paul Masters, and at least one assistant. Both Stephen and Peter-Paul were strongly influenced by Saint-Gilles, especially the Paul, a mature work of Brunus. The fact that no reflections of the upper friezes and tympana of the Saint-Gilles façade can be discerned in the Arles north gallery suggests the possiblity that the north gallery was begun before the Saint-Gilles façade was completed.

Evidence for an uninterrupted campaign starting with the northwest pier and concluding with the east side of the northeast pier is apparent in the architecture, monumental sculpture, reliefs, capitals, and ornament of the north gallery. The northwest pier, in contrast to the northeast pier, is a balanced, unified composition carried out by the Peter-Paul Master with Stephen carving the Trophîme. The western arcade with intercolumniation of .85 meters reveals a collaboration of the two major sculptors with Stephen carving the first or western pair of capitals to

318. Arles, Saint-Trophîme. Ornament over Trophîme and John, northwest pier.

319. Ornament over Peter and Trophîme, northwest pier.

320. Ornament over Stephen and Paul, northeast pier.

321. Arles, Saint-Trophîme. Ornament over Andrew and Stephen, northeast pier.

322. North-gallery corbel, ram.

323. North-gallery corbel, atlantid.

serve as model. The western intermediate pier, Christ and the two Pilgrims (Emmaus), is the work of the Stephen Master. The middle range of columns and capitals (intercolumniation of .88 meters) has only two historiated capitals by the Peter-Paul Master and at least three Corinthian-type capitals by an assistant. The eastern intermediate pier appears to be an assemblage with the Thomas, the latest work by Stephen, the Christ, the earliest work by Peter-Paul, and the James, a late work of the Peter-Paul Master. The eastern colonnade, which has a much narrower intercolumniation of .65 meters, has only one historiated capital, Moses receiving the Tablets of the Law by Stephen, which incidentally is adjacent to the Doubting Thomas, also by the Stephen Master. The rest of the capitals are by an assistant. Finally, the northeast pier contains the earliest work of the Stephen Master, namely Saint Stephen, and the latest statue of Peter-Paul, namely the Saint Paul. The east side of the pier is unfinished and has an unidentified apostle, a section of the relief, and a part of the ornamental frieze which belongs to the later campaign in the east gallery.

(2) EAST GALLERY

Greater elaboration of piers and moldings and wider and higher intercolumniations, when contrasted with the north gallery, established the east gallery as later in date (figs. 324, 241). Only the apostles on the lower part of the façade of Saint-Gilles influenced the sculpture of the north gallery, while several capitals in the east gallery reveal both stylistic connections with those of the north gallery and influences from the upper friezes of Saint-Gilles. Two statues in the east gallery portray relationships to these capitals as well as to sculpture on the façade of Saint-Trophîme. A new style, antithetical either to the north gallery of Arles or to Saint-Gilles, appears in the monumental sculpture on the piers of the east gallery and on several related capitals. Thus the homogeneity of the north gallery of the Arles cloister, in spite of the fact that two major sculptors created it, is replaced by a variety of points of view, suggesting that the east gallery was completed only during a long and interrupted period of time.

Eight of the nine inner capitals of the east gallery illustrate major scenes in the life of Christ. These scenes involve more figures than in the capitals of the north gallery, and their narrative character, often with several events on one capital, affects the sculptural-architectonic design.[4]

---

4. The historiated capitals of the east gallery are somewhat larger than those of the north gallery. North gallery (average dimensions): .28 meters wide at top; .32 meters high. East gallery: .305 meters wide; .345 meters high. Slight variations in size do not seem to be related to different hands.

The northernmost capital, Annunciation, Visitation, and Nativity (no. E1—figs. 325–327), exhibits certain similarities with those of the north gallery (see especially the Sarah—figs. 300, 301); yet it is quite clear that neither the Stephen Master nor the Peter-Paul Master carved it. The Virgin of the Annunciation (south side—fig. 325) is large and massive; thick loop folds articulate knees, while legs are indicated by wide, shallow ridge folds bordered by incised lines. The mantle covers the Virgin's head and extends over arms in long heavy folds, animated by a raised, wind-blown pattern. The angel is garbed in a tight tunic with simple collar and drilled dots. Both heads display heavy eyelids and thick lips.[5] Although the composition is obviously quite different in the Visitation on the east face (fig. 326) and in the Nativity of the north face (fig. 327), the drapery, wooden gestures, and treatment of sleeves and hands are identical. The textural interest with innumerable curving folds and the emphasis on the front plane of the capital are not found in the capitals of the north gallery, which concentrate on groups of pronounced ridge folds and greater projection of the figures.

The third capital of the north bay, the Annunication to the Shepherds (no. E3—figs. 328–330), is by the same sculptor as the Incarnation capital. Mantles are pulled across legs in frozen, wind-blown terminations, like those of the Virgin of the Annunciation. Wide, curving folds, in contrast to the thin, undulating belts of the figures on the north-gallery capitals, indicate the stomach. Although space is implied by overlapping elements such as the wings of angels, heads remain in low relief in contrast to the greater three-dimensionality of the heads on the capitals of the north gallery. No volutes, remnants of the Corinthian format, remain.

These two capitals of the north bay of the east gallery, besides appearing to be related to and modified extensions of the style of the north-gallery capitals, reveal marked stylistic relationships with sections of the upper frieze of the façade of Saint-Gilles. If the Virgin Annunciation (fig. 325) or the Angel of the Annunciation to the Shepherds (fig. 330) is compared with details of the left-hand frieze and lintel of the left portal of Saint-Gilles (figs. 78, 85), similarities in anatomical articulation and arrangement of folds over stomachs and knees and between the feet are apparent. The Soft Master, who was responsible for much of the sculpture of the left portal of Saint-Gilles, is certainly not the same artist who carved the two Arles capitals; yet the influence of the Saint-Gilles superstructure, totally absent in the Arles north gallery, has manifested itself in the east gallery.

---

5. A capital in the collection of Professor and Mrs. Meyer Schapiro of New York City is very similar in style. See C. Gomez-Moreno, *Medieval Art from Private Collections; A Special Exhibition at The Cloisters* (New York, The Metropolitan Museum of Art, 1968), 27, ill. 27.

324. Arles, Saint-Trophîme. East gallery to the south.

325. Arles, Saint-Trophîme. East (1), Annunciation.

326. East (1), Visitation.

327. East (1), Nativity.

328. East (3), Annunciation to Shepherds.

An unidentified, unfinished, apostle, 1.30 meters high (fig. 331), and attached to the east wall of the east gallery, is so badly eroded and damaged that analysis is difficult. The figure stands in a symmetrical pose with head, set against a halo, turned slightly to his right. Remains of curled hair frame his face and continue over his shoulders. His cloak falls over both arms, creating large curved folds over his right arm, and envelops his right leg, but ends above his left knee. Groups of vertically placed ridge folds flank concave strips which have pointed loop folds with varying intervals. The silhouette curves inward slightly at the bottom of the figure. There are vague connections between this figure and the reliefs of the north gallery by the Peter-Paul Master (figs. 286–291), but the closest stylistic parallels seem to be with apostles on the portal of Saint-Trophîme at Arles (figs. 381–389). Note especially the loop folds and the position of the hands.

Von Stockhausen, following Hamann's unpublished writings of 1933 which were published by Hamann in 1955, argued that this apostle originally decorated the southern corner of the northeast pier. According to him, it was part of the north gallery and belonged to the Toulousian atelier which was responsible for the two Christs, pilgrims, and Thomas of the north gallery. It was considered too archaic by the sculptors of the east gallery and was replaced by the present statue beside the scene of the Stoning of Stephen (fig. 332).[6] Since the apostle's head turns to his right, it could not have been created originally for the southern corner of the north pier, as Hamann and Von Stockhausen believed. Furthermore, the figure style seems to be closer to the later portal of Arles than to the north gallery. There is the possibility that this apostle was carved for the north corner of the southeast pier, which now displays the Gamaliel. The position of head, turned to his right, would suggest this solution. The arrival of a new artist, who created the two intermediate and south piers of the east gallery, would be sufficient cause for discarding this apostle.

This damaged apostle has some relationship to the apostle usually referred to as Saint Andrew, now on the south corner of the northeast pier (fig. 332). Both apostles have the same rigidity and frontality; yet the Andrew is squatter, and the silhouette does not become narrower at the bottom. The apostle of the northeast pier is 1.66 meters high, like the Paul on the north face, but it has a thick base plus an extra block beneath the base. It is thus a reduction of the size of the figures of the corner piers of the north gallery. Although there are some connections with the north gallery in style, it is closer stylistically to the apostles on the Arles portal. The silhouette from the side projects outward, with legs appearing to dangle (fig. 332). The head is set against a large, flat halo, unlike the curved halos of the north gallery. The stiffness

---

6. Von Stockhausen, *op. cit.*, 95, and Hamann, *op. cit.*, 209.

of pose is accentuated by truncated bundles of ridge folds bordering deep concavities with finer folds. The figure has a simple bodice of gouged folds, and the mantle is pulled tightly over his right arm by a loop grasped by his hand. Curved, undercut folds extend down the center of the figure. Below his left arm, more loop folds, which move forward and back in space, extend to the knees. Straight termination of ridge folds and their adjacent concavities over feet possess parallels with the sculpture of the west portal, especially with the Andrew (fig. 383). The head of this apostle is stark and transfixed. Hair and beard in small strands frame the eyes, which are demarcated by ridges. The head is totally different from those of the other statues in the east gallery. Von Stockhausen and Hamann believed this figure to be later than the portal.[7]

The two southernmost capitals of the east gallery (nos. E8 and E9—figs. 333–338), were carved by a different sculptor than the one who is responsible for the two historiated capitals in the north bay (nos. E1 and E3—figs. 325–339). Figures are shorter and faces more individualized and expressive. The influence of the left portal of Saint-Gilles, which is apparent in the capitals of the north bay, is intensified. The Entry into Jerusalem (no. E8—figs. 333–335), with six disciples, foal, Christ on a Donkey, Boy spreading Cloak, Two Boys with Palm Fronds, and the Walls of Jerusalem with four heads (not illustrated), is a simplified version of the lintel of Saint-Gilles (figs. 85, 87). Details such as the positions of Christ's hands, the boy spreading the cloak, the child holding the palm frond in his right hand, and the tall thin gateway—all reveal the dependence of the Arles capital on the composition of the Saint-Gilles lintel (see figs. 87 and 335). The rhythmic curves and countercurves of the Saint-Gilles lintel are absent in the Arles capital. The Saint-Gilles lintel, probably originally inspired by Early Christian sarcophagi, such as the one in Saint-Trophîme (see fig. 82), was the model for the lintel of Thines (Ardèche) as well as for several Italian lintels. At Arles the sculptor adapted the Saint-Gilles lintel to the curving bell of a small capital.

The other capital in the south bay, depicting the Dispersal of the Disciples (no. E9—figs. 336–338), exhibits the same style as in the Entry into Jerusalem capital. The shifting axes of the heads with their expressive eyes and the bunches of projecting folds appear in both capitals. The proportions of the figures and certain details of drapery, such as the disciple grasping his cloak in his right hand (fig. 336), show vague connections with the Andrew on the northeast pier (fig. 332).

Ornament on the outer capitals, abaci, and cornices of piers of the east gallery are a transformation of ornament in the north gallery. Although the Corinthian-type

---

7. *Ibid.* and Von Stockhausen, *op. cit.*, 96.

329. Arles, Saint-Trophîme. East (3), Annunciation to Shepherds.

330. East (3), Annunciation to Shepherds.

331. East gallery, Apostle against wall.

332. East gallery, north pier, Andrew (?).

333. Arles, Saint-Trophîme. East (8), Entry into Jerusalem.

334. East (8), Entry into Jerusalem.

335. East (8), Entry into Jerusalem.

336. Arles, East (9), Dispersal of the Apostles.

337. Arles, Saint-Trophîme. East (9), Dispersal of the Apostles.

338. East (9), Dispersal of the Apostles.

339. East (1), Ornamental capital.

340. East (2), Ornamental capitals.

341. Arles, Saint-Trophîme. East (3), Ornamental capital.

342. East (4), Ornamental capital.

343. East (5), Ornamental capital.

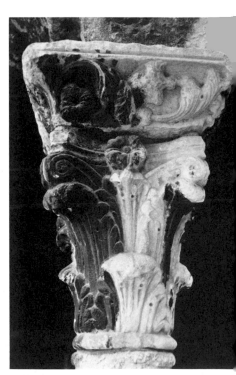

344. East (6), Ornamental capital.

345. East (7), Ornamental capital.

346. East (9), Ornamental capital.

capitals in the east gallery (figs. 339–346) are slightly larger than those in the north gallery and tend to flare out more, their organization follows the design of capitals carved by the assistant in the north gallery. However, the simplified treatment of leaves with concave surfaces, the reduction in drill work, plus the arbitrary drill holes near the terminations of leaves (see figs. 339, 343, 344), suggest that a different sculptor is involved in the east gallery; yet the quality of the carving seems lower. The inner eagle capital (no. E2—fig. 340) is a simplified version of one at Saint-Gilles (fig. 166).

The abaci, crowning the pairs of capitals, also reveal connections with the north gallery. The undulating vine and floral fillers on abaci of the two northernmost pairs of capitals (nos. E1 and E2—figs. 326, 327, 339, 340) are simplified and flattened-out variations of several abaci in the north gallery and, at the same time, are remarkably close to the cornice extending across the Andrew and relief of Stephen (fig. 321), which seem to belong to the later campaign of the east gallery, not the campaign of the north gallery. The palmette on the third abacus of the north bay (no. E3—figs. 329, 341) is a schematized variant on this motif in the north gallery.

In the middle bay (nos. E4, 5, 6—figs. 342–344) the abaci of palmettes are further simplified with scooped-out plain leaves, increased voids, and large scrolls at the corners (see nos. E4 and 5). The same type of carving can be seen in the running-vine motif above the two intermediate piers (figs. 359, 360, 362). These abaci and cornices are quite different from the abaci of the north bay and bear no relationship to ornament in the north gallery. The two abaci illustrated from the south bay (nos. E7, E9 —figs. 345, 346) are similar to the undulating vines over the two intermediate piers. Thus the ornament on the abaci of the north bay and over the Stephen relief, like the two historiated capitals, is closer stylistically to models in the north gallery, while the remaining ones exhibit a marked change. However, the eight Corinthian-type capitals remain more uniform. It would thus seem that the abaci of the central bay and cornices of the intermediate piers were carved by a different sculptor than the one responsible for those of the north bay.

The four remaining historiated capitals of the east gallery, three in the middle bay and one in the south arcade, are the work of a third, quite different sculptor. Broad, loop folds with uniform intervals and sharp edges cloak the figures of the Massacre of the Innocents, the northernmost capital (no. E4—figs. 347, 348). Drapery splays out over the feet (see Herod—fig. 348), and eyes of the large heads are accented by prominent drill holes, unlike the pupilless eyes in the capitals of the north bay. All these characteristics are seen in the capital depicting the Flight into Egypt (no. E5): Joseph (south face—fig. 349), Virgin and Child on a donkey (east face—fig. 350), the handmaiden of the Virgin driving the donkey (north face—fig. 351), and the Angel appearing to the three Kings (west face—fig. 352). Heavy garments of curved folds with pronounced edges delineate the concavities (see especially fig. 351). Undergarments make a double fold over feet, and the oval, expressionless heads have wide shallow eyes and slightly receding chins. The Angel appearing to the three Kings in a dream (fig. 352) displays the marked edges of the coverlet and heads with ornate crowns and sharply delineated eyes and mouths. This capital of the Flight into Egypt was ascribed tentatively to Benedetto Antelami by Francovich.[8]

The southernmost capital of the middle bay, depicting the Magi before Herod (no. E6—figs. 353–355), displays the same loop folds across the stomach and drapery flaring over the feet as in the Flight into Egypt capital. The transfixed heads are identical to those of the Kings in the capital just discussed, and Herod repeats the Herod in the Massacre of the Innocents capital (fig. 348). Thus, it would seem that all three capitals of the middle bay are by the same sculptor. Furthermore, this sculptor seems to have been influenced by the sculpture of the superstructure of the façade of Saint-Gilles, especially the lintel and right frieze of the right portal by the Hard Master (figs. 99–103). This relationship can be seen in the general heaviness of the drapery and the specific treatment of the folds over waist and feet.

The Adoration of the Magi and Joseph's Dream, the northernmost capital of the south bay (no. E7—figs. 356–358) must also be attributed to this same sculptor. The three Magi are almost identical to the Magi before Herod, while the enthroned Virgin recalls the east faces of all the capitals of the middle bay. The head of Joseph (fig. 358) is identical to the Joseph in the Flight into Egypt (fig. 349). The combination of the Adoration of the Magi and the Dream of Joseph at Bethlehem when an angel told him to flee to Egypt is depicted on the left tympanum of Saint-Gilles and on the tympanum at Montfrin (Gard), which was based on Saint-Gilles and Beaucaire. Gestures and costumes of the three Magi and throne with columns and crowning towers are similar in the Arles capital and the Saint-Gilles tympanum. It would thus seem that this third sculptor adapted the tympanum relief of Saint-Gilles to the curving capital, just as the second sculptor modeled his capital of the Entry into Jerusalem on the lintel of the left portal of Saint-Gilles.

The latest campaign of the east gallery consists of the Flagellation of Christ and Judas on the northern intermediate pier (figs. 359, 360), the two remaining figures on the southern intermediate pier (figs. 361, 362), and the sculpture on the southeast pier (figs. 365, 366). This sculptor and his assistant, in contrast to the three who carved

---

8. G. de Francovich, *Benedetto Antelami. Architetto e scultore e l'arte del suo tempo* (Milan and Florence: 1952), 136–137.

347. Arles, Saint-Trophîme. East (4), Massacre of Innocents.

348. East (4), Massacre of Innocents.

349. East (5), Flight into Egypt, Joseph.

350. East (5), Flight into Egypt, Virgin and Christ Child.

351. Arles, Saint-Trophîme. East (5), Flight into Egypt, Handmaiden.

352. East (5), Angel appearing to Magi.

353. East (6), Magi before Herod.

354. East (6), Magi before Herod.

355. Arles, Saint-Trophîme. East (6), Magi before Herod.

356. East (7), Adoration of Magi.

357. East (7), Adoration of Magi, Virgin and Child.

358. East (7), Dream of Joseph.

359. Arles, Saint-Trophîme. East gallery, north intermediate pier, Flagellant and Christ.

360. East gallery, north intermediate pier, Christ and Judas.

361. East gallery, south intermediate pier.

362. East gallery, south intermediate pier.

the historiated capitals, exhibit no stylistic relationships either with the north gallery of Arles or with the façade of Saint-Gilles. Figures in elaborate niches are forced into the angle of the pier. In all five statues the block is cut into diagonally, creating sharp edges on the surfaces and crisp right-angled concavities. Intervals between folds remain constant. Figures have twisting, awkward poses. Their costumes contain incised collars and wide belts, while heavy drapery terminates in tonguelike folds (figs. 360, 361). Oval-shaped heads with wide eyes have prominent heavy curls behind their necks (fig. 363). The only vague connection with the north gallery is the general shape of the head of Christ (figs. 359, 360); yet the treatment of hair and drapery relates the Christ to the master of the other four statues as well as those on the spandrels of the arcade (fig. 364).

The southeast pier (figs. 365, 366) contains a holy-water basin on the angle and a figure, Gamaliel, the teacher of Paul, on the right with reliefs in tiers in between. The Baptism and Temptation appear on the south side (not illustrated), while Christ washing Peter's Feet, the Last Supper, and Betrayal ornament the east face (fig. 366). Gamaliel (fig. 366) is 1.51 meters and taller than the figures of the intermediate piers, 1.24 meters. Although the pose of the Gamaliel is stiffer to conform to its function as impost for the transverse rib, like Peter, Paul, and John in the north gallery, the treatment of drapery in sharp edges, the staring eyes, receding chin, and flowing hair relate the statue to the sculpture of the intermediate piers. The reliefs of the southeast pier (fig. 366) show short figures with birdlike heads. The crispness of the monumental sculpture has disappeared; yet the heads echo that format of Gamaliel's face. The very low quality would indicate that these reliefs are the work of an assistant.

The figure supporting the holy-water basin (fig. 365) exhibits the same surfaces as Gamaliel with undercut folds having rounded concavities. The right arm reflects Gamaliel's left shoulder and arm in arrangement of drapery. The head recalls those of the figures of the south intermediate pier (figs. 361, 362), with oval masses and receding chins. The deep loop folds seem to be plastic versions of those of the left flagellant (fig. 359). The same rounding of the surfaces and general softness which we saw in the Gamaliel continues. A strong family relationship exists in all the sculpture of the two intermediate and southeast corner piers. The style is completely new to the Arles cloister and has no relationship with Saint-Gilles. One un-Provençal artist, probably with an assistant, seems to be responsible for the seven monumental figures and reliefs.

Sculpture in the east gallery thus seems to be the work of at least four sculptors. The first, basing his style on the north gallery plus influences from the superstructure of the façade of Saint-Gilles, carved the two historiated capitals in the north bay.

363. Arles, Saint-Trophîme. East gallery, south intermediate pier, head.

364. East gallery, spandrel of middle bay.

365. East gallery, south pier, Holy-water basin.

366. East gallery, south pier, Gamaliel.

Since the ornamental section of the Annunciation to the Shepherds (fig. 328) resembles that of the abaci of the north bay, he may have carved them as well. The second sculptor carved the two southernmost historiated capitals in the south bay and reveals the strong imprint of the left portal of Saint-Gilles. The third artist, who was responsible for four capitals, three in the central bay and the northern one in the south bay, exhibits less influence from Arles north and more from Saint-Gilles. The fourth sculptor, whose figures are clearly unrelated to the local Provençal tradition and who with an assistant finished the east gallery, carved the monumental sculpture on the southeast pier and the two intermediate piers and their superstructure. The style of these figures recalls the work on the transept portals of Chartres and therefore was not completed until the early decades of the thirteenth century.[9] Ornament on the abaci of the central and southern bay of the east gallery seems to be related to the style of this fourth sculptor.

The styles of the two apostles of the east gallery, the unidentified apostle against the east wall (fig. 331), and the Andrew (?) (fig. 332) are so closely related to the portal of Arles that further analysis must wait on the discussion of the portal. At this point, it can be stated that some of the sculpture of the east gallery appears to be earlier than the façade portal, while the work of the fourth artist definitely is later than the portal.

(3) EVIDENCE FOR DATING OF ARLES SCULPTURE

The extensive spread of dating found in the literature on Saint-Gilles-du-Gard persists in articles and monographs on Saint-Trophîme at Arles. As in the case of Saint-Gilles, the basis for dating often revolves around the priority of Provence over the Île-de-France or vice versa. Since the date of the portal of Saint-Trophîme at Arles (see Chapter 10) is often included in the discussion of the date of the Arles cloister, the following summary will include both portal and cloister.

History of Saint-Trophîme

Prosper Mérimée (1835) dated both the north gallery of the cloister and the portal in the mid-twelfth century.[10] H. Revoil (1873), who dated the façade of Saint-Gilles around 1140, argued that the portal was contemporary with the translation

---

9. W. Sauerländer pointed out to me the connection between these Arles statues and the Chartres transept sculpture.

10. P. Mérimée, *Notes d'un voyage dans le Midi de la France* (Paris: Librairie de Fournier, 1835), 290–293. E. Viollet-le-Duc, *Dictionnaire raisonné de l'architecture française du XIe au XVIe siècle*, 10 vols. (Paris: Bance, 1854–1868), VII, 417–419.

of the relics of Saint Trophîme from Saint-Honorat in 1152.[11] W. Vöge (1894) inaugurated the Provence versus Île-de-France syndrome by dating the Arles portal around 1135, earlier than Saint-Gilles, and by stating that the north gallery of the Arles cloister of the early twelfth century and the portal exerted a strong influence on Chartres.[12] R. de Lasteyrie (1902) opposed Vöge and observed that Chartres was the source of inspiration for Arles, especially the portal. Basing his conclusions on the epitaphs of canons in the cloister, four on the north wall extending from 1165 to 1203 and on the east wall from 1181 to 1239, with the respective walls finished before 1165 and 1181, he dated the arcade of the north gallery with its sculpture around 1180 and the east gallery later, citing as evidence the inscription of 1188 under Saint Trophîme on the northwest pier. Since, according to Lasteyrie, there is a stylistic relationship between the portals of Arles and Tarascon with its inscription of 1187–1197 and between the rinceau of Arles and that of Maguelonne with inscription of 1178, he dated the portal of Arles in the 1180's.[13]

L. Labande (1904) attempted to integrate the history of the building wth the dating of the sculpture. In general, he followed Lasteyrie's dating. According to Labande, the rebuilding of the nave took place between 1100 and 1140, with the architectural style related to Montmajour and Vaison-la-Romaine. The cloister changed from secular to monastic and embraced the Rule of Saint Augustine between 1153 and 1165, since a bull of 1153 made no mention of regular monastic life, while one of 1165 did. This shift, according to Labande, occurred around 1165. This regularization of the chapter caused the construction of the monastic complex.[14] In an article of 1909 Labande pushed the rebuilding of the nave to 1140–1152 and placed the portal at the end of the twelfth or early thirteenth century. He has the cloister begun a little after 1150, but the north gallery not terminated until 1180, with the east gallery later.[15]

In his 1930 monograph, Labande expanded the analysis of the architecture and sculpture. The history of the church went back possibly to the first century to Gallo-Roman subterranean chambers. There was a fifth-century basilica. No records existed between 683 and 794 during the raids by the Saracens, Danes, and Normans. Ac-

11. H. Revoil, *L'architecture romane du Midi de la France*, 3 vols. (Paris: Morel, 1873), II, 35.

12. W. Vöge, *Die Anfänge des monumentalen Stiles im Mittelalter* (Strassburg: 1894), 130-131.

13. R. de Lasteyrie, "Études sur la sculpture française au moyen-âge," Académie des inscriptions et belles-lettres, Fondation Piot, *Monuments et mémoires*, VIII (1902), 47–76.

14. L. Labande, "Étude historique et archéologique sur Saint-Trophîme d'Arles du IVe au XIIIe siècle," *Bulletin monumental*, LXVIII (1904), 22–38.

15. L. Labande, "Église métropolitaine de Saint-Trophîme," *Congrès archéologique de France*, II (1909), 218–223.

cording to Labande, the remains of a Carolingian church of the late eighth or early ninth century can be seen in the walls of the aisles and the façade. In this church, dedicated to Saint Stephen, a Council was held in 813.[16] The mid-eleventh century witnessed the reconstruction of transept, crossing, and first bay of the nave. The second reconstruction included the rebuilding and vaulting of the nave between 1078, when the body of Saint Trophîme, the first Bishop of Arles, was removed from the church and placed in Saint-Honorat, and 29 September 1152, when his relics were transferred to Saint-Trophîme. Labande believed that the nave was completed by 1152, and the crypt with its ribbed vaults was later than the nave. The designer of the portal raised the level of the nave pavement and began the sculpture around 1180.[17] This late dating of the nave follows the general theory that all Provençal architecture is later than Burgundian, Pilgrimage Road, and the Auvergne structures. There is no proof of this assumption. All ribbed vaults, like the crypts of Arles and of Saint-Gilles, are placed in the second half of the century. The cloister and its peripheral rooms such as refectory, kitchen, and dormitory were, according to Labande, constructed after the clerics submitted to the Rule of Saint Augustine and lived a communal life. Labande now dated the north gallery of the cloister between 1165 and 1180 and earlier than the portal. His dating followed the epitaphs on the north wall (1165–1203) and on the northwest pier (1188) and the adoption of the Rule of Augustine.[18]

A. K. Porter (1923) considered the portal of Arles a dated monument begun about 1142 and finished in 1152 in time for the translation of the relics of Saint Trophîme from Saint-Honorat to Saint-Trophîme and the resulting change in name of the church from Saint-Étienne to Saint-Trophîme. He argued that the portal influenced Wilhelmus Martini in Saint-André-le-Bas in Vienne in 1152. The north gallery of the cloister he dated earlier than the portal and noted its derivation from Saint-Gilles. Porter dated the east gallery before 1181 because of the epitaph of that date and the stylistic connections with Tarascon.[19]

H. A. von Stockhausen (1935 and 1936) followed the earlier conclusions of Hamann and placed the north gallery between 1120 and 1140 at the beginning of the whole series of Provençal cloisters which extend into the thirteenth century. His studies involved an analysis of the changing architectural and sculptured forms of

---

16. L. Labande *L'église Saint-Trophîme d'Arles*, Monograpies des grands édifices de la France (1930), 6–14.

17. *Ibid.*, 16–20.

18. *Ibid.*, 68–72, 86.

19. A. K. Porter, *Romanesque Sculpture of the Pilgrimage Roads*, (Boston: Marshall Jones, 1923), vol. 1, 297–299.

the seventeen preserved cloisters and three others which exist in fragmentary condition.[20]

R. Hamann (1955) agreed with Vöge and Lasteyrie that the north gallery of the cloister was earlier than the portal, since the former was influenced by the classic-imitative style of James Major and Paul of his first campaign and the latter was inspired by the completed and expanded program of Saint-Gilles. He also pointed out the influence of the Saint-Gilles crypt on the architecture of the cloister and of the Saint-Gilles façade on the iconography of the north gallery.[21]

Hamann opposed Vöge, who argued that the Arles portal was earlier than Saint-Gilles. The direct dependence of the portal of Arles on the completed façade of Saint-Gilles, both in its total design, iconography, and figure style, proved to the satisfaction of Hamann that the Arles portal corrected many of the disharmonious elements caused by the change in program of Saint-Gilles. Hamann pushed the date of the portal of Arles back before 1152. Its pre-Chartres style, the depiction of the two local saints, and his very early dating of Saint-Gilles with the entire façade finished by 1129 and the plan changes taking place in 1116—all were cited by Hamann as evidence of the dating of the Arles portal in the second quarter of the twelfth century. Both Stephen and Trophîme were associated with the church in the eleventh century, but the actual translation of the relics of Saint Trophîme in 1152 was forecast in the design of the portal, since Stephen was represented as being stoned with his soul rising to Heaven and Trophîme was depicted as a bishop being crowned. Trophîme was portrayed as in ascendancy, which paralleled the change of name of the church to Saint-Trophîme alone.[22] Finally Hamann dated the first campaign of the east gallery of the cloister in the third quarter of the twelfth century, but pointed out its strong dependence on Saint-Gilles, especially the frieze of the left portal. The late work in the east cloister he placed in the early thirteenth century.[23]

Thus, there seems to be no evidence in the history of Saint-Trophîme to date either the portal or the north gallery. Epitaphs in the north wall of the cloister (interpreted as 1165 to 1203) and one of 1188 under the Saint-Trophîme of the northwest pier, together with stylistic connections between Arles and Tarascon and Maguelonne with their inscriptions of 1187–1197 and 1178, have led scholars to date both cloister and portal in the late twelfth century. These same critics also placed the façade of Saint-Gilles late in the century. Other writers considered the portal as a dated monument, completed for the translation of the relics of Saint Trophîme in 1152, although there seems to be no internal evidence in the architecture or in the

---

20. Von Stockhausen, *op. cit.*, VII (1935), 135–190, VIII (1936), 190–198.
21. Hamann, *op. cit.*, 190–198.
22. *Ibid.*, 199–208.
23. *Ibid.*, 209–214.

sculpture of the portal to prove this assertion. W. Vöge started the Provence versus Île-de-France debate, which has confused rather than clarified the discussion.

Inscriptions in the Cloister

The seven epitaphs in the north and east galleries of the Arles cloister (figs. 367–373) have been used by Lasteyrie (1902), by Charles-Roux (1914), and by Labande (1930) as evidence for dating the sculpture of the north gallery around 1180 and the east gallery after 1181. One inscription (fig. 369) has been interpreted by these same scholars as marking the latest date (1165) for the regularization of the canons under the Rule of Saint Augustine. According to Labande, a bull of 1153 made no mention of this change, while the epitaph, which he dated 1165 (fig. 369), reads *canonicus regularis*. Since this epitaph would seem to be dated 1201 instead of 1165, the whole argument for the shift to the Rule of Saint Augustine, sometime after the middle of the century, as the reason for the construction of the cloister as well as the evidence for the late dating of the north gallery seems to collapse. Furthermore, the chapter was regularized by 1060. Six of the seven inscriptions are on blocks inserted into the outside walls, while the seventh, 1188 (fig. 368), is carved on the block under the statue of Saint Trophîme. Thus all seven epitaphs prove only that the north wall of the cloister was in existence by 1183 (fig. 367) and the east wall by 1181 (fig. 371).

The earliest inscription in the north gallery (fig. 367) is dated 1183 and is the epitaph of Canon Poncius Rebolli, who is listed as "Pons, Poncius, ouvrier," in 1180.[24] The epitaph of Jourdan (Jourdanus—G.C.N., 2551), dated 30 September 1188, was carved on the east face of the northwest pier, directly under Saint Trophîme (fig. 368). Jourdanus is listed as Dean in 1186.[25] Sufficient space exists below the inscription to allow for its carving after the erection of the pier.

---

24. J.-H. Albanès and U. Chevalier, *Gallia Christiana Novissima. Histoire des archevêchés, évêchés et abbayes de France* (Arles, Arles-Valence: 1901). It is G.C.N., 2546, and is Pons, *Poncius*, listed in the Table as *ouvrier* in 1180 (p. 1417).

    ANNO ⦂ DNI ⦂ M ⦂ C ⦂ LXXXIII ⦂ O
    BIIT ⦂ PONCIVS REBOLLI ⦂ SA
    CERDO ⦂ ET ⦂ CANONICVS ⦂
    REGULARIS ⦂ ET ⦂ OPERARI⁹
    ECCLESIE ⦂ SANCTI ⦂ TROP
    HIMI ⦂ ORATE ⦂ PRO ⦂ EO ⦂

Over the top border has been engraved later: VII KAL JANUARI

    25. *Ibid.*, 2551 and 1412 in Table.

    †II° · KAL' · OC (sfi) · OBIIT · IOR
    DAN · DECAN · SCI · TROPHIMI
    ANNO · DNI · M° · C°LXXX° · V · IIII†

The third and debatable inscription in the north gallery is the epitaph of Poncius de Barcia (G.C.N., 2572—fig. 369).[26] At the bottom of the epitaph appear M, C, a small S on its side, and I. Labande has confused the deceased with Pons des Baux, (Balcio), who is listed as Précenteur, 1153–1165,[27] whereas it seems more probable that it is the epitaph of Pons de Bars (?) (Barcia), listed under *Capiscols* as having died on 10 October 1201.[28] The 10 October, the horizontal S as another C, correspondence of name and date of death, description as head of the school of canons, and the epigraphy, especially the rendering of S's—all point to the date 1201. No evidence exists for linking this epitaph with Pons de Baux, who died in 1165. If this inscription is compared with the eight dated inscriptions in the cloister of Saint-Paul-de-Mausole at Saint-Rémy, which extend from the early twelfth century to the 1230's, the epigraphy of the one dated between 1199 and 1206 is the closest to this Arles epitaph.

The most recent epitaph on the north wall of the cloister (fig. 370) is dated 3 February 1203/1204 (G.C.N., 2582).[29]

The three inscriptions on the east wall of the east gallery span the years 1181 to 1239. The earliest, Boso, who died on 11 September 1181 (G.C.N., 2544—fig. 371), is listed as Guillaume I, Boson, Prévot (1159–1181).[30] The next epitaph, Durant, who

---

26. Ibid., 2572 and 1416 in Table.

VI IDVS OCT
IBIIT PONCIVS DE
BARCIA CAPVT SCOLE ET
CANONICVS REGVLARIS
SCI TROPHIMI ANNO
M C CI† OR . . .

This epitaph has been removed from the westernmost arcade during the recent restorations.

27. Labande, *op. cit.*, *L'eglise Saint-Trophime d'Arles*, 72, and 1416 in Table (G.C.N.).

28. Albanès and Chevalier, *op. cit.*, 1416 in Table.

29. *Ibid.*, 2582.

III ⋮ NON ⋮ FEBRVARII ⋮ DIE ⋮ FESTIVITATIS
SANCTI ⋮ BLASII ⋮ AGRESSVS ⋮ EST ⋮ VIAM
UNIVERSE ⋮ CARNIS ⋮ GUILLELMUS
GAUALLERIUS ⋮ ANNO ⋮ DOMINICE
ICARNATIONIS ⋮ M° ⋮ CC° ⋮
III ⋮ ORATE ⋮ PRO ⋮ EO

30. *Ibid.*, 2544 and 1511 in Table.

III · ID · SEPTEMBRIS · OBIIT · VI
LELM · BOSO · SACERDOS · CA
NONICVS · REGVLARIS · ET ·
PREPOSITVS · SCI · TROPHIMI
ANNO · DNI · M · C · LXXX · PRIMO

367. Arles, Saint-Trophîme. Epitaph of Canon Rebolli, 1183. North wall of cloister.

368. Epitaph of Dean Jourdanus, 1188. Under Trophîme.

369. Epitaph of Poncius de Barcia, 1201. North wall of cloister.

370. Epitaph of Guillaume Cavalier, 1203. North wall of cloister.

371. Arles, Saint-Trophîme. Epitaph of Boso, 1181. East wall of cloister.

372. Epitaph of Durant, 1212. East wall of cloister.

373. Epitaph of Guillaume de Marimes, 1239. East wall of cloister.

died on 27 May 1212 (G.C.N., 2604—fig. 372), is listed as Précenteur in 1207,[31] while the last epitaph is dated 7 November 1239 (G.C.N., 2697—fig. 373).[32] The last two epitaphs reveal the more formal, epigraphic format of the thirteenth century.

Since all the epitaphs were added to walls or carved on a block already *in situ*, as in the case of the one under Trophîme, it follows that they are not relevant to the problem of dating either the north or east gallery of the cloister.

Architecture of the Cloister

There appears to be no evidence in the architecture of the Arles cloister and its adjacent rooms to determine their dates, yet evidence does exist which helps establish the chronology of work in the cloister. The two tall rooms with pointed barrel vaults, which extend the length of the north and east cloister walks, are presently being restored (fig. 374). In the seventeenth century these rooms were converted to two storied spaces by the insertion of segmented stone vaults. Part of this vault has been removed in the western half of the north room, and some of the blind arcades between this room and the north gallery of the cloister have been opened up. These restorations reveal that the arcades in the south wall of this room do not correspond in elevation to the arcade of the north gallery, and further that the north wall of the north gallery, which is only one course of masonry in depth, must have been added to the much thicker south wall of the north room.

The arcade on the north wall of the cloister (figs. 242, 244–246) has eleven apertures which do not correspond in plan, in elevation, or in construction to the piers and three bays to the south. The northwest corner opening has been replaced by a doorway which connects the cloister and church through the vaulted, north room. The second and fourth arcades, counting west to east, were filled in until recently, while the third one is a door with an added lintel and tympanum. The system of channeled piers with flanking columns continues throughout the eleven arcades. The fifth aperture is wider and taller and serves as a second entrance to the

---

31. *Ibid.*, 2604 and 1415 in Table.
H ⋮ REQ ESCIT ⋮ DVRANT ⋮
SACERDOS ⋮ P CE T
O ⋮ T ET'CANONIC ⋮ R
SCI ⋮ TROPHIMI ⋮ QVI ⋮ OBIIT
ANNO ⋮ DNI ⋮ M° ⋮ CC° ⋮ XII° ⋮ VI° ⋮ K L' ⋮ IV
NII ⋮
32. *Ibid.*, 2697.
ANNO ⋮ DNI ⋮ M° ⋮ CC° ⋮ XXX-VIIII ⋮ ID
NOVEMBRIS ⋮ OB ⋮ UILELMUS ⋮ DE
MIRAMARS ⋮ ORATE ⋮ PRO ⋮ EO ⋮

north room. The sixth and seventh arcades correspond to arches on the south wall of the adjacent room, but the remaining four arcades were always blind, since no evidence of arcades appears on the wall of the north room.

A break in masonry with a marked edge just above the crowns of the arcades (figs. 245–247) suggests the possibility of an earlier project with a lower, unvaulted or wooden roof, yet this edge is broken by the largest doorway. In the eastern part of the north gallery this break in the masonry is replaced by holes at the same level, which are now filled in, but which perhaps originally supported timbers for a lower wooden roof.

There arc four walled up windows on the north side of the easternmost half of the north chamber. In the south side of this room one window can be seen, while others may be obscured by coats of plaster. These windows are below the springing of the barrel vault and considerably below the level of the stone roof covering the present north gallery of the cloister. They must have illuminated the north room before the present vault of the cloister was constructed. Thus there seems to be some evidence that a lower cloister, probably with a wooden roof, was planned or partially built, and then a new, higher vaulted cloister was constructed which necessitated the walling up of the clerestory windows. Thus the architecture of the north gallery and adjacent room tends to corroborate the conclusion that Stephen and Christ of the Doubting Thomas were originally carved for a smaller cloister.

In the western end of the north barrel-vaulted room (fig. 374) are two corbels of a wolf and a ram (figs. 375, 376). When contrasted with corbels in the north gallery (fig. 322), these corbels appear stiffer, more archaic, and earlier. Since these corbels are on the western end of the room with blocked-up windows which are lower than the roof over the barrel vault of the gallery of the cloister, it follows that this room was built first, then the lower arcade on the north side of the north gallery was added to it, and finally the vaulted cloister was constructed.

As already stated, the piers of the north gallery are structurally unified, although there is evidence suggesting a changing design in the eastern parts. In the northwest pier (fig. 273), the sequence of supports from cloister bench to two tiers of projecting blocks under the three statues to the three figures, and finally to their impost blocks, integrates the pier with the three ribs under the vault. In the western intermediate pier (fig. 278), as a result of the different structural situation, involving a single rib, only the central Christ projects from the wall of the arcade, while the two pilgrims reinforce the angle of the pier. This same system continues in the eastern intermediate pier; yet the smaller figure of Christ fails to unify the pier. The northeast pier (fig. 264) repeats the design of the northwest pier, but an extra block has been placed under the Stephen. Furthermore, the apostle Andrew, which is smaller than

374. Arles, Saint-Trophîme. Western end of room, north of the north gallery of cloister.

375. Corbel of room north of north gallery.

376. Corbel of room north of north gallery.

377. Arles, Saint-Trophîme. East (5), Joseph.

378. Parma Cathedral. Deposition (1178), detail.

379. Arles, Saint-Trophîme. East (5), Handmaiden.

380. Parma Cathedral. Deposition (1178), detail.

Paul, since an extra base is an integral part of it, belongs both in size and in style to the east gallery.

The supports of the open arcade are pairs of columns resting on a single base. The shafts, which are all round except one on the exterior range and octagonal and round on the inner range, are capped by a torus molding. The widths of the inter-columniations between the bases are different in each bay: .85 meters in the western bay; .88 meters in the middle bay; .65 meters in the eastern bay. The considerably narrower dimensions of the eastern bay (see plan—fig. 242) suggest an evolving design. The facts that the Paul appears to be the latest figure by the Peter-Paul Master, that the relief of Stephen is unfinished, and that the Andrew statue belongs to the campaign of the east gallery—all reinforce the argument of sequence of construction from west to east.

The east gallery (fig. 324) is longer and slightly wider than the north walk. The greater width results in a more segmental vault, while the intercolumniations of the arcade, which vary considerably, are all a meter or more in width. The entire gallery is more elaborately decorated with spandrels containing relief sculpture, undercut moldings on the arches of the arcade, more articulated exterior buttresses, and ribs with more complex profiles. Structure and surfaces point to a later date for the east gallery.

Iconography of the Cloister

Like the architecture, a study of the iconography of the north and east galleries of the Arles cloister does not lead to definite conclusions regarding their respective dates; yet the role of the façade of Saint-Gilles, as it relates to the two galleries, is important. First of all, the arrangement of figures and reliefs in the north gallery is harmoniously ordered (see fold-out plan). The main entrance to the cloister from the church was located in the northwest corner. Upon entrance, the first statue confronted is Saint Trophîme, to whom the church is solely dedicated after 1152. In the eleventh century the abbey was dedicated to Trophîme and Stephen jointly. Stephen on the northeast pier balances Trophîme, and the two thus serve as important terminations of the north gallery. Another balancing pair is Peter on the northwest pier and Paul on the northeast pier, while the intermediate piers both contain figures of Christ.

The reliefs proceed chronologically from west to east: the Holy Women buying Perfume from two Merchants and the Empty Tomb (northwest pier); Ascension and Lapidation of Stephen, the first Christian martyr (northeast pier). Christ meeting two disciples on the road to Emmaus, western intermediate pier, follows the Empty Tomb and precedes the Ascension. This subject is important both biblically and specifically in its connection with the pilgrimage to the grave of Saint James. The Doubting Thomas precedes the Ascension relief and includes the statue of Saint James, again to give emphasis to Arles as a gathering place for the pilgrimage to Santiago de Compostela.

The capitals of the north gallery are all Old Testament scenes, with the one exception of the westernmost one, which depicts the Raising of Lazarus. This capital, the relief of the Holy Women and Merchants, and Christ and Pilgrims (Emmaus) are the only scenes which can be found on the superstructure of Saint-Gilles. However, the scenes of Lazarus and the Holy Women buying Perfume are an integral part of Provençal legend and specifically related to their miraculous arrival at Les-Saintes-Maries-de-la-Mer and their subsequent role in Provence. Therefore, their presence in the Arles cloister in different sculptural contexts and with no stylistic relationships with Saint-Gilles does not necessarily prove that the superstructure of Saint-Gilles was finished before the north gallery of Arles. Furthermore, the great dependence of the Peter-Paul Master of Arles on the apostles by Brunus on the central portal and the absence of any stylistic transfer from the Saint-Gilles friezes, lintels, and tympana raise the possibility that indeed the façade of Saint-Gilles was not completed when work started on the north gallery of Arles.

In contrast to the north gallery, the subjects depicted on the east gallery parallel those on the façade of Saint-Gilles (fig. 2). At the same time, the general iconographic scheme of the east gallery both continues and complements that of the north gallery. The northernmost intermediate pier contains Christ tied to a Column flanked by a flagellant and Judas, while the southern intermediate pier, which has lost its central figure, is now flanked by a crowned female and a young man. Critics usually refer to these two as "Sheba" and "Solomon." There is the possibility that these can be read as Mary and John, originally flanking a Crucified Christ (see remains on the pier), although Mary is never, to my knowledge, depicted as crowned in the scene of the Crucifixion. If indeed this last pier did depict the Crucifixion, four Christs adorned the four intermediate piers of the two galleries of the cloister. The Flagellation decorates the upper right-hand frieze of the central portal of Saint-Gilles, and the Crucifixion is depicted on the right tympanum. There is, however, no proof of a direct influence from Saint-Gilles until the capitals of the east gallery are examined.

Starting from the north, capitals of the first bay include: (1) Annunciation, Visitation, and Nativity, (2) frontal eagle capital, (3) Annunciation to Shepherds. The second bay contains: (1) Massacre of the Innocents, (2) Flight into Egypt and the Angel appearing to the Kings, (3) the three Magi before Herod. None of these scenes is located on the Saint-Gilles façade. However, in the southernmost bay the capitals include: (1) Adoration of the Magi and Joseph's Dream, (2) Entry into

Jerusalem, (3) Dispersal of the Apostles. The first two capitals of this bay are miniature variants of the tympanum and lintel of the left portal of Saint-Gilles. Furthermore, there is a stylistic relationship between the Soft Master of the Saint-Gilles left portal and the sculptor who carved two of these three capitals. Finally, on the southeast pier are three crudely carved superimposed scenes depicting, from bottom to top, Christ washing Peter's Feet, the Last Supper, and the Betrayal—scenes which are found on the lintel and right splay of the central portal of Saint-Gilles.

Thus in the selection of subjects there is more connection between the Arles east gallery and Saint-Gilles than the Arles north gallery and Saint-Gilles. It is clear that it is the sculpture of the superstructure of Saint-Gilles which influences the sculpture of the east gallery, both stylistically and iconographically.

ARLES CLOISTER AND ITALIAN SCULPTURE

Italian and Provençal monuments are often compared to establish their chronological relationship or in an attempt to discover the origins of a new style. The pulpit by Guglielmo, carved between 1158 and 1161 for the Duomo of Pisa but installed in 1312 as two pulpits in the Duomo of Cagliari, Sardinia, is a case in point. Because several critics see stylistic connections, they cite the Guglielmo pulpit as the *terminus ante quem* for the façade of Saint-Gilles, the north gallery of Arles, and even the Arles portal. It seems to this author that the ornamental style, the short, heavy figures set against a floral ground, and the iconography of the pulpit are completely un-Provençal.

C. Sheppard (1959) warned against establishing interrelationships between monuments on the basis of similar details; he questioned the establishment of the career of an artist covering wide geographical areas or the province of birth or early training of an artist as evidence for styles dissimilar to those of works where the artist's major monuments were produced; and finally he attacked the notion of explaining away differences in style "as the result of the maturation of an artist or because the region in which a work was executed was culturally provincial." Sheppard believed that Guglielmo's style was not based on Provençal monuments, but was developed in Pisa.[33]

M. Salmi (1928) also argued that Guglielmo's style was formed in Pisa, but un-Tuscan ideas coalesced as a result of contact with Emilian artisans in the marble quarries of Carrara.[34] The only document which reveals a Pisan-Provence contact is

---

33. C. D. Sheppard, "Romanesque Sculpture in Tuscany: A Problem of Methodology," *Gazette des beaux-arts*, LIV (1959), 97–108.

34. M. Salmi, *Romanesque Sculpture in Tuscany* (Florence: 1928), 83–88.

the letter of 1156 from Pope Hadrian IV, who was formerly Abbot of Saint-Ruf in Avignon, to the canons of Pisa, requesting them to help the monks of Saint-Ruf procure materials for their cloister.[35] But this document surely does not establish a Pisa-to-Provence axis.

P. Sanpaolesi (1956–1957) produced extensive evidence to derive Guglielmo's style from earlier work on the façade of the Duoma of Pisa and from direct contacts with Roman and Early Christian sculpture.[36] The supporting lions of the Cagliari pulpits are clearly based on Roman reliefs in the Camposanto of Pisa and not on those on the portal of Saint-Trophîme at Arles. Sanpaolesi failed to prove, however, that Provençal sculpture is later than Guglielmo's work.[37] Most of the Arles sculpture can be derived from Saint-Gilles, while the Guglielmo pulpit grew out of Pisan sculpture. Saint-Gilles and Arles had Les Alyscamps; Pisa, the Camposanto; and both Provence and Pisa (Tuscany) developed originally an independent proto-Renaissance style.

The Tuscan-Provence or Provence-Tuscan syndrome is paralleled in the Provence–Île-de-France relationship. In both instances purported connections have been employed to establish the priority of one region over the other, whereas in point of fact there appear to be no stylistic similarities at all.

Having argued against any influence of Provence on Tuscany or vice versa, it may seem illogical to propose a connection between the east gallery of Arles and the Deposition of Parma by Benedetto Antelami, dated 1178 (fig. 193). But in the case of North Italian monuments the relationship with Provence is so close that the Italian sculptors must have known Provençal work, or else Italian monuments influenced sculptors in Provence. Connections between Saint-Gilles and Beaucaire and the Modena pontile have already been discussed, and mention has been made of Francovich's suggestion that Antelami might have carved the capital of the Dream of the Magi and Flight into Egypt in the east gallery of the Arles cloister (figs. 349–352).[38] As already stated, the iconography of the Parma Deposition (fig. 193) depends on the right-hand tympanum of the façade of Saint-Gilles (fig. 95); note especially the Synagogue being pushed to the ground by an angel and the presence of the elaborately garbed Church and symbols of the sun and moon.

If details of the Arles capital, such as the head of Joseph, are compared with those of Joseph of Arimathea of the Parma Deposition (figs. 377, 378) or the hand-

---

35. V. Mortet and P. Deschamps, *Recueil des textes à l'histoire de l'architecture, XII–XIII siècles* (Paris: 1929), 108–109.

36. P. Sanpaolesi, "La facciata della cattedrale di Pisa," *Revista dell'istituto nazionale d'archeologia e storia dell'arte* (1956–1957), 248–394.

37. *Ibid.*, 337–394.

38. Francovich, *op. cit.*, 136–137.

maiden of the Virgin with the Holy Women on the Parma relief (figs. 379, 380), it is evident that a close connection exists, especially in the treatment of heads of both males and females and in the drapery folds over the feet of the women. However, the sculptor of the east-gallery capital lacked the sensitivity of Antelami. It is impossible to believe that Antelami is indeed the east-gallery sculptor; but at the same time, it is impossible to argue that either the Parma Deposition or the Arles east-gallery sculpture could have been carved in isolation. Rather, it would seem as though Benedetto Antelami knew the east gallery of the Arles cloister as well as the façade of Saint-Gilles and that work was in progress in the east gallery in the years prior to 1178. More will be said about the Arles-Italy relationship at the end of Chapter 10.

381. Arles, Saint-Trophîme. Portal.

The Portal of Saint-Trophîme at Arles

THE single portal of Saint-Trophîme at Arles (fig. 381) is a stylistic paradox. Although dramatic in thematic concept, the execution is often uninspired. Duplication of forms and dullness of surfaces are vastly different from the marked individuality and bold crispness of figures in the north gallery of the Arles cloister. Whereas the Peter-Paul Master, who was inspired by the sculpture of Saint-Gilles, developed his own forceful style in the course of carving over half the sculpture of the north gallery, the four major sculptors of the Arles portal rarely escaped from their overindebtedness to the façade of Saint-Gilles. Within this derivative and repetitive ambience of the Arles portal, another paradox emerges, namely the presence of small-scaled sculpture, often of high quality, which is clearly un-Provençal.[1]

PORTAL DESIGN AND CONSTRUCTION

The single portal, added to the older façade of Saint-Trophîme, is in the form of a projecting portico supported by six short columns (fig. 381). The motif of an arch, breaking the horizontal entablature, is of Roman origin. Antiquity was

---

1. The Arles dossier in Paris (Arles, Bouches-du-Rhône, 197, 2nd dossier, Monuments historiques) contains a letter of 1921 written by the Prefect of the Bouches-du-Rhône describing his investigation of the damage to the Arles portal which was caused by the fire department who had let a new piece of equipment get out of control and had sprayed the façade.

reinterpreted by the Romanesque artist, just as the follower of Brunelleschi transformed this same form in the façade of the Pazzi Chapel in Early Renaissance Florence. In the case of the Arles portal, sufficient evidence exists to prove that the portal of Saint-Trophîme was inspired directly by the proto-Renaissance façade of Saint-Gilles-du-Gard or by the Roman triumphal arch at Saint-Rémy.

Two courses of large blocks with narrow, ornamented moldings make up the pedestallike base (fig. 381). On the front face of the portal, these bases support six columns which, in turn, sustain the sides of the superstructure. In the splays, the bases serve as footings for the four apostles with their double frieze. The setback of the splays is echoed in the flanks of the lion socles, the statue of Saint Trophîme, the relief of Saint Stephen, and the apostles behind the columns. This plane is carried up into the re-entrant angle of the upper, figured frieze.

Lintel and tympanum are supported by jambs and a trumeau. The lintel, which is the same height as the adjacent frieze, protrudes forward at its extremities and is thereby related to the capitals on the doorjambs and the ornamented border framing the tympanum (fig. 390). The elaborate archivolts are divided into three groups: the inner deep one of angels echoing the splays; the next group of moldings descending on the setback section of the frieze; the outer group with border of frontal palmettes extending to the front plane of the portal, which is continuous from bases through socles, columns, capitals, and upper frieze. The whole portal is crowned by a pedimented roof with racking cornice on corbels. Sculpture on all parts of the portal reinforces the planes by its flat, low-relief character.

When compared with the triple-portaled façade of Saint-Gilles (fig. 2), the Arles portal is a reduction and simplification of the Saint-Gilles design. At the same time, certain ambiguities of Saint-Gilles, which seem to have been caused by changes in the design as work progressed, are corrected. The extraordinary plasticity of the Saint-Gilles façade is flattened in the Arles portal. Small life-size columns replace the huge Roman monoliths of Saint-Gilles. The Arles portal is more logical in its repeated planes of architecture and sculpture; yet the forceful, experimental character of the Saint-Gilles façade has been replaced by a design which, in spite of its consistent composition, seems less inspired. Since the Arles portal is clearly influenced by the completed Saint-Gilles façade, it is of no help in ascertaining the nature of the first design for Saint-Gilles, if such ever existed.

The bases of the central portal of Saint-Gilles extend westward of the frontal planes of both the apostles in niches and of the monolithic columns. These bases were part of the earliest work at Saint-Gilles, but their function as supports for a superstructure was abandoned when the notion of the horizontal, continuous frieze was adopted. The vertical acanthus panels, flanking the central portal of Saint-Gilles,

382. Arles, Saint-Trophîme. Paul, Andrew (R1, 2).

383. Arles, Saint-Trophîme. Paul, Andrew.

384. Paul's head.

385. Saint-Gilles. Paul and James (in reverse).

386. Arles, Saint-Trophîme. Paul of north cloister.

are replaced by Trophîme and the relief of Stephen, both of which are pushed back to the plane of the apostles. Undecorated pilasters on the corners of the splays at Arles attempt, not quite successfully, to avoid the awkward, re-entrant angles over the heads of John and Paul at Saint-Gilles (see figs. 389, 395). The integration of bases, columns, and figures with the archivolts in the Arles portal resembles the design of the side portals of the Saint-Gilles façade (fig. 3). Thus the Arles portal seems to be a simplified, but somewhat mannered, version of the façade of Saint-Gilles.

APOSTLES

Eight apostles and Saint Trophîme stand on low socles in shallow, arched niches, flanked by floral pilasters (figs. 381, 382). Concave halos curve forward and impinge on the floral moldings of the capitals above. Figures are frozen in pose and relatively flat in profile. None of the crispness and massiveness seen in the monumental sculpture of Saint-Gilles, or in the north gallery of the Arles cloister, is evident in the Arles portal.

Saint Paul (R 1—figs. 382–384), exhibiting more quality than the others, served as model for six of the other seven apostles. The Arles Paul is a less sensitive replica, in reverse, of the Saint-Gilles Paul (fig. 385—Paul and James reversed). General configuration of the heads, position of hands holding scrolls, bundles of ridge folds with terminations raised over ankles, loop folds over chest, stomach, and between thighs, mantle over shoulders, wind-blown folds at sides, small indications of belts, ornamented cuffs, and wattled sleeves—all are characteristics found in both statues of Paul. The differences are qualitative. The Saint-Gilles Paul by Brunus (fig. 385) displays much more surface interest with varying intervals between ridge folds. Surfaces are crisp and firm, while the mass projects outward from the wall rather than appearing flattened into the wall, as in the Arles Paul. The bold, stark blockiness of Paul's head at Saint-Gilles is attenuated and weakened at Arles (fig. 384). Further, hands vigorously hold the scroll rather than appearing suspended in space, as do the hands of the Arles Paul. To jump ahead to the socles, the lion biting a human under Paul and lion overwhelming a ram under Andrew (fig. 382) are feeble copies of the socles under James and Paul of Saint-Gilles (fig. 67).

Paul in the north gallery of the Arles cloister (fig. 386) also exhibits stylistic connections with the Saint-Gilles Paul, but none with the Paul on the façade. However, it is not a copy; rather, the original inspiration was digested and transformed, with the result that Paul of the cloister manifests a rugged vitality which is absent in the Paul of the portal.

Andrew (R 2—figs. 382, 383) is a duplicate of Paul with different hair and with two panels of loop folds between his legs. Less folds ornament his undergarment, as the drapery is gathered in three truncated cylinders. Surfaces are more simply treated in a softer, more ropelike manner. Andrew's right hand is crudely articulated. Certain characteristics, such as the central loop folds, are reminiscent of the Andrew in the east galley (fig. 332).

The extreme right-hand apostle, Philip (fig. 387), is another replica of Paul or Andrew, but is closer stylistically to Andrew. The numerous ridge folds over thighs and legs, wattled sleeves, and number and interval of folds resemble the arrangement and treatment of drapery on the statue of Paul. Both Andrew and Philip seem to be modeled on Paul, but carved by a less sensitive assistant. James Major (fig. 387), located between the reliefs of Stephen and Philip, seems to be by the same hand as Andrew with some influence from the Saint Peter.

Saint Peter (L 1—fig. 388), with curving loop folds, twisting pose, and sharply carved drapery, is the work of a third sculptor. The quality of Peter is relatively higher than in the three statues by the Andrew Master, with more resilience displayed in the curving body and with greater variety and surface interest in the drapery. The presence of flattened ridge folds, with incised lines, is unique in the apostles on the portal. There is no model for Peter on the Saint-Gilles façade, but it does appear that this sculptor reacted to and transformed the Peter of the Arles cloister (fig. 248). Both Peters have curving folds over their right thighs and mantles falling from both shoulders. The incised folds of the cloister Peter are replaced by ridge folds. Although the ruggedness of the cloister figure is softened in Peter on the portal, there are stylistic connections between the two, especially the drapery of flattened ridges alternating with flat concavities over the legs. Heads of both statues lean to the right, but the psychological intensity of the cloister statue gives way to a relatively bland impassivity in the Peter on the portal. The Peter Master, like the Paul Master, did not carve any other apostle.

In the Saint John (L 2—fig. 388), every detail of cloak, collar, belt, and hands repeats the format of Paul (fig. 383). Drapery over the legs is concentrated in three truncated groups and two narrow panels of V folds, as in the Andrew of Arles and the Paul of Saint-Gilles (figs. 383, 385); yet the surfaces of the John are thick and heavy. From the point of view of texture, the drapery over John's legs is reminiscent of that part of John of Saint-Gilles (fig. 28). The beardless head of John is set against a curved halo, decorated with a bead-and-reel border. This detail, unique on the Arles portal, is found on the halos of John and the three apostles of Saint-Gilles by the Thomas Master. The curved halos, which are uniform on all the Arles figures, appear only on the James Major at Saint-Gilles. John's head displays the same furrowed brow, shallow eyes, long nose, and downward-turned mouth as do the three heads by the Andrew Master. As a whole, the John the Evangelist seems to be less sensitively carved than either the Paul or the Peter.

387. Arles, Saint-Trophîme. Martyrdom of Stephen, James Major, Philip (R3, 4, 5).

388. Arles, Saint-Trophîme. Trophîme, John, Peter (L3, 2, 1).

389. Arles, Saint-Trophîme. Bartholomew, James the Less, Trophîme (L5, 4, 3).

390. Arles, Saint-Trophîme. Tympanum, Christ and Symbols of four Evangelists.

The left-hand apostles, Bartholomew and James the Less (L 5, L 4—fig. 389), repeat the Paul formula of double cloak with loop folds and folded edges. The only difference consists of an extra mantle, extending from right to left. The carving of the drapery is, however, much closer to the treatment of drapery of John. It would appear that these two apostles were both carved by the John Master. With the exception of hair, beard, and a few drapery folds, these two statues (L 5, 4) are identical.

Saint Trophîme (figs. 388, 389), to whom the church was solely dedicated after 1152, is garbed in bishop's robes, holding a crozier, while angels place a tiara on his head. Surfaces of chasuble, treatment of drapery above his feet, and his head, especially the arched eyebrows and down-turned mouth, resemble those same features in John. It is therefore quite possible that the assistant who carved John, Bartholomew, and James Minor is also responsible for Trophîme.

On the right side of the portal, opposite Trophîme, is the relief of Stephen, including his martyrdom and soul being raised by angels to God (fig. 387). The head of God and the drapery of the kneeling Stephen are similar to the heads and treatment of mantles of the two apostles to the right of the relief by the Andrew Master. The lower part of the relief is a frozen version of the same scene on the northeast pier of the cloister (fig. 292), with identical composition and costumes and similar folds over Stephen's legs, while the upper half seems to be based on the Ascension on the same pier of the cloister (fig. 290).

The monumental apostles, Trophîme, and the relief of Stephen would thus seem to be the work of four artisans. The Paul Master, strongly influenced by the Saint-Gilles Paul by Brunus, carved one statue and was probably head of the workshop, since six apostles repeat the general format of his Paul. A second sculptor carved the Apostle Peter. Two less skilled assistants each carved four statues: Andrew Master—Andrew, Stephen relief, James Major, Philip; John Master—John, Trophîme, James the Less, Bartholomew. Each assistant is assigned an area on the portal, while the Peter and Paul Masters each carved one figure, the two nearest to the doorway, and then collaborated on the lintel and tympanum.

TYMPANUM, LINTEL, AND FRIEZE

Since the Christ in Majesty is surrounded by the symbols of the four evangelists, and twelve apostles appear on the lintel with the blessed and the damned on the frieze, the whole superstructure becomes the Last Judgment. In the tympanum (fig. 390), the enthroned Christ is so reminiscent of the Paul in arrangement of drapery, modeling of head, and quality of carving that it is certainly the work of the Paul Master. The Christ also recalls the tympanum figure now in the Saint-Gilles Museum (fig. 141). The Paul Master, however, by his overcomplication of folds, loses the monumental grandeur of the Saint-Gilles Christ. The angel, symbol of Matthew (fig. 390) displays the same complex surfaces as those of the Christ enthroned.

The twelve apostles of the lintel (fig. 390), with curved folds over one leg and broad belts, are similar in style to the statue of Peter (fig. 388). Several heads are very close in shape and arrangement of beard and hair to the head of Peter. Voussoirs, framing the tympanum, consist of two rows of frontal angels and three blowing long trumpets in the keystones. Raised hands, loop folds over arms, and thick belts are characteristics of the disciples on the lintel as well as the Peter. It would thus seem that the Paul Master carved the entire tympanum, while the Peter Master completed the lintel and archivolts.

The lower, figured frieze, which runs directly above the heads of the apostles (figs. 391–394), consists of the following scenes from the Life of Christ (from left to right): Flight into Egypt and Massacre of Innocents over Bartholomew and James Minor (fig. 391); three Kings before Herod over John and Peter, Dream of Joseph and Annunciation (left capital) (fig. 392); Bathing of Infant Christ and Nativity (right capital); Adoration of Magi above Paul and Andrew (fig. 393); Angel appearing to sleeping Kings over relief of Stephen (fig. 394); shepherds and their flocks over James Major and Philip (fig. 394). All the figures, with the exception of the capitals supporting the lintel, are short and wear heavy, flattened cloaks. In the scenes on the door splays, low arches on columns contain individuals or groups of figures in a manner recalling Early Christian sarcophagi.

The upper frieze, supported by six columns, is continuous across the doorway. This frieze includes the following: Adam and Eve (left-hand side—fig. 395); the saved over Bartholomew, James Minor, and Trophîme (fig. 391); angel presenting souls of blessed, already emerging from sarcophagi, to Abraham, Isaac, and Jacob, over John and Peter (fig. 392); Lazarus on the right side of the lintel (fig. 393); Michael preventing sinners from entering the Gates of Heaven over James and Andrew and around the re-entrant angle (fig. 393); the nude damned, chained together, with flames engulfing their legs, continuing across the right-hand side of the portal (fig. 394). R. Hamann interpreted the seated figure on the right of the lintel as "Lazarus in Heaven" or Lazarus raised to sainthood (fig. 393).[2] This conclusion accords with Provençal legend, but does not prove a debt to Burgundy, as Hamann stated.

The quality of the carving on the splays of the portal seems superior to the sculpture on the front plane of the portal. Curving and loop folds plus greater plasticity

---

2. R. Hamann, "Lazarus in Heaven," *Burlington Magazine*, LXIII (1933), 3–10.

391. Arles, Saint-Trophîme. Friezes, left, The Blessed.

392. Friezes, left, Souls presented.

393. Friezes, right, Lazarus and Michael preventing Sinners from entering Gates of Paradise.

394. Arles, Saint-Trophîme. Friezes, right, The Damned.

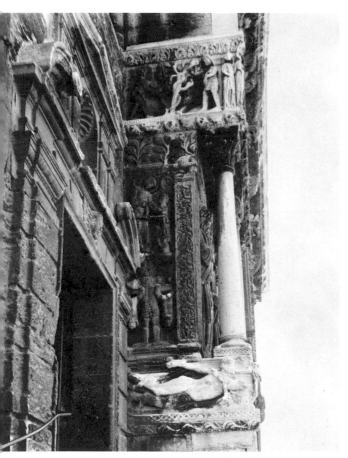

395. Left side of portal.

396. Right side of portal.

resemble the lintel and archivolts by the Peter Master. On the basis of drapery style and treatment of heads, it is tempting to assign the saved to the John the Evangelist Master and the damned to the Andrew Master.

The relief on the left side of the portal contains a swimming figure attacking a lion (fig. 395). This nude figure, wearing a lion's skin around his shoulder, is, according to F. Benoit, Hercules, a prefiguration of Christ.[3] Directly above is another nude Hercules, holding the dwarf Ceropes, and Saint Michael weighing the souls. These scenes juxtapose pagan and Christian subjects. Much of the surface of this relief is badly weathered, but the figure of Michael suggests the style of the John Master. The panel on the right side of the portal (fig. 396) depicts an enormous demon holding two damned and standing on a lizard on which sits a nude female, symbol of luxury. As Benoit indicated, these two panels plus their socles, still to be discussed, are related to the frieze of the saved and damned; they reveal how the medieval mind used pagan literary heroes, such as Hercules, for the moralistic ends of Christianity.[4]

SOCLES AND CAPITALS

Socles and capitals on the Arles portal can be divided into three stylistic groups: (1) dependent directly on Saint-Gilles; (2) related to the east gallery of the Arles cloister and possibly influencing Italian monuments; (3) work by a non-Provençal sculptor or sculptors. In several instances the quality of this small-scaled sculpture is superior to that of the monumental figures. The presence of Italians at Arles brings up again the much-argued relationship between Provence and Northern Italy. The impact of the iconography of Saint-Gilles and Beaucaire and the influence of the style of Beaucaire and Arles on such monuments as the pontile of the Cathedral of Modena and the Deposition of Parma, dated 1178 by Benedetto Antelami, has led scholars to conclude that Italian sculptors, the Campionese, traveled in southeastern France and had their apprenticeship in Provençal workshops. But the question of the nature of this Italian-Provençal relationship has remained unclarified.

In the first group, the most flagrant copying of Saint-Gilles motifs occurs in the lion socles under the apostles in the splays of the portal (figs. 382, 388). The lions biting a human under Paul and clawing a ram under Andrew are sterile, frozen replicas of the socles under James Major and Paul in the same location on the façade of Saint-Gilles (figs. 29, 67). The same insensitive plagiarism can be seen if the socles

---

3. F. Benoit, "La Légende d'Hercule à Saint-Trophîme d'Arles," *Latomus*, Revue d'études latines, IX (1950), 67–71.

4. V. Lassalle, in *L'Influence anitque dans l'art roman provençal*, Revue archéologique de Narbonnais, 2 (Paris: Editions E. dé Boccard, 1970), 170 and Plate XLVIII, compares these Hercules reliefs with their Roman sources.

under John and Peter of Arles (fig. 388) are compared with those under the same apostles at Saint-Gilles (fig. 66). At Arles extra thin socles have been placed between the major socles in an unsuccessful attempt to unify each splay. The front face of the extreme right-hand socle, depicting a ram butting an animal (fig. 387), is derived from the inner, right socle of the left portal of Saint-Gilles (fig. 64), while along the flank of the same socle (fig. 396), a centaur shooting an arrow at a lion recalls the relief on the central pedestal of Saint-Gilles.

Connections in motif and style with the east gallery of the Arles cloister include two socles and the six capitals supporting the upper frieze. The lion socles, in the middle of each side of the portal (fig. 397), are related to a corbel in the east gallery (fig. 399), which, in turn, is based on a similar but more undercut corbel in the north gallery (fig. 398). The stylistic relationship between the socles on the portal and the corbel in the east gallery points to their contemporaneity. The six capitals on the front face of the portal are symmetrically arranged (figs. 387, 389). When the four Corinthian capitals are compared with those in the north gallery of the cloister (figs. 306–317), it is clear that the latter are squatter in profile. In their more elongated and flaring shape, the portal capitals resemble those in the east gallery (figs. 339–346). The middle pair of capitals (fig. 400) have thick vines forming ovals with crisp leaves as fillers. These unusual capitals have no model at Saint-Gilles, but the much-damaged, northernmost corbel in the east gallery of Arles (fig. 401) has a similar organization and style. As noticed by many critics, the portal capitals bear a remarkably close relationship in form and carving technique to a capital on the pontile of Modena (fig. 402). The sheath which binds the main stem of the Arles capital is closer to Roman practice than is the overlapping leaf of the Modena capital.

The third group, which seems foreign both to the style of Saint-Gilles and to its transformations at Arles, consists of three socles and two capitals, all located around the doorway. The socle under the trumeau (figs. 403–405), with a seated and kneeling figure on the back and two kneeling ones on the front corners, exhibits forms which are more Italian than Provençal and are reminiscent of the atlantes figures on the pulpit of S. Ambrogio at Milan or sculpture on the portals of Modena. The head of the left, inner figure (fig. 403) harks back to the jambs of Cremona, while the gouged-out folds of the front figures reveal a carving technique atypical to Provence. The right-hand inside figure appears to be a prisoner bound by metal straps. The roughly cut folds of the kneeling figures resemble Italian sculpture, especially the socles of the Modena pontile (fig. 406). Further, the drapery style and disjointed articulation of these figures display a stylistic similarity with the flagellant of the east gallery by an un-Arlesian sculptor (figs. 359, 360). It is quite possible that this sculptor did indeed come from Northern Italy and as apprentice joined the workshop headed by the James Master.

397. Arles, Saint-Trophîme. Lion socle of façade.

398. Lion corbel in north gallery.

399. Lion corbel in east gallery.

400. Spiral capital on façade.

401. Spiral corbel in east gallery.

402. Modena. Spiral capital on pontile.

403. Arles, Saint-Trophîme. Socle under trumeau, inside.

404. Socle under trumeau, inside.

405. Socle under trumeau, outside.

406. Modena. Socle of pontile.

407. Arles, Saint-Trophîme. Socle, Samson and Delilah.

408. Modena. Socle of pontile, Samson.

409. Arles, Saint-Trophîme. Socle,
Daniel and the Lions.

410. Socle, Daniel and the Lions.

412. Modena. Socle of pontile.

411. Modena. Socle of pontile, Daniel and the Lions.

The Samson and Delilah socle (fig. 407), adjacent to Trophîme, possesses an intensity of action which does not appear on the frieze. In pose and in treatment of drapery, this socle is repeated with some variation in a corbel under the pontile of Modena (fig. 408).

On the right side of the portal, the socle of Daniel in the Lion's Den (figs. 409, 410) is so similar in composition and drapery forms to the capital on the Modena pontile (fig. 411) and the flank of the socle is so like the lions on the Modena socles (figs. 410, 412) that either the sculpture of Modena or the Arles socle must have been the model. This is not to say that the same sculptor was responsible for both, since the treatment of drapery, as well as the heads, is different. It is, however, possible to argue that an un-Provençal sculptor carved this socle on the portal under the supervision of the James Master, whose style, so totally indebted to that of Saint-Gilles, influenced him.

The corbellike capitals supporting the lintel (figs. 413–417) were also probably carved by an Italian sculptor. The left-hand one depicts the Dream of Joseph and the Annunciation, and the two faces of the right-hand corbel capital contain the Bathing of the Infant Jesus, in an unusual format, and the Nativity. The dry, angular treatment of drapery over arms, chest, and legs and the square, stark heads with eyes set close to the surface are entirely different from any other sculpture on the portal. Like the socle under the trumeau, there are some stylistic connections with the capitals by the third hand in the east gallery (figs. 347–358). Compare the heads of the Virgin of the Annunciation and of the females bathing Christ with the heads of the capitals in the east gallery. Further, the way the drapery is curved over the feet of the figures also recalls that of the capitals of the middle bay. The capitals of the portal appear more archaic than those of the cloister and seem to have more connections in style with Italian monuments, such as the Cathedral of Lodi and fragments from a pulpit in the Cathedral of Castellaquarto. Whether the same sculptor carved the capitals on the portal and the figures and capitals in the east gallery is debatable; yet both portal corbel capitals on the façade and these capitals in the east gallery of Arles are clearly outside the main stream of Provençal sculpture. Thus, there is ample evidence for the participation of North Italians in the workshop of the portal. The James Master, chief of the *chantier*, would seem to have assigned areas directly around the doorway to itinerants to decorate.

ORNAMENT

Decorative sculpture plays a larger role on the Arles portal than on the façade of Saint-Gilles; its flatness and small scale give it the character of a thin,

413. Arles, Saint-Trophîme. Corbel under lintel, Dream of Joseph.

414. Corbel under lintel, Annunciation.

415. Corbel under lintel, Bathing the infant Christ.

416. Corbel under lintel, Nativity.

417. Ornament under lintel.

two-dimensional overlay. Just as the Arles apostles are anemic versions of Saint-Gilles figures, so the ornament exhibits a hardening of the Saint-Gilles floral decoration.

Horizontal moldings are elaborately decorated with antique, geometric motifs and floral patterns. The panel, crowning the bases (figs. 382, 387–392), consists of bead-and-reel, undulating vine with fillers, a spiral, and abstract quatrefoil with circlets. The pattern is uniform across the portal with the exception of the upper molding under the Peter and Andrew, which has a pattern of squares alternating with clover forms.

In the molding above the capitals there appears an undulating vine with rolled leaves issuing from the mouths of lion masks (figs. 391–394). This motif is framed by a bead-and-reel and chevron pattern and is uniform across the portal except over Paul and Andrew, where the rolled leaves and heads are smaller and quatrefoils fill the voids. Thus in the moldings below and above Paul and Andrew, the ornament is treated slightly differently. This ornamental cornice is derived from the lower border of the frieze of the left portal, right, and the right portal, left, of Saint-Gilles (figs. 78, 104). In Saint-Gilles lion masks alternate with palmettes, and a folded ribbon or waterfall motif appears instead of the meander; yet the latter is found on the majority of the bases of Saint-Gilles. This ornamental molding is repeated in the same location on the pontile of Modena (see Daniel capital—fig. 411). Palmettes ornament the upper cornice of the frieze and lintel, the molding of the outer archivolt, and the raking cornice of the entire portal. This same motif appears on Saint-Gilles over the figured frieze and lintels of the side portals and above the corbels in the superstructure of the central portal. In Saint-Gilles the ornament possesses more variety of surfaces and more degrees of relief.

Corbels under the raking cornice consist of animal heads, frontal birds, and floral patterns (fig. 381). They continue the same format of eight corbels at Saint-Gilles (figs. 111, 112). In style the upper corbels of the portal are closer to those supporting ribs in the east gallery of the cloister than to the more undercut and more dynamic corbels in the north gallery of the Arles cloister.

Vertical panels, symmetrically composed as frames for the apostles, are elaborately ornamented with floral patterns. When seen from the side, these panels tend to detract from the importance of the monumental figures. At Saint-Gilles the narrow, channeled pilasters intensify the heroic scale of the apostles. These acanthus panels are based on the reliefs which flank the central portal of Saint-Gilles (figs. 163, 165). The latter possess more variety of axis in arrangement of leaves and greater sensitivity of surface. The same qualitative difference can be seen if the underside of the lintel of Arles (fig. 417) is contrasted with ornament under the lintels of Saint-Gilles (figs. 160–162). The thin pilaster between Paul and Andrew (fig. 382) contains a hybrid design of floral patterns interspersed with bird, winged dragon, and lion. There is no precedent for this design except possibly the horizontal cornice with beasts and reptiles at Saint-Gilles. The pilaster on the left side between John and Peter commences with a bird from the mouth of which an undulating vine with floral fillers emanates. The model for this motif is the panel framing Stephen in the north gallery (fig. 265); yet the quality of the ornament in the cloister is much higher.

CONCLUSIONS

All evidence found in the figured and ornamental sculpture leads to the conclusion that the portal was carved, in large part, rapidly by four sculptors. The completed façade of Saint-Gilles-du-Gard served as the major inspiration. As already stated, the thematic concept far surpasses the execution. The Paul Master, probably the sculptor responsible for the design, attempted to correct some of the inconsistencies of Saint-Gilles, which were caused by changes in design and concept as work progressed. The north gallery of the Arles cloister, which was influenced by the apostles by Brunus of Saint-Gilles, exhibits more originality than the portal and certainly precedes the portal in date. Accordingly, if we assume that the work at Saint-Gilles was begun in the 1140's and finished in the early 1150's, it follows that the north gallery of the Arles cloister was begun around 1150. Further, if it can be assumed that the pontile of Modena was completed by 1170 to 1175, the portal of Arles was erected in the 1160's or early 1170's. The fact that the style of the non-Provençal sculptor of the four capitals in the east gallery of the Arles cloister appears to be more advanced than the socle under the trumeau and the corbel capitals supporting the lintel of the portal suggests that the portal is earlier than parts of the east gallery. However, the capitals of the north bay of the east gallery grow out of the style of the north gallery, while two capitals in the south bay reflect the latest work at Saint-Gilles. It seems quite possible that work started on the east gallery in the early 1160's, before the construction of the portal. This campaign included the capitals just mentioned, the apostle Andrew (?) on the northeast pier (fig. 332), and the apostle now against the east wall (fig. 331). Then a new sculptor, possibly fresh from his apprenticeship on the portal, took over. He used the sculpture already carved and completed four historiated capitals and their adjacent acanthus capitals in the 1170's, while work on the monumental sculpture of the east gallery, following an interruption extended into the early years of the thirteenth century.

It could be argued, on the other hand, that the un-Provençal socles and capitals on the Arles portal were carved by North Italians, who came from the workshop of the Modena pontile, and that the portal was completed around the middle to second half of the 1170's. The fact that this Arles sculpture reveals some stylistic affinities with sculpture which can be dated earlier than the Modena pontile and the fact that the frieze of Beaucaire, of around 1160, based on that of the Saint-Gilles façade, served as partial model for the pontile of Modena—both point to a Provence–North Italian axis of influence.

418. Romans, Saint-Barnard. Portal.

419. Detail of James (R1).

420. Right side of portal.

CHAPTER 11

The Portal of Saint-Barnard at Romans

SAINT BARNARD, Archbishop of Vienne, founded a monastery at a fordable spot on the river Isère, ten miles northeast of Valence. At Barnard's death in 842, the monastery, part of the diocese of Vienne, was renamed after its founder. The original structure was destroyed by the Normans in 860 and rebuilt in the early tenth century, only to be burned by the Archbishop of Vienne in 930 to reprimand the monks for their insubordination. In 1133 the monastery and the town of Romans, which had grown up around it, were burned by Guigues Dauphin. The lower part of the present nave dates from the campaign after 1133. In the mid-thirteenth century the choir and transept were reconstructed, and lateral chapels were added in the following centuries. The interior was sacked in 1562 during the religious wars, and five years later, in the second occupation of the town, the roof was burned and the vaults and upper part of the nave walls collapsed. A restoration took place in 1718, but the vaults were not rebuilt until 1844. In 1860 the cloister was destroyed to make room for a quay on the bank of the Isère.[1]

---

1. J. de Font-Réaulx, "Saint-Barnard de Romans (Drôme)," *Congrès archéologique de France* LXXXVI (1923), 146–163. Other sources of the history of Romans are as follows: A. Nugues, "Notes sur l'église de Saint-Barnard à Romans (Drôme)," *Société d'archéologie de statistique de la Drôme, Valence,* XI (1877), 257–271. P.-E. Giraud, *Essai historique sur l'abbaye de Saint-Barnard et sur la ville de Romans,* 3 vols. (Lyon: 1856–1869). U. Chevalier, *Annales de la ville de Romans* (Paris and Valence: 1897). A. Lacroix, *Romans et le Bourg-de-Péage avant 1790* (Valence: 1897). L. Vinay, *Essai sur les monuments et les anciens édifices de la ville de Romans* (Romans: 1904). L. Vinay, *Romans archéologique* (Valence: 1911), contains a plan of the church and cloister, and a drawing of the vaulted cloister, dated 1857.

421. Romans, Saint-Barnard. Peter and John.

422. Peter and John.

423. Peter, detail.

424. Socle.

The mutilated façade (fig. 418) has lost its vaulted porch, and the superstructure of the portal is nineteenth-century. The masonry of the splays of the portal (figs. 421, 425) is so extensively weathered and patched that it is impossible to determine whether or not the lower sections, which support the columns and the paired apostles, are in their original disposition. The lack of alignment of the bases of columns and socles under the apostles, the shift in height of the capitals, and the awkwardness of the inner apostles facing a blank wall—all suggest that the paired apostles are not in their original position. However, the nature of the inner sides of the apostles nearest the doorjamb prove beyond doubt that the figures were carved for their present location. The projecting drapery on the left side of James (R 1—fig. 419), with its flat edge abutting the jamb, is ample evidence. Further, the piers which separate the portals (fig. 420) from the flanking blind arcades are homogeneously articulated. The suggestion that the paired apostles once decorated the cloister is disproved by a letter in the Archives in Paris, dated 1838 which describes the portal with paired apostles twenty-two years before the cloister was destroyed.[2]

In contrast to Beaucaire, a provincial reflection of Saint-Gilles, and in contrast to the cloister and portal of Arles, with its influence of the Saint-Gilles style, yet marked individuality, the close relationships between Romans and Saint-Gilles suggest the possibility that the four apostles may have been carved by one of the Saint-Gilles sculptors. Taken together, the Romans apostles (figs. 421–426) reveal several characteristics similar to the developed Brunus style, especially the John and Paul on the splays of the central portal of Saint-Gilles. Wattled sleeves, wave folds across abdomen, garment raised over ankles, and pronounced ridge folds framing smaller gouged folds—all can be seen on John or Paul and some of the Romans figures. However, the proportions of the Romans apostles are much slenderer, and the ponderation, especially in the Peter and John (L 2, L 1), is entirely different, with the upper part of their bodies leaning forward and knees projecting outward in a slouched pose.

Another Saint-Gilles sculptor, the Michael Master, exhibits even closer connections with the Romans apostles. The treatment of drapery over the thigh of Michael (fig. 427) resembles the same area on the James and Paul of Romans (R 1, 2—figs. 425, 426, 428), while the area from the right knee to the ankle of Paul recalls the lower part of the archangels by the Michael Master (fig. 49). The developing style of the Michael Master in the superstructure of Saint-Gilles has certain counterparts in the Romans apostles (see the pose and treatment of hems of mantles in the citizens of Jerusalem on the left portal, right frieze of Saint-Gilles—fig. 88). The same pro-

---

2. Romans, *Église St. Barnard*, *1ᵉ Dossier* (*1838 to 1902*), Drôme, 427, Monuments historiques, Paris.

jection of the knees appears in Michael and the left-hand apostles of Romans. The elongation of the Romans figures can perhaps be explained by the intrusion of Burgundian proportions. Romans is roughly midway between Arles and Saint-Gilles and Burgundy. Furthermore, capitals in the nave, such as the Annunciation (fig. 432), are Burgundian.

If indeed the Romans apostles were carved by the evolving Michael Master of Saint-Gilles, the Michael Master must have been familiar with the sculpture in the north gallery of the Arles cloister. The interlocking folds forming the collar on the Peter and Paul of Romans, the outer two apostles, are identical to the bodice of Peter and James by the Peter-Paul Master of Arles (figs. 248, 258). The mantle falling between the feet and raised over ankles can be seen in all four apostles at Romans and in John, James, and Paul by the Peter-Paul Master of Arles. The triangular arrangement of sleeve of the right-hand apostles at Romans, James and Paul, has its counterpart in Peter and the two Christs at Arles. The bent halo and emphasis on the corner of the block of all the Romans figures are close to those of James located on the re-entrant angle of the Arles east intermediate pier. In spite of their stylistic similarities, the Romans apostles do not possess the more normal proportions of the Arles figures. Their attenuation, together with a greater complexity of drapery folds, is different. Whereas the Arles statues reveal sharp, projecting edges and gouged, undercut folds, the drapery of the Romans apostles is rounded and more complex, resembling the treatment by the Michael Master of Saint-Gilles. Thus certain motifs seem to be borrowed from Arles; yet the animated nature of the surfaces with rounded, multiple folds is closer to the Michael Master of Saint-Gilles.

Under the paired apostles are badly damaged socles, each containing an animal facing outward (figs. 424, 425). On the left side a lion crushes a human, while the opposite socle consists of an ox or lion, mutilated beyond recognition. The lateral placement of single animals under paired figures does not follow the precedent of frontal animals under each apostle, as in the central portal of Saint-Gilles or the Arles portal. The Romans socles are mirror images of each other and thus give balance to the portal.

Three capitals on the central portal contain figures. On the right side, the inner capital, which is badly damaged, has bird-headed figures interlaced with frontal humans, while the outer capital has a frontal half-nude figure, perhaps depicting Luxury (fig. 430). The only well-preserved capital, the inner, left-hand one, depicts Christ meeting two Disciples (fig. 429) on the Road to Emmaus. Iconographically and compositionally, this capital is related to the western intermediate pier of the Arles cloister (fig. 279), yet stylistically, it is very close to the Arles capitals in the north gallery (figs. 296–303), although the figures are not as squat and the drapery is more complex. Since this capital (fig. 429) bears no relationship to the late work

425. Romans, Saint-Barnard. James and Paul (R1, 2).

426. Romans, James, detail.

427. Saint-Gilles. Michael.

428. Romans, James and Paul, detail.

429. Romans, Saint-Barnard. Capital, Road to Emmaus.

430. Romans. Capital, Luxury.

431. Arles, Saint-Trophîme. Cloister, capital of north gallery.

432. Romans. Annunciation capital, nave.

of the Michael Master on the frieze of the central portal of apostles at Saint-Gilles, it follows that the monumental apostles of the portal of Romans could have been carved by the Michael Master only if one assumes that an assistant carved the capitals. On the other hand, if the entire portal was the work of a single sculptor, this eclectic sculptor borrowed ideas from both the Michael Master of Saint-Gilles and the north gallery of the Arles cloister.

The heavy figures of this Emmaus capital are in marked contrast to the slender, ephemeral Gabriel and Virgin on the Annunciation capital in the nave (fig. 432). The Annunciation and other nave capitals follow the format of figures with flat folds and wind-blown terminations set against a floral ground, which is pure Burgundian, like the capitals at Vézelay. Thus the sculpture in the nave, following 1133, is a Burgundian import, while the sculpture on the façade is essentially a transformed Provençal style.

If Saint-Gilles was completed after 1150 and the north gallery of the Arles cloister can be placed in the 1150's, it follows that the Romans apostles which exhibit connections with both Saint-Gilles and Arles can be dated around 1160.[3]

---

3. All literature is in agreement that the portal of Romans followed Saint-Gilles, but the great discrepancies in dating depend on the various dates assigned to the façade of Saint-Gilles.

R. de Lasteyrie, "Études sur la sculpture française au moyen-âge," *Académie des inscriptions et belles-lettres, Fondation Piot, Monuments et mémoires*, VIII (1902), 127–128, placed Romans a little after Saint-Gilles, between 1160 and 1180.

A. K. Porter, *Romanesque Sculpture of the Pilgrimage Roads*, 10 vols. (Boston: Marshall Jones, 1923), vol. 1, 103, 275–277, 297–298, argued that Brunus was responsible for the Romans apostles after he had carved in order: Matthew, Bartholomew, James, Peter, Paul, and John of Saint-Gilles. He had Brunus moving from an archaic starkness at Saint-Gilles to a more suave and classic stage at Romans. Porter also stated that the apostles were carved for the cloister or some other location.

P. Deschamps, *French Sculpture of the Romanesque Period* (1930), mentioned the connection with Saint-Gilles, but emphasized his theory that some of the nave capitals were transported from Burgundy.

R. Hamann, *Die Abteikirche von St. Gilles und ihre künstlerische Nachfolge* (Berlin: Akademie-Verlag, 1955), 234–240, attributed the Romans apostles to the Michael Master of Saint-Gilles, a conclusion that this author had tentatively reached prior to the publication of Hamann's book. Hamann stated the relationship between the Romans and the Saint-Gilles apostles (Paul) and especially Michael, and also mentioned connections with the north gallery of the cloister at Arles. The style of the Romans figures seemed to Hamann to point toward Saint-Denis and Senlis. (Saint-Denis, finished by 1140, could hardly have been influenced by Romans, unless one follows the very early dating of Saint-Gilles proposed by Hamann.) Believing that the paired apostles of Romans are in their original location, Hamann concluded that the portal design of Romans was an intermediate stage, like the portal of Saint-Étienne in Toulouse, between Saint-Gilles and Chartres. It has now been proved that the sculpture from Saint-Étienne in Toulouse originally consisted of piers in the chapter house of Saint-Étienne, not a portal (L. Seidel, "A Romantic Forgery: The Romanesque 'Portal' of Saint-Étienne in Toulouse," *Art Bulletin*, L, 1 (1968), 33–42). Hamann's conclusion presupposed the early dating of both Saint-Gilles and Romans and the dominant role of Provence in the formation of the Île-de-France Early Gothic style of Saint-Denis and Chartres. Both of these conclusions are questionable.

433. Saint-Guilhem-le-Désert. From the south.

434. Saint-Guilhem-le-Désert. Cloister from the south.

CHAPTER 12

The Cloister of Saint-Guilhem-le-Désert

THE monastery of Saint-Guilhem-le-Désert in Hérault (figs. 433, 434), sixty-two miles west of Saint-Gilles-du-Gard, originally possessed a large ensemble of sculpture which is now exhibited in the Musée de la Société Archéologique de Montpellier, in The Cloisters in New York City, in the church of Saint-Geniez at Saint-Jean-de-Fos, and in a temporary museum in the north chapel of Saint-Guilhem-le-Désert. In contrast to the frieze of Beaucaire, to the cloister of Arles, and to the portal of Arles, in which the Saint-Gilles style predominated, much of the sculpture of Saint-Guilhem-le-Désert seems to have been created by specific sculptors who originally collaborated on the façade of Saint-Gilles-du-Gard.

The history of Saint-Guilhem-le-Désert (figs. 433–436) goes back to Carolingian times. Guillaume, Count of Toulouse, Duke of Aquitaine, Prince of Orange, and Master of the southern section of the Carolingian Empire, was Charlemagne's lieutenant in the campaign against the Moors in Spain. His fame as warrior was spread across Europe by the popular *chansons de geste*. In 804, on the advice of Benoît, first Abbot of Aniane, Guillaume constructed a monastery in the barren gorge of the Verdus on the left bank of the Hérault, the desert of Gellone, five miles northwest of Aniane.[1] Two years later Guillaume became a monk and the same year attended

---

1. J. Vallery-Radot, "L'église de Saint-Guilhem-le-Désert," *Congrès archéologique de France*, CVIII (1951), 156–158. E. Bonnet, *Cartulaire de l'abbaye de Gellone* (Montpellier: la Société archéologique de Montpellier, 1898). L. Vinas, *Visite rétrospective à Saint-Guilhem-le-Désert* (Montpellier: Sequin, 1875), 76–82.

the meeting at Thionville during which Charlemagne established the succession of his sons. Charlemagne opposed Guillaume's disavowal of his titles, but to no avail. Guillaume asked for and received a sacred relic of the True Cross.

The monastery grew rapidly after Guillaume's death in 812, largely as a result of the fame of this hero of the *chansons de geste* and the presence of the relic at Gellone. In the eleventh century, perhaps as early as 1030, a new church was begun which may have been destroyed by a fire which took place before 1066. The earliest work of the existing structure is the lower part of the westernmost bay of the nave. The rest of the nave was probably completed by the dedication of 1076, while an enlarged east end and the first floor of the cloister were finished around 1100.[2] The plans of the ground floor and first floor (figs. 435, 436), made by Robert Plouvier, a Maurist monk, show the layout of the monastery in 1656.[3] Excavations conducted in 1960 unearthed a crypt under the present choir which, according to Vallery-Radot, antedated the nave, but predated the new larger east end of the church.[4] The second floor of the cloister was erected in the second half of the twelfth century. The sculpture with which we are concerned belongs to this relatively late campaign.

In the twelfth century the name of the monastery was changed from Gellone to Saint-Guilhem-le-Désert. It became a recommended resting place on the southern pilgrimage route to Santiago de Compostela. The pilgrims stopped to venerate the famous relics and to recall the deeds of the renowned founder of the monastery. In 1569 the monastery was sacked by the Calvinists, and in 1624 the dilapidated condition of the cloister, chapter house, refectory, and dormitory was described by the visiting prior of the monastery of La Grasse. In the seventeenth century the monastery was reformed under the congregation of Saint-Maur.[5] During the revolution the abbey was sold, and a mason acquired the cloister and used it as a quarry. Pieces of sculpture were scattered in surrounding villages. An inundation of the Verdus River in 1817 further damaged the abbey.[6] A considerable amount of decorative sculpture ended up in the garden of the Justice of Peace of Aniane from where it finally was purchased through several intermediate transactions by the American sculptor George Grey Barnard in 1906 and then acquired by the Metropolitan Museum of Art in 1925 for The Cloisters (see fig. 456).

Three reliefs in the Musée de la Société Archéologique de Montpellier, one relief in Saint-Guilhem-le-Désert, and a fragment in the church of Saint-Geniez at

---

2. Vallery-Radot, *op. cit.*, 159–175.

3. E. Lambert, "Monuments disparus et documents d'archives," *Phoebus*, I (1946), 16–22.

4. J. Vallery-Radot, "Fouilles romanes," *Art de France*, IV (1964), 275–277.

5. Vinas, *op. cit.*, 148–160.

6. *Ibid.*, 57–63.

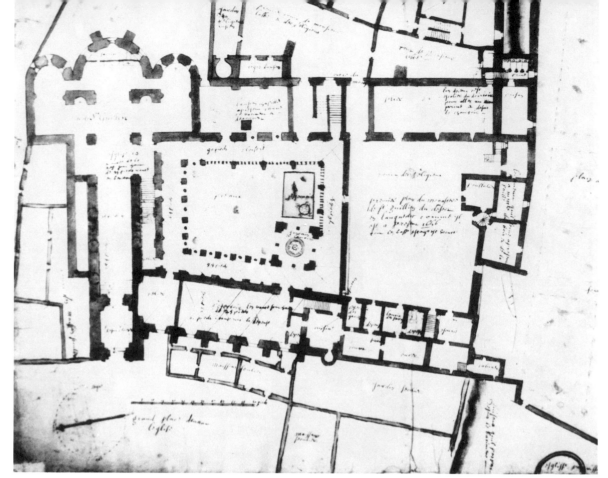

435. Saint-Guilhem-le-Désert. Plan of ground floor (1656).

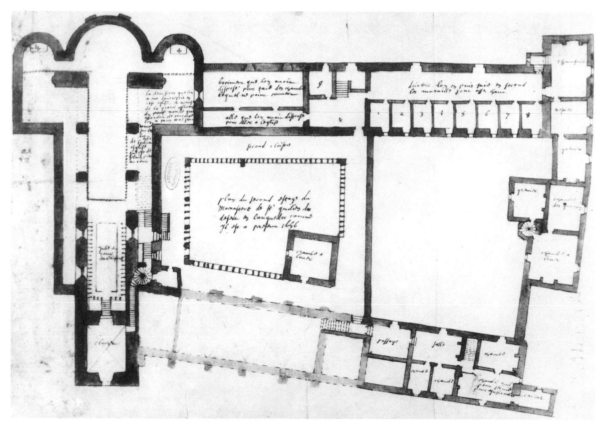

436. Plan of first floor (1656).

437. Saint-Guilhem-le-Désert. Relief with three Apostles. Montpellier, Musée de la Société Archéologique.

438. Relief with three Apostles (detail).

439. Saint-Gilles. CP.R 3 Apostle. Soft Master.

440. Saint-Gilles. Frieze of CP, Christ's Prophecy of Peter's Denial.

Saint-Jean-de-Fos comprised the known figured sculpture from Saint-Guilhem-le-Désert over and above small pieces which will be discussed later. The relief with three apostles in Montpellier (figs. 437, 438), which is 1.02 by .48 meters, resembles sculpture by the Soft Master of Saint-Gilles (figs. 439, 440). Although only one-half the size of the monumental apostles of Saint-Gilles, the relief exhibits the same slouched ponderation, similar arrangement and style of drapery with varied intervals of folds, geometric designs on collars, and related treatment of folds over the feet as seen in the apostle by the Soft Master of Saint-Gilles (fig. 439). In spite of the differences between heads in the round and heads in relief, the treatment of eyes, beard, and hair is similar to that of the central portal (CP.R 3) by the Soft Master (see fig. 439). Many stylistic parallels exist between this relief from Saint-Guilhem and the later sculpture of the superstructure of the façade of Saint-Gilles by the Soft Master, such as the left-hand frieze and lintel of the left portal (see figs. 78, 79) and Christ's Prophecy of Peter's Denial on the central portal, which is the last work by the Soft Master at Saint-Gilles (fig. 440). In the latter, the drapery over the legs of Christ is very close to that on the apostles of the Saint-Guilhem relief, while the head of Christ resembles that of the three on the relief. The motif of an apostle grasping his beard can be seen on both the Saint-Gilles and Saint-Guilhem reliefs. Some stylistic connections can be found between this Saint-Guilhem relief and the fragment of the Last Judgment tympanum in the Maison Romane at Saint-Gilles (fig. 142); yet in the latter the figures are squatter and heavier and, as stated earlier, are the work of an assistant of the Soft Master. In spite of the somewhat elongated proportions of the figures, this Saint-Guilhem relief seems to be the work of the Saint-Gilles Soft Master.

The damaged rectangular sculpture in Montpellier, containing three apostles and the figure of Christ (1.02 by .34 meters—figs. 441–443), is different from the relief with three apostles (fig. 437), since the figures are not set within a frame, but animate three sides of a block. In arrangement and style of drapery, in pose and gestures, in overlapping of figures, and in the soft surfaces, this relief resembles the one with three apostles. Heads are set against curving halos, with the halo of the corner figure of Christ displaying the remains of a cross. Certainly the same sculptor who carved the relief with three apostles, the Saint-Gilles Soft Master, was responsible for carving this relief.

The third relief in Montpellier (1.02 by .47 meters—fig. 444) has five apostles facing to their right. Every detail echoes the relief with three apostles and, in turn, is related to the two monumental statues by the Soft Master of Saint-Gilles and his work on the upper frieze of the façade of Saint-Gilles, especially the preparation for the Entry into Jerusalem on the left portal and Christ's Prophecy of Peter's Denial on the central portal (fig. 440).

Against the north wall of the north chapel of Saint-Guilhem-le-Désert stands a relief of two apostles holding palm fronds (1.02 meters high—fig. 445). The thick, curving fold across the thigh of the right-hand apostle recalls the relief of the Payment of Judas by an assistant on the central portal of Saint-Gilles (figs. 136, 137); yet the quality of the carving is higher in the Saint-Guilhem relief. With the exception of the thick fold, the rest of the details of drapery, the heads, and the nature of the surfaces resemble the three reliefs in Montpellier. Thus it would seem that the Soft Master of Saint-Gilles was responsible for all three reliefs in Montpellier and this relief at Saint-Guilhem-le-Désert.[7]

A headless statue, holding a palm frond (?) (.80 meters high—figs. 446, 447), is located in the church of Saint-Geniez on the outskirts of Saint-Jean-de-Fos, three miles south of Saint-Guilhem-le-Désert.[8] In size and style it is connected with the four reliefs from Saint-Guilhem-le-Désert; yet this relief was not carved by the Soft Master of Saint-Gilles. The stance of the figure, the arrangement of the cloak buckled at the neck, the wattled sleeves, the flowing cuffs, the accentuated articulation of arms and hands, and especially the crisp, rugged surfaces—all are quite different from the three reliefs in Montpellier and the two apostles in Saint-Guilhem-le-Désert. At the same time, many common denominators can be seen between this relief and the Michael of Saint-Gilles (fig. 448) or reliefs in the superstructure by the Michael Master, such as the Citizens of Jerusalem on the left portal (fig. 449) or the Christ before Pilate. On the basis of these stylistic relationships it can be argued that this figure was carved by the Michael Master of Saint-Gilles-du-Gard.

---

7. R. Hamann, in *Die Abteikirche von St. Gilles und ihre künstlerische Nachfolge* (Berlin: Akademie-Verlag, 1955), 240–251, derived the style of the relief of five apostles from his Andrew Master (the CP.R 3 apostle of Saint-Gilles) from the Entry into Jerusalem on the left portal and the Prophecy of Peter's Denial on the central portal of Saint-Gilles. Thinner proportions and more ordered drapery reminded him of Chartres West and the east gallery of the Arles cloister. Comparing the relief of three apostles with the Virgin and Child of the left tympanum of Saint-Gilles, Hamann argued that it was carved by a less sensitive hand. He related the damaged piece with Christ to the relief of five apostles, but related the relief with two disciples in Saint-Guilhem-le-Désert to the Michael of Saint-Gilles and the Burgundian tradition. Since all sections of the frieze of Saint-Gilles mentioned by Hamann seem to this author to have been carved by the Soft Master of Saint-Gilles (CP.R 3, 4 apostle) and since the differences in quality among the three reliefs in Montpellier appear non-existent, it follows that all three were carved by the Saint-Gilles Soft Master. The two disciples at Saint-Guilhem have more stylistic connections with the three reliefs in Montpellier than with the Michael of Saint-Gilles. Furthermore, the only stylistic relationships between the Saint-Guilhem reliefs and the paired apostles of Romans are the bent halos. Hamann's insistence on the influence of the Arles cloister and Arles portal, especially the reliefs of Trophîme and the Stoning of Stephen, seem to be unfounded.

8. Marcel Gouron, Chief Archivist of the Department of the Hérault, discovered this statue. He kindly informed me of its location. After the local locksmith failed to find a key to the church, the mayor of Saint-Jean-de-Fos broke the lock.

441. Saint-Guilhem-le-Désert. Christ and Apostles, Montpellier, Musée de la Société Archéologique.

442. Christ and Apostle.

443. Christ and Apostle.

444. Relief with five Apostles. Montpellier, Musée de la Société Archéologique.

445. Two figures.

446. Saint-Guilhem-le-Désert. Apostle (?). Saint-Geniez.

447. Apostle (?), detail.

448. Saint-Gilles. Saint Michael.

449. Saint-Gilles. Citizens of Jerusalem (LP.R).

Three pairs of figures, Elders of the Apocalypse (.61 by .30 meters—figs. 450–452), are exhibited at the Musée de la Société Archéologique at Montpellier.[9] The first pair (fig. 450) is very similar stylistically to the three reliefs in Montpellier by the Soft Master of Saint-Gilles. The other two (figs. 451, 452) exhibit a markedly different style with more numerous, thick, parallel folds and with zigzag borders and hems of cloaks (hands, heads, and parts of musical instruments are modern). The last two are clearly not by either the Soft Master or the Michael Master of Saint-Gilles, but have some features reminiscent of the sculpture of Perpignan and Arles-sur-Tech in southwestern France. As V. Lassalle quite correctly pointed out in a recent article, these two pairs of Elders of the Apocalypse show a strong stylistic relationship to the cloister portal of the Cathedral of Tarragona.[10] On the basis of a study of the sculpture of Tarragona, Lassalle argued that this master had an intimate knowledge of Provençal monuments, especially the portal of Arles, that he possibly knew Italian sculpture, and that during his apprenticeship in France he could have carved these two reliefs.[11] Certainly these two pairs of elders are the work of an un-Provençal sculptor who has come under the strong influence of Provençal art.

On the main staircase of the Faculté de Médecins at Montpellier are displayed a pair of socles with lions clawing and biting humans (.65 by .50 meters—fig. 453). These socles recall those on the portal of Romans (fig. 424). The drapery style resembles reliefs by the Saint-Gilles Soft Master, while the treatment of the lion's mane is similar to that of the socles under the James Major and Paul at Saint-Gilles (fig. 67).

Is it possible to determine the original location of these reliefs? It must be assumed that a great deal of the sculpture was either lost or destroyed or remains hidden in nearby towns.[12] Hamann, incorporating all the existing sculpture except the Elders of the Apocalypse and the fragment from Saint-Geniez, and at the same time adding some he made up, published an elaborate, wide portal with reliefs set between projecting pilasters and the apostles of the rectangular block upheld by the lion socles on the doorjambs.[13] His reconstruction seems to be based partially on the portal at Romans and, like the portal of Romans, is one of the steps in portal design which, according to him, lead from Provence to Chartres. The width and the convexity of the

---

9. Hamann, *op. cit.*, 250, compared these figures with the corbels of the Arles cloister and argued that they supported the vaults opposite his reconstructed portal, to be discussed later.

10. V. Lassalle, "L'influence provençale au cloître et à la cathédrale de Tarragone," *Mélanges offerts à René Crozet* (Poitiers: 1966), 873–877.

11. *Ibid.*, 878–879.

12. Vinas, *op. cit.*, 62–64. It is more than likely that many fragments from Saint-Guilhem-le-Désert still exist.

13. Hamman, *op. cit.*, 245–246, fig. 317.

lion socles make their function as supports for existing sculpture impossible. Furthermore, the plans of 1656 (figs. 435, 436) reveal the fact that no portal of Hamann's dimension ever existed. The rib-vaulted narthex under the west tower was constructed in the last one-third of the twelfth century and has insufficient room for a sculptured portal. The plan of the ground floor of the monastery reveals no large portal connecting the cloister and the church. Some sculpture, including the lion socles and lost statues, may have decorated the door leading into the chapter house.

The three reliefs of apostles in Montpellier (figs. 437, 441–444), all 1.02 meters in height with similar moldings, contain eleven disciples and Christ. The three, taken together, seem to form a unified composition, with the relief of the three figures facing the right, the damaged piece with Christ in the center, and the relief with five figures looking to their left on the right. It is possible that these reliefs once decorated the corner and intermediate piers of the north gallery of the second floor of the cloister (see fig. 436), growing out of the format of the reliefs in the Moissac cloister or those in the cloister of Santo Domingo de Silos crossed with the Arles cloister solution of figures and reliefs. Since the upper gallery of the Saint-Guilhem cloister was unvaulted, there was no necessity of having single figures supporting transverse and diagonal arches, as in the cloister of Saint-Trophîme at Arles. The relief in Saint-Geniez (figs. 446, 447) could also have adorned an intermediate pier, while the apostles in the chapel of Saint-Guilhem-le-Désert, like the rectangular block with Christ, may have adorned the other corner pier. The fact that the ornamental sculpture in the cloister of Saint-Guilhem-le-Désert in New York City and the ornamental sculpture at Saint-Guilhem-le-Désert, still to be discussed, is 1.02 to 1.03 meters in height suggests perhaps that the figure reliefs were originally part of the cloister of Saint-Guilhem-le-Désert.

On the floor of the north chapel of Saint-Guilhem-le-Désert rest the remains of a sarcophagus with figures on four sides which purports to be the receptacle in which the relics of Saint Guilhem were placed in 1138, according to the archives of the sixteenth century (figs. 454, 455). In 1925 Richard Hamann discovered many fragments then separated from the sarcophagus. His son Richard Hamann-MacLean assembled several figures from these pieces.[14] In spite of the antique overtones, Hamann believed that all the sculpture was Romanesque, reminiscent of the style of Toulouse. Further, he argued that the origin of the sculpture was the proto-Renaissance of Saint-Gilles as exemplified in the Entry into Jerusalem on the left portal and the Prophecy of Peter's Denial and the Christ before Pilate on the central portal.

---

14. R. Hamann, "Ein unbekannter Figurenzyklus in St. Guilhem-le-Désert," *Marburger Jahrbuch für Kunstwissenschaft* (1926), 71–89.

450. Saint-Guilhem-le-Désert. Elders of Apocalypse.
Montpellier, Musée de le Société Archéologique.

451. Elders of Apocalypse. Montpellier.

452. Elders of Apocalypse. Montpellier.

453. Socle. Montpellier, Faculté de Médecins.

454. Saint-Guilhem-le-Désert. Virgin and Child. Sarcophagus.

455. Sarcophagus.

456. Saint-Guilhem-le-Désert. Cloister. The Cloisters, New York.

According to Hamann, the Saint-Guilhem sculpture represented the stage between Saint-Gilles and the sculpture of La Charité-sur-Loire and Chartres.[15]

In the early 1930's the fragments were fitted to the preserved base of a sarcophagus and interpreted by H. von Schoenebeck as dating mostly from the fourth century.[16] Walter Horn devoted a section of his book on Saint-Gilles to the sarcophagus, which he considered the high point in the proto-Renaissance of southern France. He added several pieces to the reassembled sarcophagus and agreed with von Schoenebeck that the themes and their groupings were Early Christian. However, since the sarcophagus does not conform to any Early Christian format and since the style of some of the figures is Romanesque, Horn related the figure style of Saint-Gilles especially to the scenes of the Betrayal, Carrying the Cross, and the Flagellation. Horn's Flagellation Master of Saint-Gilles was possibly the sculptor of part of the sarcophagus, and in his opinion, he carved the sarcophagus in 1138 after the completion of the side portals of Saint-Gilles, but before the completion of the central portal.[17]

R. Hamann, in his monograph on Saint-Gilles, divided the figures of the sarcophagus into three styles: one an antique style related to the Saint Paul of Saint-Gilles, the second a Toulousan style (Magi before Herod?—fig. 455) connected with the Christ before Pilate of Saint-Gilles, and a third, weaker style, the Virgin and Child (fig. 454), dependent on the other figures of the sarcophagus. Hamann used Horn's date of 1138 to confirm his date of 1129 for the completion of the entire façade of Saint-Gilles and reaffirmed his arguments that Saint-Giulhem-le-Désert was a stage in the evolution from Saint-Gilles to Chartres.[18]

The two sections of the sarcophagus, which are illustrated (figs. 454, 455), revealed some stylistic connections with both the reliefs from Saint-Guilhem-le-Désert and the frieze of Saint-Gilles. If compared with the four reliefs by the Soft Master of Saint-Gilles (figs, 437, 441, 444, 445), it is clear that the illustrated parts of the sarcophagus were carved by different hands. None of the elongation of figures nor the soft surfaces of drapery can be found in the sarcophagus. Rather, figures are squatter, more massive, and more articulated with overtones of the late antique. However, remains of the heads of the two fragments recall those in Christ's Prophecy of Peter's Denial (fig. 440), the latest work by the Soft Master at Saint-Gilles. Costumes, greater anatomical articulation, crisp projection of folds, and animated gestures of the sarcophagus figures recall the disciple from Saint-Guilhem in the church of Saint-

15. *Ibid.*, 73–85.

16. H. von Schoenebeck, "Ein Christlicher Sarkophag aus St. Guilhem-le-Désert," *Jahrbuch der Arch. Instituts*, XLVII (1932), 97–125.

17. W. Horn, *Die Fassade von St. Gilles* (Hamburg: Paul Evert, 1937), 81–89.

18. Hamann, *Die Abteikirche von St. Gilles*, 254–258.

Geniez (fig. 446) by the Michael Master of Saint-Gilles and sculpture at Saint-Gilles by the same master. The style of drapery of the reliefs of the sarcophagus is much simpler than that of the more animated figures on the reliefs by the Michael Master at Saint-Gilles, such as the Citizens of Jerusalem on the frieze of the left portal (fig. 449), Christ before Pilate, and the Flagellation on the central portal. The curved and projecting loop folds on the legs and arms of one fragment (fig. 455) do not possess the complex double profile of drapery folds as seen on the figures of Christ before Pilate at Saint-Gilles. Rather, the cruder, stiffer Saint-Guilhem figures seem to be simplified variants of the late work by the Michael Master of Saint-Gilles. Thus in contrast to the reliefs of the apostles in Montpellier and Saint-Guilhem-le-Désert and the figure in Saint-Geniez which were carved by the Soft Master and Michael Master of Saint-Gilles, respectively, the twelfth-century fragments of the sarcophagus appeared to be a somewhat provincial reflection of the latest work of the Michael Master and not carved during the evolution of work on the façade of Saint-Gilles, as Horn argued,[19] but after the completion of the central portal. The date of 1138, proposed by both Hamann and Horn, for the completion of the sarcophagus would seem to be considerably too early in the light of the stylistic connections between the sculpture of Saint-Gilles and Arles, Beaucaire, and Modena.

Pieces purportedly from the cloister of Saint-Guilhem-le-Désert were purchased by The Metropolitan Museum of Art in New York from George Grey Barnard in 1925 and installed in The Cloisters in Fort Tryon Park in 1938 by the late James J. Rorimer, then Director of The Cloisters (fig. 456).[20] The actual provenance of all this sculpture is doubtful because in the garden of the Justice of the Peace of Aniane (five miles southeast of Saint-Guilhem-le-Désert) sculpture from Saint-Guilhem became mixed with fragments from the Abbey of Aniane. However, measurements of capitals, ornamental pilasters, and figured reliefs do correspond in height to suggest that most of the sculpture did indeed come from Saint-Guilhem-le-Désert and originally was located on the second floor of the cloister (see plan—fig. 436). Following the French Revolution, the cloister and monastic buildings housed unsuccessfully a spinning mill and a tannery before being purchased by a mason, who used the structures as a quarry. Pieces became scattered in surrounding towns, with many arriving at Montpellier and in Aniane.[21]

The small Saint-Guilhem-le-Désert cloister in New York includes columns,

---

19. Horn, *op. cit.*, 88.

20. The list is as follows: 35 capitals, 17 abaci, 14 semiengaged capitals, 25 columns, 39 bases, 1 pilaster, 2 blocks of stone, 1 voussoir, 10 *chaperons de muraille*.

21. Vinas, *op. cit.*, 62. This author found columns in the garden of a house and a keystone over the entrance door of another house in Montpeyroux. However, several pieces mentioned in Vinas are presently lost.

capitals, abaci, and pilasters which are similar in style and dimensions to fragments preserved at Saint-Guilhem-le-Désert and in the Musée Archéologique de Montpellier. Several capitals in the west gallery, as reconstructed in New York, are clearly Gothic in form. This later sculpture suggests that the large upper cloister at Saint-Guilhem was completed only after protracted campaigns.

Three historiated capitals from Saint-Guilhem, one in Montpellier (fig. 457) and two in The Cloisters (figs. 458, 459), exhibit three quite distinct styles. All three are .30 meters in height. The Montpellier capital, Christ with Disciples performing a Miracle (?), seems to be a free and plastic variant of the low reliefs from Saint-Guilhem by the Soft Master of Saint-Gilles. The same slender proportions, undercut loop folds, and accented gathering of drapery across the waists can be seen on capital and reliefs. The gouged-out folds with rounded tops, the ease of pose and gesture, and the use of drill work in the hair recall the Prophecy of Peter's Denial relief, the last work of the Soft Master at Saint-Gilles (fig. 440). The second capital (The Cloisters—fig. 458) has two frontal, stiff figures on two faces, one face with palmette, and a fourth badly damaged. The complexity of folds suggests Provençal sculpture in general, while the thick fold below Christ's right knee recalls sculpture around Vienne (Rhône Valley).[22] The third capital, depicting the Presentation in the Temple (The Cloisters—fig. 459), reveals a totally different style. Stocky figures, oval heads, use and treatment of corner scrolls, and the type of drapery—all recall the style of the capitals in Saint-Sernin of Toulouse. However, this capital exhibits many features of the sculpture at Saint-Gilles by the Thomas Master, who served his apprenticeship in southwestern France. The treatment of the mantle of the High Priest (not illustrated) resembles that on the left-hand socle of the right portal of Saint-Gilles (figs. 58, 59), while the serrated terminations of cloaks and articulation of legs (fig. 459) appear to be plastic versions of the Cain and Abel relief at Saint-Gilles (fig. 52). On the other hand, the round heads and flowing beards are reminiscent of those in the choir capitals of Les-Saintes-Maries-de-la-Mer.

A floral pilaster at Saint-Guilhem-le-Désert (fig. 460) and one in The Cloisters in New York (fig. 461), both 1.03 meters high, exemplify the exuberant character of the ornament at Saint-Guilhem. The first exhibits an undulating vine with complex floral fillers growing out of secondary stems. The surface is extensively undercut, while floral fillers have concave leaves and accents of drill work. In general this ornamented panel recalls the bottom of the lintels of the Saint-Gilles façade, especially under the left portal (fig. 160), although the greater complexity is closer in style to

---

22. Willibald Sauerländer suggested to me the possible relationship of this capital to sculpture in the middle Rhône Valley.

458. Capital. The Cloisters, New York.

459. Capital. The Cloisters, New Yo

457. Saint-Guilhem-le-Désert. Figured capital, Montpellier, Musée de la Société Archéologique.

460. Floral pilaster.

461. Floral pilaster. The Cloisters, New York.

462. Wave pilaster.

463. Wave pilasters. The Cloisters, New York.

464. Saint-Guilhem-le-Désert. Floral capital. Montpellier, Musée de la Société Archéologique.

465. Floral capital. The Cloisters, New York.

466. Capitals. The Cloisters, New York.

467. Capitals. The Cloisters. New York.

the vertical panels flanking the central portal of Saint-Gilles (figs. 163–165). These Saint-Gilles panels exhibit similar interweaving of secondary stems and similar arrangements and surfaces of the radiating floral fillers. The pilaster in The Cloisters (fig. 461) is a stiffer and more plastic variant of the one in Saint-Guilhem. Both of these reliefs have no stylistic connection with the flat and dull ornament of the Arles portal, but appear related to reliefs on the façade of Saint-Gilles.

A thin, wavelike pilaster at Saint-Guilhem (fig. 462) has several counterparts in the Saint-Guilhem cloister in New York (fig. 463). The pair of capitals and abaci of the latter, which do not belong with the pilasters, contain frontal and curving palmettes which are closer to ornament on the Saint-Gilles façade than to any on the cloister or on the façade of Saint-Trophîme at Arles.

Two capitals with oval vines and leaves on each face, one in Montpellier (fig. 464), the other in The Cloisters (fig. 465), both .30 meters high, recall capitals of similar format on the façade of Arles, in the east gallery of the Arles cloister, and on the pontile of Modena (figs. 400–402). The Saint-Guilhem capitals appear to be schematized versions of the more naturalistic capitals at Arles and Modena. At Arles, undivided leaves are separated by grooves, while in the Saint-Guilhem capitals, raised edges demarcate the leaves. In the latter, drill work is used more extensively than in the Modena capital.

The Corinthian-type capitals from Saint-Guilhem-le-Désert (figs. 466, 467) possess none of the massiveness and plasticity of capitals flanking the side portals of Saint-Gilles. At the same time, they are totally different from the squat capitals of the north gallery of the Arles cloister. The gouged and drilled concavities are new; yet the general format and shape of the capitals are reminiscent of some of those in the east gallery of Arles.

On the basis of pilasters and capitals in The Cloisters, of the reliefs and capitals in Montpellier, and of the pieces still at Saint-Guilhem-le-Désert, all of which certainly do not comprise all the original cloister sculpture, it is possible to see the workmanship of two sculptors from Saint-Gilles, the Soft Master and the Michael Master. If indeed the Presentation capital came from Saint-Guilhem, an un-Provençal sculptor, either from southwestern France or related to the Thomas Master in Saint-Gilles, was a member of the workshop. Further, an itinerant, either of Spanish origin or else migrating to Spain, carved two pairs of the Elders of the Apocalypse. The style of the ornament points to Saint-Gilles, but similarities with Arlesian sculpture in some pieces do exist. Most of the sculpture, except the clearly Gothic capitals of the early thirteenth century in The Cloisters in New York, would seem to have been created in the 1150's or as late as the early 1160's.

Bibliography

The following books and articles are listed in chronological order of publication within each section.

SAINT-GILLES-DU-GARD

Monographs and Articles

Labande, L. H. "L'Église de Saint-Gilles." *Congrès archéologique de France*, LXXVI, I (1909), 168–181.

Fliche, A. *Aigues-Mortes et Saint-Gilles*. Petites monographies des grands édifices de la France. Paris: Laurens, 1925.

Gouron, M. "Dates des sculptures du portail de l'église de Saint-Gilles." *Bulletin de la Société d'histoire et d'archéologie de Nîmes et du Gard* (1933–1934), 45–47.

Aubert, M. "Petrus Brunus, sculpteur à Saint-Gilles-du-Gard." *Bulletin de la Société nationale des antiquaires de France* (1934), 138–139.

Hamann, R. "The Façade of Saint-Gilles: A Reconstruction." *Burlington Magazine*, LXIV (1934), 19–29.

Schapiro, M. "New Documents on St.-Gilles." *Art Bulletin*, XVII (1935), 415–431.

Aubert, M. "Les dates de la façade de Saint-Gilles à propos d'un livre récent." (R.H.L. Hamann, "Das Lazarus-Grab in Autun." *Kunstgeschichtliches Seminar*, Marburg, 1935.) *Bulletin monumental*, XCV (1936), 369–372.

Horn, W. *Die Fassade von St. Gilles. Eine Untersuchung zur Frage des Antikeneinflusses in der südfranzösischen Kunst des 12. Jahrhunderts*. Hamburg: Paul Evert, 1937.

Schapiro, M. "Further Documents on Saint-Gilles." Notes in *Art Bulletin*, XIX (1937), 111–112.

Gouron, M. "Découverte du tympan de l'église Saint-Martin à Saint-Gilles." *Annales du Midi*, LXII (1950), 115–120.

Gouron, M. "Saint-Gilles-du-Gard." *Congrès archéologique de France*, CVIII (1951), 104–119.

Hamann, R. *Die Abteikirche von St. Gilles und ihre künstlerische Nachfolge.* 3 vols. Berlin:Akademie-Verlag, 1955.

Books and Articles Discussing Saint-Gilles

Mérimée, P. *Notes d'un voyage dans le Midi de la France.* Paris: Librairie de Fournier, 1835, 336–345.

Viollet-le-Duc, E. *Dictionnaire raisonné de l'architecture française du XIe au XVIe siècle.* 10 vols. Paris: Bance, 1854–1868, VII, 417.

Revoil, H. *L'architecture romane du Midi de la France.* 3 vols. Paris: Morel, 1873, II, 47–66.

Vöge, W. *Die Anfänge des monumentalen Stiles im Mittelalter.* Strassburg: 1894, 47ff, 101ff.

Marignan, A. "L'école du sculpture en Provence du XIIe et XIIIe siècle." *Le Moyen Âge*, III (1899), 1–64.

Lasteyrie, R. de. "Études sur la sculpture française au moyen-âge." L'Académie des inscriptions et belles-lettres, Fondation Piot, *Monuments et mémoires*, VIII (1902), 80–115.

Porter, A. K. *Romanesque Sculpture of the Pilgrimage Roads.* 10 vols. Boston: Marshall Jones, 1923. Saint-Gilles: vol. 1, 273–298; vol. IX, Plates, 1302–1330.

Priest, A. "The Masters of the West Façade at Chartres." *Art Studies*, I (1923), 28–44.

Hamann, R. *Deutsche und Französische Kunst im Mittelalter. Südfranzösische Protorenaissance und ihre Ausbreitung in Deutschland auf dem Wege durch Italien und die Schweiz.* Marburg: Kunstgeschichtliches Seminar, 1923.

Aubert, M. *French Sculpture at the Beginning of the Gothic Period.* New York: Harcourt, Brace, 1929, 56–58.

Deschamps, P. *French Sculpture of the Romanesque Period, Eleventh and Twelfth Centuries.* New York: Harcourt, Brace, 1930, 83–89.

Gardner, A. *Medieval Sculpture in France.* Cambridge: University Press, 1930, 164–171.

Lassalle, V. *L'influence antique dans l'art roman provençal.* Revue archéologique Narbonnaise, 2. Paris: Éditions E. de Boccard, 1970, 73–74, 76–79, 90–92, 99–102, 104–105, 114.

History, Documents, Restorations

D'Éverlance, L'Abbé P. *Saint Gilles et son pèlerinage.* Nîmes: Jouve, 1881.

Goiffon, L'Abbé. *Bullaire de l'abbaye de Saint-Gilles.* Nîmes: 1882.

Puech, A. "Documents pour servir à l'histoire de l'abbaye de Saint-Gilles." *Bulletin du Comité de l'art chrétien*, IV (1890), 253–284.

Nicholas, C. "Documents inédits sur Saint-Gilles." *Bulletin du Comité de l'art chrétien du Diocèse de Nîmes*, VI (1895), 435–453.

Nicholas, C. "Construction et réparations de l'église de Saint-Gilles." *Mémoires de l'Académie de Nîmes*, XXIII (1900), 95–149.

Nicholas, C. "Notes de M. Delmas sur l'église de Saint-Gilles 1843." *Mémoires de l'Académie de Nîmes*, XXV (1902), 95–122.

Charles-Roux, J. *Saint-Gilles. Sa légende, son abbaye, ses coutumes.* Paris: A. Lemerre, 1910.

Bligny-Bondurand, E. *Les Coutumes de Saint-Gilles (XIIe–XIVe siècles).* Texte latin critique, avec traduction, notes, introduction et tables. Paris: Picard et fils, 1915.

Vielliard, J. *Le Guide du pèlerin de Saint-Jacques de Compostelle.* Macon: Protat Frères, 1963, 35–47.

Saint-Gilles, Église 1ᵉʳ Dossier, (Gard, 506), Monuments historiques, Paris, 1839–1883–1926.

Roman and Early Christian Sources
LeBlant, E. *Étude sur les sarcophages chrétiens antiques de la ville d'Arles*. Paris: 1878.
Wilpert, J. *I sarcofagi cristiani antichi*. 4 vols. Rome, 1929.
Benoit, F. *Sarcophages paléochrétiens d'Arles et de Marseille*. Paris: 1954.
Lassalle, V. *L'influence antique dans l'art roman provençal*. Revue archéologique de Narbonnaise, 2. Paris: Éditions E. de Boccard, 1970.

Iconography
Sanover, G. "Iconographie de la Bible d'après les artistes de l'antiquité et du moyen-âge." *Bulletin monumental*, LXXX, (1921), 212–238.
Janson, H. *Apes and Ape Lore in the Middle Ages and the Renaissance*. London: 1952, 47, fn. 87.
Seiferth, W. *Synagoge und Kirche im Mittelalter*. Munich: Kosel-Verlag, 1964.
Blumenkranz, B. "La polémique antijuive dans l'art chrétien du moyen-âge." *Bulletino dell'Istituto storico italiano per il medio evo e Archivio Muratoriano*, LXXVII (1965), 41–42.
Blumenkranz, B. *Le juif médiéval au miroir de l'art chrétien*. Paris: Études Augustininiennes, 1966, 66.
Golb, N. "New Light on the Persecution of French Jews at the Time of the First Crusade." *Proceedings of the Academy for Jewish Research*, XXXIV (1966), 1–63.
Kobler, F. "Das Pisaner Affenkapitell in Berlin-Glienicke." *Minuscula discipulorum;* Kunsthistorische Studien Hans Kauffmann zum 70. Geburtstag 1966 (Berlin: Hessling, 1968), 157–164.
Kraus, H. *The Living Theatre of Medieval Art*. Bloomington and London: Indiana University Press, 1969, 22–23, 150–155.
Colish, M.L. "Peter of Bruys, Henry of Lausanne, and the Façade of Saint-Gilles." *Traditio*, XXVIII (1972), 451–460.

Reconstructions of Portals and Façade
Hamann, R. "The Façade of Saint-Gilles: A Reconstruction." *Burlington Magazine*, LXIV (1934), 19–29.
Horn, W. *Die Fassade von St. Gilles*. Hamburg: Paul Evert, 1937.
Hamann, R. *Die Abteikirche von St. Gilles und ihre künstlerische Nachfolge*. 3 vols. Berlin: Akademie-Verlag, 1955.
Gouron, M. "Saint-Gilles-du-Gard" *Congrès archéologique de France*, CVIII (1951), 104–119.
Lassalle, V. "La façade de l'abbatiale de Saint-Gilles. Essai de restitution." *Bulletin de l'École antique de Nîmes* (1966), 79–89.

Saint-Gilles and Related Monuments
Porter, A. K. "Condrieu, Jerusalem, and Saint-Gilles." *Art in America*, XIII (1924–1925), 117–129.
Vallery-Radot, J. "L'église Saint-André-le-Bas de Vienne et ses rapports avec Saint-Paul de Lyon, Notre-Dame d'Andance et Notre-Dame de Die." *Bulletin monumental*, XCVII (1938), 145–172.
Albrand, E. *L'église et le cloître de Saint-André-le-Bas à Vienne*. Vienne: 1951.

Gardner, A. *Medieval Sculpture in France*. Cambridge: University Press, 1930, 171–179.

Deschamps, P. *French Sculpture of the Romanesque Period, Eleventh and Twelfth Centuries*. New York; Harcourt, Brace, 1930, 84–86.

Von Stockhausen, H-A. "Die Romanischen Kreuzgänge der Provence. Teil I: Die Architektur." *Marburger Jahrbuch für Kunstwissenschaft*, VII (1933), 136-145, and "Teil II: Die Plastik," VIII, IX (1936), 89–97. Offprint, 1932, 4–13, 59–67.

Francovich, G. de. *Benedetto Antelami. Architetto e scultore e l'arte del suo tempo*. Milan and Florence: Electa Editrice, 1952, 136–137.

Hamann, R. *Die Abteikirche von St. Gilles*. 3 vols. Berlin: Akademie-Verlag, 1955, 190–198, 209.

Sanpaolesi, P. "La Facciata della cattedrale di Pisa." *Rivista dell'Istituto Nazionale d'Archeologia e Storia dell Arte*, 1956–1957, 248–394.

Sheppard, C. "Romanesque Sculpture in Tuscany: A Problem of Methodology." *Gazette des Beaux-Arts*, LIV (1959), 97–108.

Lassalle, V. *L'influence antique de l'art roman provençal*. Revue archéologique de Narbonnaise, 2. Paris: Éditions E. de Boccard, 1970, 32–33, 76–79, 82–84, 90–94, 98–99, 102–104, 111–117.

ROMANS, SAINT-BARNARD

Monographs, Articles, Documents

Giraud, P. *Essai historique sur l'abbaye de Saint-Barnard et sur la ville de Romans*. 3 vols. Lyon: 1856–1869.

Nugues, A. "Notes sur l'église de Saint-Barnard à Romans (Drôme)." *Société archéologie de statistique de la Drôme, Valence*, XI (1877), 257–271.

Chevalier, U. *Annales de la ville de Romans*. Paris and Valence: 1897.

Lacroix, A. *Romans et le Bourg-de-Péage avant 1790*. Valence: 1897.

Vinay, L. *Essai sur les monuments et les anciens édifices de la ville de Romans*. Romans: 1904.

Vinay, L. *Romans archèologique*. Valence: 1911.

Font-Reaulx, J. de. "Saint-Bernard de Romans (Drôme)." *Congrès archéologique de France*, LXXXVI (1923), 146–163.

Romans, Église Saint-Barnard, 1st dossier (Drôme, 427), Monuments historiques, Paris, 1838–1902.

Books and Articles Discussing Romans

Lasteyrie, R. de. "Études sur la sculpture française au moyen-âge." L'Academie des inscriptions et belles-lettres, Fondation Piot, *Monuments et mémoires*, VIII (1902), 127–129.

Porter, A. K. *Romanesque Sculpture of the Pilgrimage Roads*. 10 vols. Boston: Marshall Jones, 1923, vol. 1, 103, 275–277, 297–298.

Deschamps, P. *French Sculpture of the Romanesque Period*. New York: Harcourt, Brace, 1930, 43, 47.

Hamann, R. *Die Abteikirche von St. Gilles und ihre künstlerische Nachfolge*. 3 vols. Berlin: Akademie-Verlag, 1955, vol. 1, 234–240.

SAINT-GUILHEM-LE-DÉSERT

Monographs and Articles

Renouvier, J. "Histoire, antiquités et architectonique de l'abbaye de Saint-Guilhem-le-Désert." *Monuments de quelques anciens diocèses de Bas-Languedoc*, 1837, Plates XIII, XIV, XV.

Thomassy, R. "L'ancienne abbaye de Gellone." *Mémoires de la Société des Antiquaires de France*, XV (1840), 307, Plates VIII, IX.

Vinas, L. *Visite rétrospective à Saint-Guilhem-le-Désert*. Montpellier: Sequin, 1875.

Bonnet, E. *Cartulaire de l'abbaye de Gellone*. Montpellier: la Société archéologique de Montpellier, 1898.

Bonnet, E. "L'église abbatiale de Saint-Guilhem-le-Désert." *Congrès archéologique de France*, LXXIII (1906), 384–440.

Hamann, R. "Ein unbekannter Figurenzyklus in St. Guilhem-le-Désert." *Marburger Jahrbuch für Kunstwissenschaft* (1926), 71–89.

Schoenebeck, H. von. "Ein Christlicher Sarkophag aus St. Guilhem-le-Désert." *Jahrbuch der Arch. Instituts*, XLVII (1932), 97–125.

Schneider, H. "The Acanthus at The Cloisters." *Bulletin, The Metropolitan Museum of Art*, New York, June, 1945, 248–252.

Lambert, E. "Monuments disparus et documents d'archives." *Phoebus*, I (1946), 16–22.

Jourda, P., Rudel, J., and Christian, M. *Saint-Guilhem-le-Désert, vallée inspirée du Languedoc, son site—son abbaye—son cloître—son héros de légende—son saint*. Montpellier: 1947.

Vallery-Radot, J. "L'église de Saint-Guilhem-le-Désert." *Congrès archéologique de France*, CVIII (1951), 156–180.

Vallery-Radot, J. "Fouilles romans." *Art de France*, IV (1964), 275–277.

Books and Articles Discussing Saint-Guilhem-le-Désert

Revoil, H. *L'Architecture romane du Midi de la France*. 3 vols. Paris: March, 1873, II, 37–39, Pl. XXXVIII–XLIII.

Lasteyrie, R. de. "Études sur la sculpture française au moyen-âge." L'Academie des inscriptions et belles-lettres, Fondation Piot, *Monuments et mémoires*, VIII (1902), 131–132.

Porter, A. K. *Romanesque Sculpture of the Pilgrimage Roads*. 10 vols. Boston: Marshall Jones, 1923, I, 279, Plates 1397–1402.

Deschamps, P. *French Sculpture of the Romanesque Period, Eleventh and Twelfth Centuries*. New York: Harcourt, Brace, 1930, 89.

Rey, R. *La sculpture romane languedocienne*, Toulouse: Edouard Privat, 1936, 320–321.

Hamann, R. *Die Abteikirche von St. Gilles und ihre künstlerische Nachfolge*. Berlin: Akademie-Verlag, 1955, 240–258.

Horn, W. *Die Fassade von St. Gilles*. Hamburg: Paul Evert, 1937, 81–89.

Lassalle, V. "L'influence provençale au cloître et à la cathédrale de Tarragone." *Mélanges offerts à René Crozet*. Poitiers: 1966, 873–877.

Index

As this book concentrates on five monuments, the usual purely alphabetical index would be less useful to the reader than the one devised. This index will consist of three parts: the five major monuments; other monuments in and outside Provence; and authors.

(1) FIVE MAJOR MONUMENTS

(3) AUTHORS

The Facade of Saint-Gilles-du-Gard
was composed in Baskerville and Bulmer type faces by
the Eastern Typesetting Company. The text and plates
were printed in fine-screen offset lithography by The
Meriden Gravure Company. The binding is by the
Chas. H. Bohn Company.

Designed by Raymond M. Grimaila